the visceral logics of decolonization.

The Visceral Logics of Decolonization.

NEETU KHANNA

Duke University Press *Durham and London* 2020

© 2020 Duke University Press
All rights reserved
Designed by Aimee C. Harrison
Typeset in SnagBleu Republic and Avenir by Copperline Books

Cataloging-in-Publication Data is available
at the Library of Congress
ISBN 9781478005179 (hardcover)
ISBN 9781478006787 (pbk.)
ISBN 9781478009009 (ebook)

Cover art: Mithu Sen, detail of *Charcoal of the mind!!*, 2014. Mixed media collage and watercolor on Japanese Kozo paper on light box. Courtesy of the artist.

CONTENTS

Acknowledgments. vii

Introduction.
The Visceral Logics
of Decolonization. 1

1. Agitation. 35

2. Irritation. 60

3. Compulsion. 85

4. Evisceration. 109

Coda. Explosion. 132

Notes. 151

Bibliography. 161

Index. 175

ACKNOWLEDGMENTS

Words cannot express my gratitude to my extraordinary graduate mentor, Jenny Sharpe, for her unequivocal support, brilliance, guidance, inspiration, compassion, humor, and friendship throughout the years. Jenny has modeled for me a rare form of academic mentorship, and I thank her for gently challenging me to take the paths I am afraid to take. She has taught me what it means to be a committed feminist scholar and reminds me of the importance of what we do in the crucial moments when I despair.

The profound influence of Aamir Mufti's brilliant work paves the way for this book. I fell in love with the Progressive Writers in Aamir's office. I thank him for continually challenging me and for his mentorship and friendship through these years. He has taught me about the pleasures of working with passion.

Anyone who knows the dazzling work of Sianne Ngai will also see her imprint all over these pages. I was so fortunate to have Sianne's support in the formative stages of this project, and she was a vital source of both inspiration and mentorship.

Eric Hayot was instrumental to shaping this project in its early stages. I thank him for his mentorship, and for his help untangling ideas and cultivating a way of speaking and thinking about the visceral. Ali Behdad and Purnima Mankekar also provided crucial feedback on the project in its dissertation stages.

This book also grew out of the classrooms of and conversations with Ali Behdad, Yogita Goyal, Gil Hochberg, Rachel Lee, Nouri Gana, Arthur Little, Esha Niyogi De, and Richard Yarborough. Richard Yarborough is both the reason I pursued a graduate career at UCLA and the reason I survived.

He continues to be the mentor and educator I hope to become, and I can never repay him for the warmth, support, and inspiration he has provided me throughout the years.

My years at USC have been a dream. I could not imagine a more intellectually fulfilling and supportive environment, and I have cherished my time and the friendship of my colleagues immensely. First and foremost, I would like to thank Panivong Norindr for his incredible mentorship, his brilliance, kindness, humor, and unflagging support. Panivong, Natania Meeker, Olivia Harrison, and Devin Griffiths pored over innumerable drafts of the book, and there are no words to express my gratitude for their invaluable feedback and intellectual generosity—I feel so blessed, above all, to have found in these brilliant colleagues such wonderful friends. One of my greatest joys since joining USC has been working with the postcolonial faculty reading group, whom I want to thank for their comments on the book and for filling my home in LA with so much joy. For reading or listening to various iterations of the book and providing critical feedback, friendship, and support, I would also like to thank Peggy Kamuf, Edwin Hill, Akira Lippit, Jack Halberstam, Nayan Shah, Dorinne Kondo, Kara Keeling, Sarah Gualtieri, Macarena Gomez-Barris, Karen Tongson, Nitin Govil, Shana Redmond, Robeson Taj Frazier, Aniko Imre, Anna Krakus, Julie Van Dam, Guilan Siassi, Michaele DuPlessis, Erin Graff Zivin, Veli Yashin, Julian Gutierez-Albilla, Roberto Diaz, Samuel Steinberg, Jessica Marglin, James McHugh, and John Carlos Rowe. This book could not have been written without the institutional support I received at USC and UCLA, most notably the USC Zumberge Research and Innovation Award and the UCLA dissertation year fellowship.

This book benefited immensely from a series of generous invitations to share my work. I am grateful to Ann Cheng for inviting me to the Critical Food Studies conference at Princeton University, Catherine Sameh and Attiya Ahmad for inviting me to the Transnational Feminisms conference at Barnard, Aamir Mufti for inviting me to the Bandung Humanisms conference at UCLA, Hala Halim for inviting me to present at the Bandung, Afro-Asianness, Non-Alignment, Tricontinentalism, and Global South Comparatism panel at ACLA, Purnima Mankekar for the invitation to the Center for India and South Asia at UCLA, Jeannine Murray-Roman for inviting me to the The New Scholars series at Reed College, and Hentyle Yapp for inviting me to present at multiple panels at the ASA over the years and for inviting me to join the LA Queer of Color Critique reading group.

Finally, I am deeply grateful to Macarena Gomez-Barris, not only for her mentorship over the years, but for organizing the most incredible workshop for the manuscript in its final stages at the Global South Center at Pratt. I especially want to thank Maca, May Joseph, and Julietta Singh for their meticulous feedback, as well as for their solidarity and compassion when I needed it the most.

I am especially grateful to Sonali Chakravarty, Eirene Visvardi, and Jill Morawsky for inviting me and so warmly welcoming me to the Center for Humanities at Wesleyan University as a Mellon Postdoctoral Fellow to join the faculty seminar Visceral States: Affect and Civic Life—one of the most intellectually gratifying and memorable years of my life. There are so many that I have to thank for making Wesleyan such a vibrant intellectual space as well as my home that year, but I am especially grateful to Sonali, Eirene, David Coombs, Jo Fitzpatrick, Angela Naimou, Robyn Autry, Kathleen Coe Roberts, Kachig Tololyan, and Kehaulani Kauanui for their kindness, intellectual exchange, and humor, trips to the Shadow Room, parent-trap plots, aggressive turkey videos, and essential music mixtapes. I am grateful to Sonali in particular for her wisdom and the sisterhood we have sustained over the years.

Conversations with the inimitable Ruthie Wilson Gilmore over an unforgettable two weeks at the American University of Beirut were profoundly transformative for me, and I thank her for her fierce brilliance, warmth, and solidarity in a moment when I most really needed it. I also thank the organizers of the UCHRI seminar at the American University of Beirut and the wonderful friends I made there for their profound impact on my thinking. Parama Roy and Kyla Tompkins were key in vitally resuscitating this project in a moment of despondency, when one of its older lives was coming to an end. This book is fundamentally indebted to their pathbreaking work. Parama patiently read the entire manuscript from start to finish and guided me in reshaping it; the current iteration of the project is in no small part due to her brilliance and what she could see in it. Kyla was the one to see in this project that it was about new and old materialist thought, an insight that profoundly transformed the theoretical architecture of this book.

I must also thank the incredible group of graduate students who took my Colonial Affect seminar over the years. They were instrumental in bringing this book into being. I want to especially acknowledge the brilliant graduate students who have served as my research and teaching assistants: my RA, Chinmayi Sirsi, who gathered research and worked with me on translation, and my TAs Sylvie Lydon, Mina Ichigo Kaneko, and Athia Chaudhry, who taught much of this material with me and contributed their marvelous perspectives.

I am deeply grateful to Ken Wissoker for his incisive vision and guidance—for understanding this project immediately in a way no one had, including myself. I thank Ken for his wisdom and enthusiasm about the book and for encouraging me to pursue a potential I would not have had the courage to otherwise. The two anonymous reviewers at Duke were the ideal readers for this book, and I continue to be awed and humbled by the care and precision with which they read my work and provided truly transformative feedback. I would also like to thank Danielle Kasprzac and the anonymous reviewers at Minnesota University Press, as well as the anonymous reviewers at Oxford University Press for their detailed comments. A special thanks to Colleen Jancovic for her meticulous copy editing throughout the writing of this book. Earlier versions of chapters 2 and 3 appear in the *Journal of Postcolonial Writing* and *Postcolonial Text*, and I thank the editorial staff of these journals for permission to republish and for providing a platform to refine many of the ideas in this book.

None of this would have been possible, or at all pleasurable, without the comradery and support of my writing partners: Myrna Douzjian, Jeannine Murray-Roman, Laffitte Lamberto-Egan, Dorinne Kondo, Macarena Gomez-Barris, Olivia Harrison, Aness Webster, Kinohi Nishikawa, and Chinyere Osuji. Their guidance, encouragement, and companionship brought so much pleasure and much needed support. I owe a special thank you to one of my longest writing partners, Jeannine Murray-Roman, she has helped me make sense of every thought in this book from its most incomprehensible iterations, and her brilliance is all over these pages. And to Myrna Douzjian who has been a daily writing companion, helping me through insurmountable impasses with love and humor: I have no idea what I would do without you. Finally, there are no words to express my gratitude to Naomi Greyser and Ladonna Parker, who coached me through all of this— this book is inconceivable without their skilled guidance, wisdom, and the depth of their intellectual and emotional support.

I am unspeakably grateful to the fierce feminist pack of wolves who have gathered around me and sustained me through the writing of this book. To these friends, there are not enough pages in the world to convey my love and gratitude to you, your unflagging patience, encouragement, and enthusiasm about this book mean more to me that you'll ever know: Jesus Hernandez (my partner in crime with whom I began and survived this journey), Tina Beyene, Khanum Sheikh, Sharmila Lodhia, Azza Basarudin, Christina Heatherton, Marian Gabra, Myrna Douzjian, Talar Chahinian, Lisa Felipe, Melissa Valdez, Jeannine Murray-Roman, Jason Goldman, Hentyle Yapp, Megan Asaka, Jake Peters, Nisha Kunte, Aness Webster, Kelly Krulisky, and LAcommune, especially Jo Suh, Joanna Villanueva, Annette Kim, Michelle Sriwongtong, and Diana Won. Above all, none of this would be possible without the fierce love, sisterhood, and the collective stupid-genius of Tina Beyene and Khanum Sheikh, they were and continue to be my lifeline.

The largest debts I owe to my family. My family has provided me with the greatest source of love, strength, and support throughout my career, and there simply are no words to express my gratitude and how much they mean to me. The physical and emotional burden of my writing this book and pursuing this line of work fell fully on them. My mother, Neelam Soni Khanna, was the first activist I knew and remains my most intimate interlocutor in this world; she has taught me the importance of fighting and of living with passion. My father, Satish Kumar Khanna, is in some ways the first feminist I knew, and he has taught me about the pleasures of perseverance and loving what you do. None of this would be possible without their love and encouragement, their sacrifices, the dreams they dreamt on my behalf, and their backbreaking labor, and so I dedicate this to them.

I was so lucky to meet my love, Brian, in the middle of writing this book, and I thank him for his humor and quiet brilliance and for the joy he has brought to my life. He has read every single word and has heard every incoherent, agonized iteration of this book. He also took it upon himself to read the authors and philosophers I work with so that he could become fluent in the languages I think (and live) in. He has selflessly and quietly carved out a space in this world for me to think and dream expansively. The lovingness of these gestures will never be lost on me. And I thank my Nishad, who exploded into this world as an unstoppable force of nature, of the most visceral kind. This book is for you two, also.

I would also like to acknowledge the Sonis, the Khannas, and the Blackwells, scattered across the globe, and the postcolonial histories they map, and for the stories I inherited on their behalf. I thank Veronica San Diego, Brian Sr., David Blackwell, and Pritesh Sampat for their love, excitement, and encouragement through the years—it has meant so much to me. I must also thank my cousins, Sushant and Kartik Soni for the most loving tech support anyone could ask for. This book could literally not have been written without them. I would also like to acknowledge the large and loving (and loud) diasporic Punjabi community that raised me in LA, and who still drop by unannounced with *ladoo*s when there is news.

Finally, I dedicate this book especially to my sister, Rohini, the most incredible woman, activist, and thinker I know. She has remained my greatest inspiration, advocate, and support throughout my life, and none of this would have been possible without her. This book is as much hers as it is mine. As anyone who has ever met me knows, we are two inseparable parts of a whole. Ro, this is for you; I hope it makes you proud.

Introduction.
THE VISCERAL LOGICS OF DECOLONIZATION

> We can feel new feelings. We can learn to be aware with a
> new awareness. We can envisage the possibility of creating new races
> from the latent heat in our dark brown bodies.
> —Mulk Raj Anand, *Untouchable*

The interrogative impulse of this book emerges from a set of questions about how a racialized sensibility sediments in the reflexes of the colonized subject. If the unfinished project of decolonization demands we dismantle the enduring ideologies that continue to sustain the legacies of empire, I ask: How are we to account for and disrupt the ways in which the colonized subject becomes complicit with these social regimes? What would it mean to decolonize these deeply gendered sensibilities— to undo these emotive lessons in the habits of mind and memory of the postcolonial subject? How are we to feel new feelings? This study opens up a new pathway for thinking through the critical problematics of decolonization by exploring a dense and knotted set of relations between embodied experience and political feeling—a set of relations we may understand as *visceral*.

An itch, a craving, a tingling sensation, waves of nausea, the heat of anger, convulsions of ecstasy, the pull of emotive contagion—often staged through the bowels, digestive tracts, and viscous textures of the body— these richly phenomenological figures that characterize the visceral aesthetics of this archive drive my study of revolutionary feeling. *Visceral Logics* is a feminist study of the political forces and historical materialities that bring forth a series of complex affective forms in the apocalyptic moments of decolonization and the rise of modern nationalism. In what follows, I turn to an archive of Marxist anticolonial writers who provide a remarkable experimental staging ground for a materialist exploration of racialized emotions. I take as my primary case study a collective of Muslim internationalist authors who shared a commitment to Marxist literature and art as a source of progressive transformation for the Indian nation and the consciousness of its new citizens. These writers, active from the 1930s through the 1960s, joined the world's literary intelligentsia by writing in dialogue with the Bloomsbury Group of London, the modernists of Paris, the Soviet socialist realists, the Afro-Asian Writers Association, and members of the Third World Marxist movements seeking to transform the global social order. *Visceral Logics* returns to this critical prehistory to the Bandung cultural moment of the 1960s.

Thinking with the visceral poses a particular challenge to our theories of empire and decolonization, which have largely focused on the discursive and ideological contours of colonial violence and power. This embodied interface confounds distinctions between thought and feeling, habits of mind and the habituated reflexes of the body, the ideological and the intuitive, the involuntary and the desired. The visceral traffics between the materiality and metaphor of bodily life. Any endeavor to think these dimensions of decolonization will necessitate an engagement not only with the discursive practices of empire, but also with how these habits of mind are secured by emotive ones. If our political and scholarly practices aim to dismantle colonial habits of thought and ideologies, we must be able to engage the multiple sites in which these enduring ideologies continue to operate. We must be able to attend to that fraught and unruly relationship between feelings and what we obscurely refer to as "consciousness." Tracing a constellation of bodily actions and reactions, I theorize the visceral as a critical dimension of Marxian theories of revolutionary consciousness, an anticolonial political thought born of the internationalist moment.

Scholars of decolonization have long been preoccupied with understanding the violence colonialism enacts on the mind and body of the colonized subject. Frantz Fanon famously refocused for us the definition of "decolonization," revising psychoanalysis to theorize the affective trauma of colonization within a "stretched" Marxist political philosophy and a phenomenology that imagines collective liberation along with a sustained critique of bourgeois historicism. As Gerard Aching writes, "The complexity of [Fanon's] use of the term *decolonization* emerges precisely from his powerful combination of psychoanalysis, political philosophy, strategies of national liberation, and the critique of political elites" (25). One of the challenges Fanon lays out for us in his vision of decolonization in *Les damnés de la terre* (*The Wretched of the Earth* [1963]), especially when read through his earlier writings in *Peau noire, masques blancs* (*Black Skin, White Masks* [1952]), is that a collective revolutionary consciousness must both arise from and transform the psychic trauma of racialization. Decolonization in this conception draws on the experiential energies of a fractured psychic life to mobilize it into the very engine of an emancipatory consciousness.

In the writings of Fanon, as well as those of the Indian Marxist authors in this study, the visceral response of the colonized subject is imagined as that catalyst for this transformation. These authors pose vital questions about how the psychological trauma of colonial subjugation can become the resource and engine of a collective liberation. Thus, while my use of "the visceral" certainly draws on many familiar understandings—such as the body's intuitive, "gut" reactions and emotive response—what I mean by the term is quite specific to the political tradition under scrutiny in these chapters. Colonial and revolutionary affect both derive from the same emotive energetic. That they derive from the same substance, in the Spinozan sense, animates problematics of decolonization in this study. The visceral, as a *logic* of decolonization, interanimates the energies of both colonized and revolutionary affects within the physiological responses of the racialized subject; it is imbued with the potentiality of a radical affective reconstitution.

This book takes as a case study the Marxist movements within Indian nationalism, what has been called the "progressive" legacy in the history of Indian aesthetic and cultural production featuring the aesthetic experiments of the largely Muslim literary intelligentsia of India, including Ismat Chughtai, Khwaja Ahmad Abbas, Mulk Raj Anand, and Ahmed Ali. These writers placed questions of gender and sexuality squarely at the center of their debates on social transformation and decolonization. Writing primarily in Urdu, Hindi, and English, many of these writers organized formally under the title of the All-India Progressive Writers' Association (PWA) and the Indian People's Theater Association (IPTA). As Priyamvada Gopal characterizes these writers, they were "English-educated, fluently bilingual colonial subjects strongly committed to anti-colonialism; members of relatively elite social groupings invested in a variety of Marxist and socialist projects; littérateurs who were devoted to the literary craft while urgently concerned with social and political transformation; and, last but not least, Muslims who were engaged in a critique of Islamist orthodoxy even as Hindu majoritarianism threatened to exclude Muslim communities from the life of the Indian nation" (*Literary Radicalism in India*, 7). *Visceral Logics* charts the artistic experiments of India's progressive political movements, from the utopian visions of the secular nation through the violent aftermath of independence and partition, to reveal how these authors reached for alternative, gendered sensibilities of national belonging. These imaginings, I argue, were predicated on a radical transformation of the emotive life of the gendered colonial—and increasingly "communal"—Indian citizen subject.

As the prevailing trauma of colonial violence remains lodged in the racialized sensibilities of our postcolonial world, what would it mean to undo the visceral lessons of colonialism in the habits of mind and emotive reflexes of the postcolonial subject? In pursuit of this question, I turn to the internationalist political thought of the decolonizing world of the 1930s through the 1960s, because, as I argue, these very questions were at the center of the artistic experiments and global debates on national liberation, albeit in poetic and aesthetic registers of racialized feeling that we have yet to fully understand. While Fanon's writings on decolonization remain a cornerstone for this project, I map an alternative feminist genealogy of the visceral in this book, one that both provokes and exceeds the questions Fanon has left in his wake. Studying progressive aesthetics through the lens of the visceral surfaces imaginaries of decolonization that are fundamentally driven by transformations of normative gender subjectivities through the reimagining of corporeal inhabitance and bodily being.

The visceral repositions our approach to the scene and study of affect by centering the somatic life of the body as a fundamental site of colonial subjugation and corporeal control. This study of decolonization necessitates that we shift our inquiries from the psychoanalytic unconscious to the somatic unconscious. I take the physiological reflex as our point of entry into the study of the colonized psyche as constitutive rather than merely expressive of thought and feeling. Thinking with the visceral, in other words, requires that our theories of consciousness and liberation contend with the involuntary and automated reflexes of the body—realms that are largely relegated to the instinctual or innate; seen as biologically programmed and therefore outside the reach of cultural critique. In fact, this study began by tracing a peculiar pattern of densely affective, explosive figures specific to the foundational writings of the anticolonial philosopher Frantz Fanon. These bodily responses of laughter, weeping, trembling, nausea, and vomiting—both involuntary and emotive, bodily and cerebral—appear within the distinctive stylistics of Fanon's writings not simply as metaphors but, to borrow from Raymond Williams, hovering at "the very edge of semantic availability" (134). Why have these affective responses evaded sustained analytic inquiry? What are they being called on to do within the anticolonial theorizing of this moment? This book asks how we can "read" the visceral of this transnational aesthetic and how a rethinking might address deep and sedimented problematics of postcoloniality anew.

One of the best-known and most widely studied scenes of colonial affect remains Fanon's depiction of the colonized black subject's encounter with a young white child on the train. The child exclaims to his mother, "Mama, see the Negro! I'm frightened," setting off the existential crisis of the narrator: "In the train it was no longer a question of being aware of my body in the third person but in a triple person.... I existed triply: I occupied space. I moved toward the other ... and the evanescent other, hostile but not opaque, transparent, not there, disappeared, nausea" (*Black Skin, White Masks*, 112). The Sartrean figure of nausea here renders the painful existential fragmentation and tripling of consciousness set in motion by the gaze and incisive speech act of a young white child on a train. In the chapters to come, I propose that we rethink this nausea through this scene's peculiar body logics: "'Mama, see the Negro! I'm frightened!' Frightened! Frightened! Now they were beginning to be afraid of me. I made up my mind to laugh myself to tears, but laughter had become impossible" (*Black Skin, White Masks*, 112). How may we read the sign of failed laughter within Fanon's race theories? For what begins as the unfulfilled desire for laughter ends in this state of nausea—a visceral transference of yet another frustrated desire for a cathartic release. I argue that it is in fact the narrator's thwarted desire for laughter—the explosive and vibratory logics of a colonized laughter—that sets in motion this visceral figure of nausea. Reading nausea in terms of failed laughter begins to open up the way in which these psychosomatic figures summon the accruing energies of the body. These visceral figures, I contend, are central to Fanon's theorizing of the black colonized consciousness as well as his theories of decolonization.

To magnify the peculiar bodily activities of Fanon's famous scene on the train through the lens of the visceral is also to focus the volatility of gendered bodily response within the theater of colonial power, and to center our attention on the energetic life of emotions that cannot be wholly explained by the logics of the mind or language. This phenomenological rendering of the colonized consciousness places a certain ontological pressure on dominant conceptions of the body and its role in organizing the logics of decolonization. As Fanon's now canonical scene of colonial crises continues to unfold, there is another intriguing transference of the convulsive body of laughter:

> Look at the nigger! ... Mama, a Negro! ... Hell, he's getting mad.... [L]ook, a nigger, it's cold, the nigger is shivering, the nigger is shivering because he is cold, the little boy is trembling because he is afraid of the nigger, the nigger is shivering with cold, that cold that goes through your bones, the handsome little boy is trembling because he thinks that the nigger is quivering with rage, the little white boy throws himself into his mother's arms: "Mama, the nigger is going to eat me up!" ...
>
> I sit down at the fire.... I felt an easily identifiable flood mounting out of the countless facets of my being. I was about to be angry. The fire was long since out, and once more the nigger was trembling. (*Black Skin, White Masks*, 114)

In this scene of psychosomatic dynamics between the white boy and the black man, a scene of terror and (mis)recognition and of semantic ambiguities and slippages (is he trembling in fear or anger, or is he cold? Who is afraid, angry, cold?), the psychic interiorities of the black subject resonate through the vibratory logics of his body. How do we read the trembling subjects of this scene of power and psychic violence?

Focusing the affective energetics that animate this scene, I ask how the black male subject and the handsome young white boy are "moved" (physically and emotionally) in this moment of colonial encounter. What bodies "tend to do," Sara Ahmed writes, are "the effects of history" ("Orientations: Toward a Queer Phenomenology," 553). Underwritten by the materialist philosophies and scientific imaginaries of the historical moment in which Fanon is writing and thinking decolonization, these affects are a kind of energy accumulating within and between these bodies, the intensity of the trembling rising as the two bodies "heat up": *I sit down by the fire.... I was beginning to be angry.* The narrator recounts a tense phenomenology of racialized anticipation, the not yet of a racialized rage, compounded in mounting energies between the black subject and the white child—*an easily identifiable flood mounting out of the countless facets of my being.* If, for Spinoza, affects are characterized by states between motion and rest, for Fanon, colonial affects are inscribed within temporalities of momentum and states of (agonized) suspension and anticipation. In the mirroring of these two trembling subjects—a peculiar synchronicity—the theater of a colonial power struggle plays out between the adult black man and white child, complicating a simple binary opposition. Like tuning forks, the somatic responses of this scene focus the energies vibrating between subjects. Their energies animate and enervate the subjects in ways that synchronize their physical responses, even as the scene seeks to stage the violence of colonial power and difference.

An affective reading of this scene reveals a rich and complex dynamic of colonial power and relation as Fanon brings to focus a peculiar phenomenon of emotive contagion and transmission. The transfer and transaction of emotive energies orchestrates these two bodies. Trembling in tandem, these two subjects seem to have little control over a certain affective manipulation organizing their bodily responses and setting in motion this colonial drama. Inextricable from the psyche and consciousness of the racialized subject, what is the nature of this *visceral* manipulation in somatic logics seeming to go awry? The corporeal logics of this scene tether the colonial subject to the colonizer. But it is the affective dynamic vibrating between them that binds them, interanimating these bodies in what Arun Saldanha terms the "event" of race, a historical force that operates through the "dynamic physicality of human bodies" (8). This volatility and interanimation of Fanonian affect are central features of the anticolonial imaginary that I analyze in this book. The visceral offers a materialist analytic that recasts the scene of racialized affect through the energetic dynamic that reverberates between two bodies, animating and activating racialized repositories in automated response.

It is in such volatile scenes of colonial encounter that a transformation of consciousness is imagined, precisely because this is where racialized logics in visceral responses begin to misbehave. These involuntary bodily responses archive and automatize a deep and violent history of colonial subjugation. The visceral logics orchestrating this scene cannot, however, simply be disrupted or overturned by a psychic intervention, even as they are intimately linked with a condition of consciousness. These sites of affective manipulation—where the colonial (dis)ordering of the gendered body secures psychic logics in somatic action—are just as crucial to the study of colonial power as the discursive logics we have tended to privilege in postcolonial scholarship. Embodied repositories of racialized memories continue to play out recursively *because they remain unrecognized*. It is thus my contention that any study of colonial power must make legible the visceral logics of the colonized subject so that we may interrupt their incessant repetitions.

Our postcolonial pasts are exploding upon us in the present in the forms of militant nationalisms across the globe. The visceral, as I develop the concept in this book, is an analytic for the violent landscapes of our postcolonial present, shaped as they are by these traumatic pasts. What the visceral allows me to think (and, in fact, I argue that we cannot think without) are a set of questions imperative to the critique of postcolonial nationalisms, as well as their recruitment of diasporic communities. How does the nation-state, in its various colonial and postcolonial configurations, gain complicity from its gendered subjects? How are these conditions of "consciousness," these "structures of feeling," locked in the automatic reflexes of the body under modern regimes of subjection? How are colonial traumas and their structures of feeling inherited, their emotive genres passed down through generations?

This book argues that the biopolitical interface I call "visceral" was at the center of the anticolonial political debates surrounding the revolution of consciousness in the first half of the twentieth century. By mining the visceral, I seek to uncover an undertheorized dimension of a global Marxist aesthetics that emerged with particular force during the era of decolonization. Its literatures of decolonization are saturated with the kinds of biological and corporeal details I work through in the chapters that follow. Sartrean figures of nausea and Bakhtinian tropes of the grotesque, lingering at the abject sites where the body opens to the world, for example, are some of the most familiar visceral grammars of this era. Achille Mbembe writes about the colonial imaginary, "Beyond specifically the mouth, belly, and phallus, the body is the principal locale of the idioms and fantasies used in depicting power" (7). This study brings into focus the theoretical labor in which these figures engage within the global materialist imaginaries of decolonization. With readings spanning the canonical writings of Fanon and Muslim internationalists, I aim to draw out a philosophical through line that underwrites these writers' anticolonial imaginaries.

This book draws on and extends the modes of inquiry opened up by the feminist and queer theory branches of affect studies and new materialisms for how they give name and form to the affects of late capitalism and their role in violent regimes of normative desire, "that place where appetites find a shape in the predictable" (Berlant, *Cruel Optimism*, 2).[1] I am indebted to the work of Sianne Ngai who argues, drawing on Fredric Jameson, that we need new emotive epistemes or "affective ideologemes" for the forms that emerge under these conditions of modernity and late capitalism (7). However, affect studies has largely failed to establish within postcolonial studies the traction it has gained in studies of gender and sexuality. We may understand this gap as due to the difficulty of theorizing the conditions of racialization and colonialism through the lens of affect, which has largely relied on Western archives and has often slipped into universalizing abstractions of embodied experience.[2] Such theories of affect risk eliding the historical and sociological specificities of the subject under the conditions of colonialism, as well as the epistemological assumptions underlying the theory of affect. Grounded in its challenge to universalizing tendencies of theory and criticism, postcolonial studies defined itself from its inception as a project of decolonizing knowledge production. What happens to our theories of affect when we shift our aesthetic focus to the colonial context, to non-Western literary and linguistic traditions, and to the era of decolonization rather than the aesthetics of late capitalism in the West that have tended to dominate affect studies archives?

While the recent "turn" to affect has become richly generative of new academic genres, reading practices, and modalities of intellectual discourse with which we may engage modern legacies of race and colonialism, much of affect theory, inflected by various schools of psychoanalysis, has largely relied on what Teresa Brennan calls the emotively contained subject as "the last bastion of Eurocentrism in critical thinking" (2).[3] In other words, theories of affect tend to rely on an imaginary of the individuation and self-containment of the emoting individual. Brennan locates this dynamic of emotive contagion as a crucial missing piece in the critical and scientific literatures in Western psychology—what she calls the transmission of affect. Throughout this study, we will find that the visceral appears only in moments of encounter—in other words, in the dynamics that "set off" or trigger the visceral response of the racialized subject. The somatic response is triggered by the proximity and presence of other bodies: bodily energies and actions inscribed in dense relations of power and alterity. Indeed, as we will find, the "event-ness" of race, to borrow from

Saldanha, becomes the very condition for the emergence of the visceral's appearance on the stage of a revolutionary history. Rejecting the fiction of the bounded individual, such an understanding of racialized embodiment requires a study of affect through the relations of colonial subjectivity and the experiences of the relational self and its inscriptions in power.[4]

Attending to the visceral grammars of colonial and postcolonial politics, I propose, is a task of retooling our reading practices. The questions of the chapters are refracted through one of the central questions of the Marxist anticolonial movements gaining momentum across the globe in the first half of the twentieth century: What roles do political art and aesthetics play in disrupting and reconditioning the visceral logics that sustain the projects of empire? Key political contestations—over decolonization and the nascent nation, between religion and secularism, regarding caste and heredity, or in regulating intimacy and sexuality, to name a few—are consistently hashed out in the cavities and tissues of the visceral. This book approaches the aesthetics of affect and embodiment within these texts as particularly saturated nodes of historical and representational predicament in a decolonizing world. Here I follow Ngai, drawing on Rei Terada, in her approach to the aesthetics of affect and emotion as densely knotted "interpretations of predicaments": "signs that not only render visible different registers of problem (formal, ideological, sociohistorical) but conjoin these problems in a distinctive manner" (3). The visceral is a concentrated site of postcolonial crises where the contradictions of colonial and postcolonial modernity are most violently at play. To borrow from David Eng, "These structures of feeling, to cite a concept from Raymond Williams, are those emergent social forms, ephemeral and difficult to grasp or name, that appear precisely at a moment of emergency, when dominant cultural norms go into crises" ("The End(s) of Race," 1486).

With this book I join a range of scholars who have sought to capture and explore the complexity of the Progressive Writers' aesthetic insights into Indian national politics, including Ulka Anjaria, Ben Conisbee Baer, Jessica Berman, Toral Gajarawala, Priyamvada Gopal, Gayatri Gopinath, Rakshanda Jalil, Aamir Mufti, Tahira Naqvi, Alex Padamsee, Geeta Patel, and Snehal Shingavi.[5] I am indebted to these scholars, and particularly to the South Asian feminist work that reveals the Progressive Writers' Movement's nuanced engagements with gender and sexuality as a site of radical transformation.[6] But this study diverges from previous projects on the Progressive Writers in significant ways. While the Progressive Writers' Movement has been studied largely in terms of Indian national politics, to which my analysis is greatly indebted, the visceral logic of my study repositions this movement by drawing out its materialist philosophy—an index of its internationalist dimensions. The analytic I develop in this book reveals how progressive aesthetics provide the sites through which these writers mined the dense interplay between gendered colonial embodiments and a Marxian revolutionary consciousness. The aesthetics of the visceral emerge from the dense internationalist cross-traffic of philosophies and aesthetics: the hybridizing of European modernisms with Soviet realisms and Urdu literary forms, and of Western philosophical traditions (from existentialism to psychoanalysis) with Sufi metaphysics, Sanskrit texts, and indigenous religious performance genres. The visceral as a materialist logic of decolonization invokes both the historical materialism, the Marxism of the movement, and the materialist traditions of thinking through the energetic life of bodily matter: Freudian psychoanalysis, phenomenology, and the monism attributed to Spinoza.

These readings of the visceral shift the frame through which the Progressive Writers have been conventionally read in terms of both national politics and Marxist philosophy. Viscerality demands that we recognize materialism at play in their internationalist political thought. As Snehal Shingavi notes, the politics of progressive writing in India during this period have largely been explained "through nationalist figures rather than the internationalist genealogies of Marxism, realism, and modernism or vernacular genealogies" ("When the Pen Was a Sword," 9). The visceral, as an optic of anticolonial thought, sharpens our understanding of the role these writers played in the internationalist development of anticolonial political thought. The aesthetic and philosophical links between the Progressive Writers and the canonical writings of Fanon that bookend this study gesture toward the internationalism surfaced by the visceral.[7]

To consider the visceral figures in Fanon's canonical writings is also to ask what it means to understand the explosive and vibratory logics of a colonized laughter—its logics of pleasure and pain—as crucial mediators between his language and politics. While the vibratory logics of the body organize Fanon's revolutionary subject, it is the convulsive logics of a mass euphoria, of political agitation, that I center in this study of nationalist ecstasy. If it is the poetics of political "agitation" that organize the relationship between religious and nationalist euphoria within an Indian Muslim internationalism, it is the tactile poetics of "irritation" that guide my inquiries into the Dalit subject of India. In a chapter on colonial cravings, the compulsive logics of the body caught in the dialectic of desire and disgust guide my feminist inquiries into the violent regimes of colonial hygiene and sexual discipline. And while touch and tactility come to organize the imagined liberation of the casteized subject, this tactile palate is expanded to questions of texture for my interrogation of colonial disgust.

That I turn to the unlikely source of Marxist literature to explore these questions of emotive experience is a central intervention of this book. *Visceral Logics* intentionally reengages a Marxist category that seems to have become obsolete—dismissed as naïve or passé within contemporary postcolonial debates—so as to conjugate contemporary studies of affect with Marxian theories of consciousness.[8] The visceral inquiries of this book open up a far more complex and incisive mobilization of the revolutionary consciousness than previously understood. For that reason, my study constitutes a renewed engagement with materialist articulations of the revolutionary consciousness that were so central to the anticolonial literatures of this era.

Ann Stoler reminds us that colonial violence operated through two interrelated sources on the colonized body: "one that worked through the requisition of bodies . . . and a second that mold[ed] new structures of feeling—new habits of heart and mind" (2). In other words, the production of modern colonial subjects was carried out through both the management of physical bodies, sanctioned through racial grammars of difference, and the emotive conditioning and molding of the colonized subject. Colonial disciplinary regimes sought to train the proper sensibilities of taste and "comportment" in colonial subjects, and these structures of sentiment functioned as dense "transfer points" for the consolidation of imperial power (Stoler, 4). Education in the British colonies, for example, which was famously couched in Victorian obsessions with gendered and sexual propriety, was naturalized in the powerful "gut" reflexes of the colonized subject.[9] Parama Roy writes compellingly about the molding of new notions of appetite, health, and hygiene in colonial India—new forms of disgust that naturalized the cultivation of what Stoler identifies as taste and comportment. As Roy writes, drawing on Gayatri Chakravorty Spivak's formulation of the imperial project of "soul making"—transforming "the heathen into a human": "The projects of epistemic overhaul involved in making heathens human occurred in several registers concurrently. For one thing, they were irreducibly somaticized; souls in the making were more often than not incarnated in bodies whose appetites, expressions, and comings and goings had to be rigorously fashioned. *Soul making and body shaping, physiology and epistemology were intimately conjugated*" (7).[10] The visceral theories of this book explore the nature of this conjugation.

In a powerful internationalist vision of decolonization, the anticolonial writer and activist Mulk Raj Anand, a leading figure in the progressive Marxist movements in India, writes in 1935 that we can "feel new feelings." "We can learn to be aware with a new awareness," Anand writes (*Untouchable*, 153). What is so remarkable about this articulation of revolution is its imagining of a human collective whose very ways of feeling could be a site of radical transformation. In this vision, what we obscurely refer to as a racialized awareness could be a site of radical relearning. These emotive and embodied repositories of the body must be the sites of revolution precisely because empire has already monopolized them. Asking what it could mean to feel new feelings, to borrow Anand's poetic doubling, opens up a series of materialist engagements with the elusive space in which "the instinctual is subjected to the social," where colonial discourses are naturalized in the automated reflexes of the body (Gopal, *Literary Radicalism in India*, 71).[11] In this book I think with these artists and activists as they were debating the transformative potentialities of various visceral states that motivate "progressive" feeling: the convulsions of nationalist ecstasy, the heat of a righteous rage, the compulsions of forbidden cravings, the erotics of colonial disgust, the spasms of an ecstatic terror.

Poetics of Progressive Feeling

The PWA traces its genesis to a group of four Urdu writers who published a collection of short stories in an anthology titled *Angarey* (Embers, or Burning Coals). The collection openly criticized the religious orthodoxies of their Muslim communities and challenged their era's social mandates on gender and sexuality. It created such outrage and backlash that the anthology was banned by the British government six months after its publication (Gopal, *Literary Radicalism in India*, 15). Each of these writers—Ahmed Ali, Rashid Jahan, Sajjad Zaheer, and Mahmudazzafar Khan—became a leading member of the PWA four years later.[12]

While one line of the association's genealogy is rooted in a rebellious generation of the Urdu literary intelligentsia of India that placed gender and sexuality at the center of debates on decolonization and progressivism, the PWA also understood its movement as deeply entrenched in the European modernist movements against imperialism and fascism, as well as in the global Marxist movements of this period. With its members writing primarily in Urdu, Hindi, and English, the PWA was established in London in 1935. It was influenced by the recent formation of the International Association of Writers for the Defense of Culture, an antifascist organization initiated in Paris by European modernists such as André Malraux and André Gide (Gopal, *Literary Radicalism in India*, 23).[13]

Adopting much of the vocabulary that emerged out of the 1935 congress for the Association of Writers for the Defense of Culture, Mulk Raj Anand described the PWA as "one of the largest blocs for the defense of culture" ("On the Progressive Writers' Movement," 2). The dissemination of progressive literature was conducted through the establishment of PWA libraries and through poetry and story recitals, including the organization of peasant poetry conferences. In addition to experimenting in a wide variety of literary genres, including short stories, novels, poetry, and plays, the Progressives worked in an array of artistic forms, including sculpture, dance, and politicized indigenous performance genres; they also experimented in radio and popular film (Gopal, *Literary Radicalism in India*, 123–24). They sought to bring about radical conditions through workshops, translation projects, seminars, conferences, and collaborative publications in the form of periodicals, books, and pamphlets (Gopal, *Literary Radicalism in India*, 25–26).

Anand drafted the PWA's manifesto on December 24, 1938, outlining the shared objectives of the newly born organization. Adopted at the second All-India Progressive Writers' Conference, the manifesto forecast how progressive artists and intellectuals would redefine the art and literature of India. Progressive literature was to have a pivotal role in awakening and transforming the collective consciousness of the nascent Indian nation:

> Indian literature, since the breakdown of classical culture, has had the fatal tendency to escape from the actualities of life. It has tried to find a refuge from reality in baseless spiritualism and ideality.... It is the object of our Association to rescue literature and other arts from the conservative classes....
>
> We believe that the new literature of India must deal with the basic problems of our existence to-day—the problems of hunger and poverty, social backwardness and political subjection. All that drags us down to

passivity, inaction and un-reason we reject as re-actionary. All that arouses in us the critical spirit, which examines institutions and customs in light of reason, which helps us to act, to organize ourselves, to transform, we accept as progressive. ("Amended Manifesto," 20–21)

Framed in the language of a universal rationalism, the definition of progressive literature emerged in opposition to what the group saw as the escapist and opiatic forces of religion—what it termed "cultural reaction." The Progressive Writers sought to counter these reactionary forces in Indian culture and society—the "narrow nationalists, revivalists, the priest craft or orthodoxy," in the words of Anand ("On the Progressive Writers' Movement," 18). For the Progressive Writers' Movement, as we will see, anticolonial critique does not fall into the same colonial Manicheism of Fanon's nationalist writings. Rather, it imbricates and layers in critiques of "indigenous" or precolonial institutions such as caste, class, gender, and religion with critiques of colonial modernity and a platform for national liberation. As captured in the language of Anand's manifesto, however, what constituted literature as "progressive" was not defined in strict aesthetic or ideological terms. Instead, it was measured by "the spirit" it was to awaken in the reader. This definition of progressive writing, in fact, articulates a vague, undefined—in fact, yet-to-be-defined—relationship among ideology, consciousness, and political "action." What would define progressive literature for this group, and which political sentiments it should arouse in its members' readers, remained an object of experimentation and debate from the movement's inception. In fact, the case studies of this book reveal how PWA inquiries into what defined art as revolutionary or "progressive" bring to light the extraordinary ways in which the possibilities of national revolution are underwritten by the visceral poetics of revolutionary feeling.

Driving the emergence of the Marxist revolutionary subject in these imaginaries of decolonization are feelings and emotions that energize or awaken the body, those that *move* the body and mind of the protagonist of History to new registers of consciousness and political action. The affects that motivate this ascension are volatile, emotive energetics. These imaginaries of revolution, inflected by psychoanalytic theory, are channeled through the drives and impulses, the visceral reflexes, of the gendered colonized body. The visceral actions and reactions further organize and orchestrate the historical imaginary of revolution within the artistic experiments I examine. I uncover their role in the emplotment and the unfolding of a revolutionary horizon as imagined within the social realist novel—the literary form that became the contested staging ground for the utopian visions of a decolonizing world.

For example, conceived through emerging scientific and medical epistemologies of the time, from psychoanalysis to thermodynamics, the visceral reflex of anger is debated in Mulk Raj Anand's novel as a potentially revolutionary energetic in its capacity to vitalize, indeed viscerate, the revolutionary subject to an "ascendance" of political consciousness.[14] The role of political anger in impelling a transformation of consciousness, a topic long debated from Aristotle to Audre Lorde, appears in Anand's novel as a way of thinking the place of rage in mobilizing revolutionary transformation. In the aesthetics of the Indo-Soviet filmmaker Khwaja Ahmad Abbas, however, I take up the question of revolutionary rage to consider its ecstatic dimensions—the place of ecstasy in this nationalist form of rage and terror—by focusing on how its contagious and convulsive dimensions shape its mass emotive form. These novels reveal emerging vocabularies and discoveries not only in psychoanalysis, but in fields such as thermodynamics, quantum physics, and electro-conductivity, which influenced how these authors imagined the possibilities of emotive transformation as energetic. They foreground the ways in which the transmission and transformation of feeling is conceptualized through an imaginary of human emotion as a volatile, unstable energy.

Within these political imaginings, the affective energies of the revolutionary subject ignite the political consciousness of the nascent nation. Such explosive affects are thus predictably driven to catharsis, an inevitable bodily release. At stake in the cathartic release, we will find, is not simply an ascendance of consciousness, but a violent historical rupture, as I theorize in the coda of the book. This affective release is a key organizing logic of the revolutionary subject and the political imaginaries of these chapters. The volatile engine of a revolutionary transformation of consciousness, a "latent heat," in the words of Anand, housed in the visceral response of the colonial and subaltern subjects. This heat powers the unfolding of a revolutionary history.

Organized by a Marxist historical teleology, the social realist novels of this study—what Aamir Mufti terms the "national realist" novel—chart the utopian "ascension" of consciousness of the peasant or proletariat figure, which became the literary form for the vast array of artistic visions of social transformation in the Progressive Writers' Movement. As Mufti argues about the Progressive Writers' Movement's adopting of the social realist novel, "The protocols of social realism, first formulated as a program at the Soviet Writers' Congress in 1934 and adopted as official Popular Front policy in 1935, undergo a transformation in being transplanted to a colonial setting. What the language of realist aesthetics now seeks to define is a specific relationship between writing and the nation so that it is more accurate to speak of *national realism* in this context" (183). Each progressive novel uses the bildungsroman form to trace the "coming of age" of its protagonists against the coming of age of the nascent nation. While many of the historical protagonists of this study are subaltern figures—the prostitute, the untouchable, the orphan, the vagrant—the socialist realist project of representing the subaltern was hotly debated among the Progressives, and many chose instead to center middle class subjects that mirrored their own experiences.

The diverse literary styles of these novels bear the mark of the PWA's aesthetic experimentations and the transnationalism of the movement, such that, in the case of many of the novels examined in this study, in the heightened sensory aesthetics of Chughtai or Anand for example, contemporary readers may not recognize that it is "realist" writing that they are reading. We will find, for example, the simultaneous influence of both social realism and European modernisms within the diverse literary styles of the PWA, in ways that trouble conceptions of literary modernism as a corrective to realism within European literary trajectories. One also finds the unmistakable melodramatic inflections of an emerging Bombay popular cinema in the social realist dialogues of these novels, as many of the Progressives earned their living as scenarists and scriptwriters for the film industry. I take as my starting point Gajarawala's important insight that, for authors writing in the colony in the 1930s, "the newness of the novel, the presence of indigenous forms of narrative, social, and political radicalism, and various types of experimentalism meant that realism and modernism often functioned side by side and sentence by sentence" (72). Mining the visceral in this study requires that the reading practices through which we engage the literature of the Progressives be able to attend to the diverse array of generic codes at play, as well as to how their fiction re-works the aesthetic practices of modernism and realism when transplanted to the colony. As Anjaria compellingly argues of realist aesthetics in India during this era of nationalism, "against common perceptions, realism in the colony is highly metatextual, founded on variegated textual fields and constituted not by ideological certainties but by contradictions, conflicts, and profound ambivalence as to the nature of the real world being represented, and the novel's ability to represent it" (*Realism in the Twentieth-Century Indian Novel*, 5).

My focus on the Progressive Writers movement begs the question: Why return to the moment of decolonization or this anticolonial movement at all, when both are marked by failure? To draw on David Scott, the "problem space" of the anticolonial moment in which the Progressives were debating the role of art in social transformation, the nature of the hopes and desires invested in revolution, have since shifted in the historical present (6). Scott calls for a rigorous rethinking and historicizing of our "past hopes" and "anticipated futures" after Bandung. In shifting from their historical present to ours, the task is to retool the very questions we ask of the revolutionary struggle. This book explores the richness and overlooked complexity of the transnational life of the Socialist and social realist novel as it hybridizes with global modernisms, for their materialist inquiries into (post)colonial affective genres and forms. I argue for the indispensable nature of this internationalist body of literature for understanding our violent postcolonial present as well as the past. Beyond simply revealing the Progressive Writers' Movement's experiments in thinking colonial affect—their questions, desires, and debates about the progressive or reactionary effects of certain impulses upon an emergent national consciousness—I aim to theorize the affective genres that emerge from within the historical moments of their formation and refurbish these genres as critical tools for the present. In other words, I am not advocating a particular affective platform for liberation. Rather, I am interested in how an understanding of the materiality and vitality of affective impulse and response provides a much-needed theoretical agility in grappling with the visceral impasses of our violent postcolonial present.

Visceral Logics

The visceral logics of decolonization explore the dynamic intra-action between psychic and somatic activities for where these energetics go astray. The revolutionary potentiality of the visceral is characterized by the volatility and unpredictability of its energetic activity, and how it unfolds in unruly and erratic ways. We only need to recall the trembling subjects of the Fanonian train scene with which we began. To dwell for a moment on an extended example, in an extraordinary experiment in realist sensory aesthetics written in the 1940s, the Urdu feminist writer and anticolonial activist Ismat Chughtai depicts the struggles of a distinguished male artist commissioned by a museum to paint the portrait of a young peasant girl from a small village. The short story "Til" (The Mole) centers on the artist's frustrated attempts to render this subaltern figure in his painting. The artist continually struggles unsuccessfully to find the right hues and textures with which to paint her—the shades of her skin, the tint of her eyes—and thus to represent the girl in her "realistic" dimensions. Far from a cooperative subject for his portrait, the girl is characterized as boldly defiant, stubborn, temperamental, and brazenly coquettish, launching the artist repeatedly into bouts of uncontrollable rage. In one such scene, Chughtai depicts the frustrations of the artist, Chaudhri, as the young subject of his painting, Rani, refuses to sit in the instructed pose, balancing a pitcher on her shoulder:

> [Rani]: "Didn't you hear me say I'm tired? I will throw down the pitcher if you don't listen to me." ...
>
> [His] feet set apart, the muscles in his face quivering with anger, Chaudhry glared at her. His grizzly beard fluttered like a sailboat flapping wildly in the storm, and tiny beads of perspiration appeared on the surface of his bald, smooth head.
>
> "My back hurts from sitting for such a long time." Scared, Rani quickly eased back into position. Then she burst into tears.
>
> "Boohoooo..." Her lips flapped as she blubbered.... Chaudhry widened his eyes and glared at her again. Whenever she started crying, the muscles in Chaudhry's jaws quivered violently, the bridge on his nose went askew, the brushes in his hand danced like firecrackers, and the colours on his palette flowed into a muddle and lost their glow. ("Til," 112–13)

The artist's inability to discipline his subaltern subject, to manage or contain her, is repeatedly articulated through his inability to represent her. Chaudhry's artistic frustrations are yoked within the short story to his battle with his own repressed sexual desire for the object of his painting, as the subject of his painting taunts him for the obscenity of his gaze.

In staging this subtle scene of power between the male artist and his female subaltern subject, Chughtai brings questions of realist aesthetics into crisis through a feminist lens sharply attuned to visceral dynamics of the erotics of power and subversion. What I highlight in this scene, however, is the corporeal drama that is taking place, recalling the trembling subject of Fanon's writings. This scene of convulsion and contagion, however, is staged not between colonizer and colonized, but between male bourgeois artist and female subaltern, foregrounding within the anticolonial project a feminist critique of a masculinist anticolonial nationalism—a double-edged critique that is a defining characteristic of much of the Progressive Writers' literature.

Against the scene of the artist's failed mimetic endeavor—his inability to capture the girl in her "realistic" dimensions—there emerges, once again, this peculiar mirroring of these two trembling bodies. The artist's quivering jaw and fluttering beard are mirrored in the young girl's lips as she is caught in convulsive sobs, and he, conversely, is trembling in anger. In this scene of power and struggle, rendered on the terrain of aesthetic representation and staged between the frustrated bourgeois painter and the defiant subaltern subject, Chughtai amplifies the affective dynamic vibrating between these two bodies. The girl's defiance, the artist's frustration, his anger, her fear, her tears, his rage—this power struggle, staged on the grounds of both gender and class, is thus represented somatically through this back-and-forth ricocheting of their opposing emotive reflexes.

Chughtai maps questions of feminist representation onto this highly eroticized scene of domination and resistance: as the girl breaks into convulsive sobs, the artist begins trembling, and as her tears begin to flow, so do the colors on his canvas. The artist's project is not simply disrupted by this spectacle of emotion. In fact, the mimetic endeavor is strangely reversed: the subject of the painting orchestrates the body of the painter. With a characteristic sense of subtle self-reflexive humor and irony, Chughtai frames her short story with a scene that turns the bourgeois male artist's aesthetic project on its head. The story poignantly critiques the exotification of this artistic project, which, in Chughtai's opinion, characterized many of the works of her own male friends and comrades within the Marxist anticolonial movement.

The unruliness of the visceral energetic, its reckless contagion and erratic nature, becomes the site of Chughtai's feminist inquiry into both power and resistance. Scenes of viscerality expose how disruptive and nonnormative forms of gender and sexuality propel decolonization precisely because this is *where these affective energetics go awry*.[15] In other words, it is where visceral logics misbehave, where the volatility and "mindedness" of the somatic unconscious is most vividly on display (to borrow from Elizabeth Wilson) that the possibilities of decolonization are imagined. It is also from these sites of somatic crises that I derive the visceral concepts I theorize in the chapters that follow: convulsion, compulsion, irritation, agitation, evisceration, explosion.

The visceral requires the body of the "other" to set off its somatic response. Perhaps one of the reflections cited most often from Deleuze on Spinoza: "We know nothing about a body until we know what it can do, in other words what its affects are, how they can or cannot enter into composition with other affects, with the affects of another body, either to destroy that body or be destroyed by it, either to exchange actions and passions with it in composing a more powerful body" (Deleuze and Guattari, 284). Convulsion, a logic of (de)colonization that will return to us throughout this book, focuses the dynamics of affective exchange that interanimate bodies inscribed in logics of power and alterity, for it is in this encounter that the affective recomposition of the subject becomes possible.

Chughtai's agitated bodies, in contrast to Fanon's, reveal spasms isolated in localizable parts and particulate matter—lips flapping, beard fluttering, convulsive sobs, secretions of sweat—their motion escalating in intensity and speed as "relations of motion and rest, of speeds and slowness," in the words of Deleuze (12). The visceral, in Chughtai's writing, attunes our eye to a lower frequency of affective register, subtle somatic arousals that often are barely perceptible, and in so doing opens up a rich and subtle landscape for feminist inquiry. This materialist conceptualization of bodily matter and affective energy is inflected by vocabularies of energy and flows of matter, from thermodynamics and quantum physics to psychoanalysis and phenomenology, locating the biopolitics of empire in the "circulations of energy, affects, atoms, and liquidity in its accounting of the soma" (Lee, 7).[16] I draw these scenes of convulsion in tandem to begin the work of this book: I read this scene in Chughtai's "The Mole" as a feminist counterpoint to Fanon's famous train scene, one that demonstrates a shared materialist philosophy but also opens up an alternative feminist genealogy of viscerality that exceeds the imaginative horizon of Fanon's masculine and Manichean subjects. While the visceral in Fanon's writings draws the colonial subject into an affective exchange with the colonized—a game of destroying or being destroyed, in Spinoza's words—the somato-poetics of the Progressive Writers open up a more nuanced imaginary of corporeal relations, imaginaries of gender reconstitution and modes of collective bodily being that arise from these moments of affective encounter and exchange.

The visceral is thus held in the minor, in the minutiae. While I argue for its importance within the revolutionary imaginary of each of these social realist experiments, the phenomenological moments that I mine emerge as extremely minor and marginal bodily details: the friction of a wool coat on the skin of the untouchable subject; a twitch in the tensed muscle of the politically agitated subject; the improper cravings of our feminist revolutionary subject who, while watching her sewing machine needle cut across the cloth, experiences an exhilarating tingling in her teeth. The affective forms I theorize in each chapter are woven of a subtle somato-poetics.

These tiny visceral expressions emerge out of anticipatory moments within the national realist arc of theses novels. They indicate early somatic arousals; low-grade, threshold moments that eventually will be driven to an explosive release, to what I theorize as a historical catharsis in my concluding chapter on Fanon. As I further explore in the concluding chapter, the possibilities of revolution are housed not simply in the visceral encounter, then, but more precisely in the anticipatory temporalities that precede the cathartic release. I linger in their temporalities and trace their emplotments in these revolutionary imaginings to open up their peculiar historical registers and imaginaries of revolution. In this sense, this project carries important resonances with the Marxist historiographers of subaltern studies. Gyanendra Pandey asks how we can write the histories of those who inhabit the realm of "unreason"—the unarchivable underbelly of reasoned and state history: "When and how do we archive the body as a register of events; or gestures, pauses, gut-reactions; or deep-rooted feelings of ecstasy, humiliation, pain?" (7). The tiny somatic arousals I mine in this study are inflected by a Marxist preoccupation with the materiality of the colonized body in relation to colonial modes of production and exploitation: how we labor on and in bodily and environmental matter; how we shape, consume, and exploit it in conjunction with the social and economic structures through which the everyday conditions of colonial modernity are produced and reproduced.

My readings of the visceral linger on a strange narrative immersion in the materiality of these mundane details—details that render the intended narratives of these texts unfamiliar and strange. While motivating the revolutionary arcs (or social realist trajectories) of these novels, the visceral emplotments I draw out also rupture and refuse the traditional trajectories of the "national realist" narratives—they queer or disorient the national frame of the novel form. I trace these unruly visceral plots for how they consistently refuse and derail the normative fantasies and frameworks that stabilize national discourses, mobilizing what Ann Cvetkovich has described as an immersive reading that focuses "the sensation and feeling as the register of historical experience" (*Depression*, 11). This involves a crucial "slowing down," as Cvetkovich emphasizes, "so as to be able to immerse [oneself] in detail ... turning the ordinary into scenes of surprise" (*Depression*, 11). Tiny corporeal details estrange the intended frame, much like the Barthesian "punctum" or, perhaps, like Arundhati Roy's millipede, curled up in the heel of the boot as the boot, crashing down on the skull of the untouchable character, appeases the god of Big Things and effaces the impossibilities of History.

The instability intrinsic in the visceral, both corporeal and temporal, orchestrates scenes of visceral crises that organize the political inquiries of these chapters. These crises, states of what Lauren Berlant and Ann Cvetkovich might term affective "impasses," are both the lubricants of and threats to the very possibility of revolution (*Depression*, 20). The scenes of crises rupture and remap the nationalist politics of these texts in important ways, forming a second conceptual arc of the book. If Spinozan bodies are distinguished by their affects in relations of motion and rest, speed and slowness, the visceral activates relations of energetic buildup and accumulation and, eventually and inevitably, its affective release. Convulsion, a visceral logic of the politically agitated subject, presents us with crises of the reflex inscribed within a problematic of affective momentum. Scenes of historical crises—of reflex and trigger, of bodily suspension and momentum—cluster around the explosive release of revolutionary affect. These corporeal and historical contradictions, for example, underwrite the paired Fanonian figurations of laughter and nausea with which I began, figures for the crises of momentum and suspension. Against a linear, "empty and homogenous" rationalist historical teleology, the visceral in these novels inhabits a full, disruptive, and erratic temporality (Benjamin and Arendt, 261).

Crises of convulsion underscore how the vitality and contagion of the somatic unconscious orchestrates a political dynamic that does not predictably correspond to conscious action or will and thus "dislocate[s] agency as the property of a discrete, self-knowing subject," in the words of Diane Coole and Samantha Frost (20). By focusing on the spasmodic logics of the politically agitated subject, these scenes often feature visceral states and feelings that move the body to such extreme heights of stimulation that it is caught by the recursive movements of its compulsion or muscular spasms—a series of bodily suspensions that disrupt and dislocate the progressive movement, the utopic ascension, of the revolutionary subject. This dynamic somatic threshold appears between that which moves the body and that which crosses over to such intensity that the subject is conversely immobilized, convulsing—whether in a state of rage, terror, or grief or in the throes of ecstatic pleasure. These corporeal states and thresholds bring into focus a series of problematics of human agency and historical determinism that are intrinsic to the ecstatic logics of (de)colonization and nationalism.

While convulsion is a kind of visceral momentum that stages a loss of control over the reflexes of one's own body, nausea is the figure par excellence of another visceral (historical) crisis. The trope of nausea is a figure for a thwarted or "suspended" state of agency, a tense but stalled energetic state, that reoccurs throughout the chapters of this book, albeit in a surprising variety of permutations (Ngai, 1). While convulsion is a body logic of momentum, nausea is inscribed within a temporality of suspension: the frustrated desire for a cathartic release. And while convulsion is a figure for the problem of the vitality and volatility of the somatic reflex, nausea stages a crisis of the trigger. In the Fanonian train scene, the failure of laughter is a failure to access the trigger that would set off the bodily response. While laughter is a physiological response, it is dependent on a psychic trigger; the psychological block is the condition of colonial discourse for Fanon. It is in this sense that nausea emerges as a figure for the crisis of colonial consciousness, housed in the thwarted access to the visceral response (and release).

Nausea reappears in this study to continually remind us that the visceral is as much about the semantic refusals of the body as it is about its diagnostic promise. These racialized renderings of nausea replace the more abstracted Sartrean figure of existential nausea with a deeply embodied and often biomedical representation of the colonial subject's struggle with the automatized reflexes of the body, reflexes that fashion taste and desire. With nausea, whether focused through the mimetic contractions of the bowels in witnessing another's disgust or through the subject's fear (desire) of proximity and intimacy with the object of repulsion, we find that this trope becomes the sign of an agonized anticipation. Scenes of nausea focalize the involuntary reflexes of a body that refuses to comply with the will: the anxious search for the body's psychosomatic triggers. When linked to its biomedical conception, nausea will also bring us to the disorientation of the colonial subject—the loss of balance, orientation, proprioception—vertigo.

The visceral (as with nausea) layers and refracts the material and metaphorical semiotics of the body at once. The aesthetics of bodily knowledge refract and unravel in unexpected ways. In fact, the unruliness of the body in language becomes a crucial site of precarity, but it also opens the possibility of feeling new feelings—located in the gaps between sensation and language.

The energetic force of these visceral eruptions carries an unmistakable likeness to such Spinozan theories of affect as energy, intensity, and the capacity to move and be moved. Spinoza's monism famously challenged Cartesian and idealist distinctions between mind and body and human and nonhuman matter, which positioned matter as inert and human consciousness as the sole site of agency and knowledge of the self and nature. A recent return to Spinozist philosophy in the humanities restores an understanding of the energetic life of the body. Indeed, the anticolonial archive of the Progressives anticipates some of the "new" materialist trends in theorizing affect and corporeal materiality. Drawing materialism to the fore within the Progressive Writers' archive, I show how the aesthetics of decolonization and political transformation center the "vitality" of visceral matter as volatile, lively, productive, and self-organizing, independent of the mind's capacity to act on it (Coole and Frost, 20).

While the visceral's volatility and energetic behavior, as well as its centering of bodily actions and reactions, are key components of Spinoza's monism, particularly as invoked by the Deleuzian poetics of affect, I diverge from the Spinozist notion of affect as prelinguistic, outside of language and subjective experience—a "suspension" of meaning. For the Progressives, the visceral explores the relations between habits of feeling and habits of thought and discourse. I share Kyla Wazana Tompkins's concern about the inability of much of new materialism to address the legacies of colonialism. Like many working in materialisms at the intersections of postcolonial, critical race, and Marxist theory, I understand the relationship between "discursivity and materiality [as] circular and, in Karen Barad's terms, intra-active" (Tompkins, "On the Limits," 1). I join critical race and postcolonial scholars in situating the new materialism as one of many philosophical traditions and cosmologies that are grappling with the "animacy" of matter, to draw from Mel Chen, always inscribed in relations of power, and the "'thingness' of the human," viewing the circulations and exchanges of consciousness, feeling, and the energy of human bodies as "shared social phenomena as they rise out of the substance of the world" (*Animacies*; Tompkins, "On the Limits," 1).

How do we study affect in a way that is attentive to geopolitical difference? It is with this problematic in view that the visceral moves between theory for decolonization writ large, and the sociopolitical particularities of affective forms. Each chapter sheds light on a different dimension of the visceral as it emerges out of revolutionary political thought—its dynamics of affective release and transfer, for example, crises of the reflex and trigger, problematics of touch and texture, proximity, intimacy. These problematics are explored here through sociopolitical loci specific to the South Asian context, such as caste, gender, and religion, through which each affective form is excavated and theorized. Most prominently, the visceral—as an optic of contemporary postcolonial violence and trauma—emerges largely out of the prophetic visions of the Muslim intelligentsia. The visceral forms in this book are also powerful insights into the structures of feeling of what Mufti has termed the "minoritization" of the Muslim in India and the "crises" of modern secularism in Indian postcolonial society (2).

The study of racialized sensibilities through the lens of their visceral logics attunes us to the specific geohistories that produce their affective forms in gendered sensibilities. The range of visceral logics themselves—appetite and aversion, musculature and ecstatic excitation, longing and melancholy, touch and erotic texture—index very particular geohistories of colonial racial formation. They emerge out of an array of colonial and pre- and postcolonial institutions, from colonial regimes of hygiene and taste (desire and disgust), colonial experiments in medicine and gynecology (female bodily texture), Brahmanical codes of purity and pollution (touch and tactility), and the politicizing of Islamic spiritual practices under erasure by Hindu majoritarianism (ecstasy). These historical conjunctures reveal a very different history of racialization from the one theorized, for example, by the visceral logics of "epidermalization" in Fanon's canonical theories of black ontological crises. I point to these divergent geohistories to emphasize the visceral's utility in thinking across archives of racial and gender formation rather than to make the case for the irreducible particularity of the Indian context. Ania Loomba argues that the conflation of race with color or "biology" has created a false division between "scientific" (racial) and religious or cultural forms of discrimination, including caste and communal difference in India: "The histories of anti-Semitism, Islamophobia, and caste-prejudice cannot then be fully connected to those of slavery, bonded labor, plantation labor, and color prejudice" (516). Attending to the somato-poetics of race connects without conflating imbricated global histories of colonial oppression. As Loomba writes, "Thinking across periods, and across regions, allows us to understand better why colonial race ideologies took the forms they did, and how they drew from other forms of oppression globally" (516).

Each distinct somatic logic in this book—agitation, irritation, compulsion, evisceration, explosion—animates a range of dense entanglements between gender sensibilities and racialized consciousness. In this study, I show how decolonization, as a transformation of racialized consciousness, is always contingent on the radical reconstitution of normative gendered subjectivities precisely because gender provided the grounds of colonial subjection through corporeal refashioning. Visceral regimes of gender (re)fashioning in "taste" and sensibility are produced out of, and therefore inextricable from, colonial and postcolonial regimes of racialization. The writers I examine in this study use the bildungsroman form, for example, to chart the psychosexual development of a range of subjects under the violent processes of gendered discipline (heavily influenced by the writings of Freud) under both the colonial civilizing mission and the imperatives placed on the citizen subject by a nascent nationalism. The visceral aesthetics of the Progressive Writers emerge from their sustained preoccupation with gendered processes of affective and corporeal fashioning in their fiction— the conjugations of physiology with epistemology, of "soul making and body shaping" (to borrow from Roy), through which racialized habits of thought and feeling sediment in gendered sensibility and comportment, and thus provides the site of their revolutionary undoing.

It is in this sense that this book charts an alternative feminist genealogy of viscerality that counters Fanon's canonical writings on colonial affect that locate the pathology of blackness in emasculation (or what he terms "castration") as defined by normative gender binaries. In contrast, studying progressive aesthetics through the lens of the visceral lays out theories of decolonization as fundamentally linked to a transformation of normative gender subjectivities. The diverse ways in which gender epistemologies of the visceral sediment, reconstitute, or disrupt racialized consciousness in somatic response is precisely what is at stake in the visceral inquiries across chapters. For example, inquiries into nationalist ecstasy in Abbas's *Inquilab* reveal the reimagining of normative patriarchal masculinities produced out of experiences of colonial violence in what I term "ecstatic terror." Related questions of revolutionary rage in Anand's *Untouchable* work through an aestheticized (and eroticized) hypermasculinity to overturn the abjection of caste. In chapter 3, "disgusting" female bodily textures set off femme cravings that explore the undoing of lessons in proper femininity at the places where colonial and nationalist regimes of obscenity give way to women's erotic desire, as Ismat Chughtai and Rashid Jahan explicitly expose and challenge the masculinist assumptions of their male comrades.

Decolonization is thus necessarily grounded in disruptive formations of gender and sexuality, whether in the unruliness of women's desire that refuses normative gendered regimes of propriety and "taste" or (to borrow from Edward Said) in masculine affiliations that refuse patriarchal inheritance (*The World, the Text, and the Critic*, 23). In fact, the historical protagonists of PWA novels are often figures that disrupt or pervert normative patriarchal logics. Figures of familial illegitimacy such as the prostitute, the bastard, and the orphan disrupt the filial attachments organized by the nation.[17] Some of the most insightful scholarship on the sensorial investment of the Progressives emphasizes their gendered critiques of national belonging and filiation. For example, Gayatri Gopinath explores forms of queer desire that disrupt national configurations of femininity that refuse sedimentations into fixed identities in the writings of Chughtai, while Gopal charts the "reconstitution of bodily being" and the making of the modern gendered "habitus" in the writings of Jahan and Chughtai (*Literary Radicalism in India*, 54). Mufti reads the gendered figure of the prostitute in Saadat Hasan Manto's Urdu short stories as a reworking of the classical trope of the *tavaif* or courtesan that disrupts and perverts the filial organization of affect and attachment demanded by the (Hindu) nation (as mother) and thus as a figure for the crises of secular modernity and the minoritization of Muslims in India. Building on these insights but also reorienting our critical gaze to their somato-poetics, I propose that the Progressive Writers do something quite remarkable with the very category of gender in locating colonial discipline in somatic response, at the embodied sites where the innate and intuitive are subjected to the social. These novels furnish new ways to understand the complex processes through which racialized sensibilities develop through physiological reflex.

The Somatic Unconscious

The visceral repositions our approach to the scene and study of affect by centering its dynamics of affective release and transmission, which is also to say, the somatic life of the body. As Parama Roy writes, "Colonial politics often spoke in an indisputably visceral tongue.... [T]he stomach served as a kind of *somatic political unconscious* in which the phantasmagoria of colonialism came to be embodied" (*Alimentary Tracts*, 7, emphasis added). Borrowing from and extending Roy's provocative term beyond the "gastropoetic" valences of the visceral to a range of sensory realms, I refocus our inquiries into the colonized subject in this book from the psychoanalytic unconscious to the "somatic unconscious."[18]

Whether it is the heat of anger, the pull of the erotic, or the spasms of ecstasy, the visceral locates the vitality of bodily matter in the somatic response. Taking the somatic as our point of entry into the study of colonial affect, rather than the other way around, the visceral inquiries of this study take seriously Roy's provocative charge that the violence of colonization involved the "somatizing" of subjects, invoking the trafficking in the life of the mind and the life of the bodily, culture and biology, "epistemology and physiology" (*Alimentary Tracts*, 7). This materialist understanding of the radical reshaping and reconstitution of bodily life that characterizes the colonial project remains central to this study of colonial affect and the possibilities of its transformation.

The nondualistic understanding of the complex and dynamic relationship between the social and biological developed by feminist and race scholars working in food studies is something I seek to bring to our studies of colonial affect and the biopolitics of empire. Working at the intersections of food studies and postcolonial and critical race studies, Parama Roy's *Alimentary Tracts* and Kyla Tompkins's *Racial Indigestion* provide important supplements and provocations to Stoler, and these thinkers remain critical interlocutors for theorizing the visceral logics of colonialism. While Stoler locates the workings of colonial power in the ordering and reordering of intimate spaces to explore how the macropolitics of imperialism play out in the microeconomies of the everyday, Roy's and Tompkins's feminist work on the racial and colonial politics of appetite and aversion allows us to read the ordering and disordering of visceral logics: the "imaginative shaping of the matter we experience as body and self," to borrow from Tompkins, "fus[es] biology and culture" (*Racial Indigestion*, 1).[19]

Attending to the somatic life of the colonized subject, however, entails a reorientation to dominant imaginaries of the body. Taking seriously the visceral logics of subjugation that are so central to this materialist tradition of thinking decolonization places a certain ontological pressure on much of our body theory. The somatic is not simply inert bodily matter, merely expressive of affective or psychic stimulus, but, rather, an agent within the energetic life of the somatic unconscious, always already inscribed within a relation of power. The somatic, as vibrant matter, is brought into focus in these texts as self-organizing, unpredictable, and volatile, refusing causality between either the mind's instrumentalization of the somatic (the psychosomatic) or, conversely, the somatic's animation of psychic life.[20]

What distinguishes my reading of the Progressive Writers is what I distill from their sensory aesthetics, what I call the "somatic vitality" of the visceral response. Scenes of somatic vitality expose decolonization—the transformation of racialized consciousness—as inextricable from the disruptive and nonnormative forms of gender and sexuality precisely because it is where visceral logics misbehave (where the vitality of the somatic unconscious is most vividly at work) that the possibilities of decolonization are imagined.

In emphasizing the "somatic vitality" of the visceral, the book makes a key postcolonial contribution to feminist and queer theory. Scholars such as Eve Sedgwick, Elizabeth Wilson, and Rachel Lee argue for the necessity of more nuanced and sophisticated models of the biological in feminist accounts of embodiment and affect, against the "anti-biologism" of feminist theories that equate biology with gendered essentialisms. The somato-poetics of the Progressive Writers highlight the colonial context as a crucial testing ground for visceral regimes of modern gender subjection, instrumentalized in the name of civilizational and racial difference (the "making of heathens into human"). Within these theories of the visceral the somatic reflex does not merely express the "inward" activities of racialized and gendered thought and feeling, but has a much more dynamic and dialectic relationship with them. Drawing on an array of Asian American artists, Rachel Lee centers the fragmentation and disaggregation of the biological body into a vital "ecology" of parts and processes under racial capitalism, a rich reworking of biopolitics for a postcolonial and critical race (particularly Asian Americanist) critique, but one that also explores the creative energy of biological matter and processes without seeking to restore the racialized subject to a fictive state of wholeness or integrity. Lee writes, "Recognizing the distributed agencies of body parts represents a mode of inquiry attuned to a more complex, networked notion of bodily intelligences" (25). As Lee notes, drawing on Wilson's *Gut Feminism,* Wilson challenges "the false divide" in trauma theory and psychoanalysis "of the separation and hierarchy of psychic over somatic phenomenon." The visceral poetics of the Progressive Writers emerging in the moments of decolonization in India reveal a suggestive resonance with Wilson and Lee, writing in the contemporary field of feminist technoscience in the American context. In one of the most counterintuitive emplotments of the visceral within this study, for example, we will find a set of inquiries into the somatic unconscious of the subject by turning to logics of touch and tactility. What does it mean to understand touch, a logic of skin and surface, as visceral, imagined to reside within the deepest of bodily depths? In the writing of Anand, the visceral will force us to approach the epidermal arousal of the casteized and racialized subject, not as inert matter, motivated by sensations "beneath" the dead skin, but involving the very arousals and awakenings at the level of skin as the revolutionary impetus. The untouchable subject comes alive to his own tactility.

I rework visceral touch through a feminist lens that theorizes queer erotic bodily texture in the writings of Rashid Jahan and her student, Ismat Chughtai. I consider how female bodily texture activates and animates bodily appetites, both gastronomic and erotic, which becomes key to excavating disgust as a powerful aversive reflex that secures moralizing regimes through the cultivation of taste, hygiene, and propriety. Both touch and texture rely on the confusion and doubled invocation of metaphor and materiality, what Steven Connor calls the "sign and stuff" of our "material imagination" (40). The very possibilities of the feeling of new feelings, in fact, in making the body "mean" differently, are housed in the semantic splintering of the visceral. Touch and texture impel a gendered reconstitution of the sensorial and affective nodes of the racialized body within the epistemic overhaul of the imaginary, a reconstitution that includes the disorganization of the metaphorical and material registers of the body.

These readings are enabled by the range of documents and artistic experiments that I include, through which the visceral becomes readable as a crucial node of Marxist aesthetics and politics. The minute somatic details I examine in the novels of these chapters become legible in their poetic and historical registers only by reading the full corpus of each author's oeuvre, juxtaposing less well-known writings with the most acclaimed fiction, opening these authors up to new understandings of their political visions. Their visceral figures are set into relief by a rich array of archival materials and artistic experiments, including manifestos, pamphlets, public lectures, personal letters, memoirs, and journalistic writings, as well as indigenous performance genres, radio plays, and popular films. The full range of these artistic forms makes possible readings of the fiction that take seriously the experimentation of their artistic endeavors, as well as their collaborative modes—how, in other words, these artists were thinking through and against one another.

Overview of the Book

The chapters of the book are organized by distinct visceral logics through which the revolutionary subject is imagined to be liberated within this cluster of Marxist literature. Each visceral preoccupation indexes the way it has been conceptualized through and against the energetic and affective forms of the others. By mining the corporeal imaginaries of these anticolonial works, each chapter leads us through various dimensions and visceral crises of the revolutionary problematic: what would it mean to decolonize when the racialized sensibilities of the postcolonial subject are so deeply automatized in the visceral responses of the body?

Chapter 1, "Agitation," contemplates the place of ecstasy and political euphoria in impelling the momentum and contagion of mass revolutionary emotion. By centering the convulsive logics of the political agitator, the chapter explores the double-edged character of affective transmission and corporeal manipulation, which is characteristic of visceral affect and its inevitable release. Positioned at the moments in which national euphoria begins to dissolve into communal violence in India, the chapter recalls familiar images of the masses caught under the spell of a revolutionary emotionalism—a collective longing and anticipation that recalls progressive political protests and rallies, as it does the threat of fascism. The specter of fascism that haunts the imaginaries of nationalist emotion is a master plot across the book's chapters. Tracking the cinematic and literary aesthetics of Khwaja Ahmad Abbas, most famous for his neorealist collaborations between the Bombay popular film industry and the state-sponsored film industry of Russia in the 1950s and '60s, the chapter probes Abbas's grappling with the relationship between nationalist and religious ecstasy.

Chapter 2, "Irritation," asks the questions at the heart of this project: what would it mean to feel new feelings when one's complicity with the colonial regime of thought has become naturalized in the automatized reflexes of the body? The chapter takes up this question surrounding the possibilities of transformative emotion and the revolutionary stimulant through the fiction of the anticolonial activist and author Mulk Raj Anand.

Whereas chapter 1 follows the political agitator to theorize the possibilities and pitfalls of nationalist ecstasy, the revolutionary subject of chapter 2 is an irritated one. The chapter centers the poetics of touch and feeling at the embodied interface between the surface and depths of the "untouchable" class. I focus on Anand's experiments in the poetics of touch and feeling in his famous social realist novel *Untouchable*, written in English and published in 1935 with the help of the Bloomsbury modernists Virginia and Leonard Woolf. "Irritation" in this chapter mobilizes its double meaning at the surface and depths of the revolutionary subject. Connoting a mild abrasion of the skin, as well as a slight or undeveloped anger, "irritation" conjugates the tactility of the skin, the site of both racial and caste oppression for Anand's subaltern subject, with the internal engine of a revolutionary rage—the "latent heat" of the revolutionary subject of India.

Chapter 3, "Compulsion," complicates the energetic trajectory of the previous chapters by underscoring the dialectic of attraction and repulsion that underwrites the visceral and its role in the production of colonial affect. While in the previous chapters the visceral stimulants of political rage and nationalist emotion are invested with the potential to energize the colonial subject to various states of consciousness and political action, disgust is a peculiar energetic within this context. The phenomenology of disgust in this study is theorized through its relationship with its dialectical other, desire. Disgust and desire, as energetic forces of repulsion and attraction, return us to the crises of the reflex and trigger. The question of how the body is "moved" viscerally in this chapter raises the additional question of how texture animates and activates bodily appetites, both sexual and gastronomic, through the compulsive figure of craving. Drawing on the socialist feminist writings of Rashid Jahan and her student, Ismat Chughtai, I offer a queer feminist critique of the traditional phenomenology of disgust by analyzing the codes of erotic texture produced out of histories of colonial hygiene and bourgeois sexual discipline in late colonial India. Both women were known for their incendiary gender critiques of both colonialism and the Indian Muslim orthodoxy, and Chughtai is now perhaps better known for the obscenity charges waged against her by the colonial government for the homoerotic content of her literature. Their femme figures of craving bring us to the instability and unruliness of the visceral energetic in this chapter; however, it is also from within the push and pull of the dialectic that these feminist writers locate the possibility of progressive feeling in the very affects harnessed by violent disciplinary regimes of taste and propriety. "Compulsion" is a materialist exploration into how the female body—her erotic curvatures and grotesque protuberances, her sticky and viscous textures and fluids—become the focalized object of what I term the "erotics of colonial disgust."

In the early chapters of the book I trace a range of experiments in imagining the visceral subject, thought experiments that probe the emotive dimensions of decolonization. Chapter 4, "Evisceration," is about the erasure of the visceral, a flattening of affect through which the pitfalls of nationalist emotion, the fear of fascism, are represented and theorized. The novels of the Muslim internationalist author Ahmed Ali unsettle the Marxist teleology that structures the social realist novel form and perform a self-conscious rewriting and inversion of the visceral tropes we have explored thus far. With this rewriting, Ali's novels issue a prophetic warning against the forms of violent nationalism that were emerging out of the emotive genres of decolonization. Chapter 4 thus takes up the visceral as a logic of time, inextricable from the historical genres deployed in these anticolonial imaginings. Ali's novels replace and displace the visceral energetics of the previous chapters, which "move" and vitalize the body through a transformation of consciousness. In this way, they provide a self-conscious political critique that brings "the crises" of the potential Muslim citizen subject of India into view (Mufti, 2).[21] I propose we read this flattening of the visceral as an aesthetics of evisceration—holding in tension the double valence of the term: to disembowel and deprive of essential meaning or vital content.

I close with Fanon and his canonical writings on decolonization in a coda that articulates a foundational premise of the book: anticolonial writing demands that we understand the visceral dimensions of consciousness to be underwritten not only by racialized feeling, but also by a Marxist historical temporality, wherein the contradictions of colonial and postcolonial modernity are most violently at play. "Explosion" concludes with a call to think Marxist *history as visceral logic*, retracing my theories of the visceral energetic through the question of historical temporality. Meditating on a constellation of explosive bodily figures that appear throughout the anticolonial writings of Fanon—laughter, nausea, vomiting, shivering, ejaculation—I posit the visceral as a critical theory for Marxian revolutionary consciousness and liberation.

1. Agitation

Days after India gains independence, the internationalist journalist and filmmaker Khwaja Ahmad Abbas publishes an entry in his weekly column in *Blitz Magazine* titled "Letter to a Child Born on August 15, 1947." Written as a letter addressed to India's "midnight's children," Abbas's piece reflects on the difficulty and even impossibility of conveying the emotional experience of this historical moment and projecting it into the future for the next generation of Indians born into freedom. "You will learn the historical significance of this date," Abbas writes, "but it is improbable that the spirit of this day ... , its tempo and tempestuous pageantry, can ever be fully conveyed to you" (*Bread, Beauty, and Revolution*, 3). As Abbas reflects on his incapacity to capture "the spirit" of this historical moment, it is both the feeling of this moment and the feeling of its progressive momentum that defy representation in language. He writes:

> August 15, 1947: How is one to describe the mood of a day that was not a day but the concentrated essence of what a whole people have worked for and fought for and yearned for and prayed for in the course of centuries? How is one to analyze the emotional complex formed out of the hopes

and aspirations and yearning—and may one add, the frustrations?—of a whole nation? (*Bread, Beauty, and Revolution*, 3)

The moment of radical rupture here is conceived of as emerging from the collective yearnings and longings of the colonized people, as Abbas stages his struggle to capture in writing the distinct contours of this "emotional complex" that brings the Indian nation into being. The moment of independence for Abbas as a punctuated and precise unit of history here is not so much a temporal unit or measure—*a day that was not a day*—as some other kind of experiential category altogether, born out of the collective emotive energy of the formerly colonized nation. The saturation of these collective emotions, these anticipatory affects inscribed within the immanent temporality of the nation, are configured here as the very force that impels or wills the nation into being. Abbas renders the collective yearning of the nation as an explosive historical energy, inscribed within the surging rhythms—the tempo and temporality—of the emergent nation: "Here was the biggest news of our times, but it could only be covered with clichés.... The reporter could reduce to writing the surging mass emotion of August 15 no more successfully than you can bottle a typhoon or enclose a volcanic eruption" (*Bread, Beauty, and Revolution*, 3). Here, within Abbas's writing, this force is conceived of as the radical drive of a revolutionary History.

This chapter begins the visceral inquiries of this book by exploring the form and phenomenology of this explosive collective expression of nationalist emotion as it emerges in the struggles for decolonization. I open with this passage taken from the news archives of a newly born India, but the phenomenon it describes is now a familiar trope of the historical moments of decolonization within a transnational postcolonial imaginary. This vision of the colonized masses synchronized under the spell of a heightened patriotism is ingrained in our nationalist memories and mythologies of decolonization and continues to inflect our imaginings of political transformation and activism. As our contemporary historical present is increasingly defined by the global rise of militant ethnonationalism, I ask in this chapter, how are we to understand the visceral contours of this heightened nationalist devotion, whether it is celebrated as the collective force of a revolutionary history or feared for an explosive emotionalism that may too easily slide into a regime of fascism and fanaticism? What is the nature of this collective longing and desire—what Abbas calls the "emotional complex" through which the nation is imagined to be born?

Tracking the cinematic and literary aesthetics of the Indo-Soviet filmmaker and journalist Khwaja Ahmad Abbas, this case study probes Abbas's grappling with the relationship between nationalist and religious ecstasy. This chapter recalls familiar images of the masses caught under the spell of a patriotic emotionalism, an image that recalls the promise of social transformation as well as the threat of fascism. I explore how the visceral may open up the affective forms of this nationalist longing and patriotic emotionalism. Abbas's inquiries into the nature of revolutionary affect brings us to a set of inquiries surrounding what it means to be moved to political action, rendered through a series of ecstatic political subjects in the postindependence moments in which national euphoria begins to dissolve into communal violence. This visceral preoccupation is underwritten, I argue, by an aesthetics of political agitation.

As Sianne Ngai writes, in its connotations of emotive disturbance or disruption, or even of a vigorous shaking, the affect of agitation "underlies the contemporary meaning of the political agitator or activist," one who rouses the crowd, seeks to "stir" or "shake" public opinion to political action, while classic understandings of agitation are "used in the philosophical discourse of emotions to designate feeling prior to its articulation into a more complex passion" (31). My inquiries into the poetics of progressive feeling in Abbas's artistic experiments take us to a series of bodies in a range of agitated states: convulsing, seizing, vibrating bodies; bodies caught in spasms, as a body is moved when subjected to an electric "shock." The agitated subjects of this chapter take us to a vital threshold between a stimulant that moves a body to political action, on the one hand, and an excessive excitation that renders the body, paradoxically, immobile, suspended in convulsions, on the other. By focusing on the figure of the political agitator, and the affects of political agitation, I explore the revolutionary possibilities and dangers imbued in the contagion of ecstasy. This approach allows us to revise Anderson's notion of the nationalist experience of "simultaneity" as I work it through psychoanalytic film theory on the spectacle and contagion of the body in ecstasy.

To make sense of the contemporary iterations of anticolonial nationalism, the emotive forms we have inherited from the moments of decolonization, we must find ways to understand their ecstatic expressions. In this chapter, I argue that we must understand this "emotional complex," an experience of nationalist synchronicity that Benedict Anderson has theorized as a "simultaneity" so central to anticolonial nationalism, as one that is conjured not simply through a collective experience of time—here a time of yearning and hope—but through a collective experience critically mediated by what Linda Williams terms "ecstatic excess" (149). In what follows, I interrogate the euphoric dimensions of this mass mobilization of nationalist feeling and devotion. I think with Abbas as he contemplates the place of ecstasy in impelling the momentum of revolution.

In centering political agitation, we locate the visceral unconscious in the quivering muscles of the ecstatic subject. The ecstatic body, Williams reminds us, is both moved and moving. Focusing the tensed musculature of the politically agitated or revolutionary subject, we will find, is to bring to focus the unruly and erratic dimensions of affective release and contagion characteristic of the visceral, as well as its logic of prolonged and frustrated release. This becomes indispensable to the vision of decolonization that I elaborate in the chapters that follow. Foregrounding the visceral as a distinct structure of feeling and historical time within Marxian theories of revolutionary consciousness, I conclude the chapter by returning to the famous revolutionary writings of Frantz Fanon in *The Wretched of the Earth* and centering the place of the ecstatic body in Abbas's and Fanon's theories of national revolution. Agitation, as a visceral logic of decolonization, interanimates the ecstasy of longing with the ecstatic terror of anticolonial violence.

Nationalist Ecstasy

As a dedicated socialist author, journalist, and lawyer and a renowned film director, Abbas was one of the most prolific and versatile members of Muslim internationalist artist circles in India. As Priyamvada Gopal writes of Abbas, "In some ways, he was the quintessential translator, translating his work and the work of other authors into English or Hindi, turning his fiction and that of others into films, making English novels out of his Hindi screenplays, and interpreting films for the general public in his capacity as a film critic" (*Literary Radicalism in India*, 128). From adapting socialist literature to the local stage or the international screen to his trilingual weekly column in *Blitz* (published in Urdu, Hindi, and English), Abbas experimented with a vast array of artistic media to reach a mass audience. Abbas was a founding member of the Indian People's Theater Association in 1942 and was able to reach a broader audience in the face of a 10 percent literacy rate in India by politicizing indigenous performance practices, staging plays, and eventually adapting the Progressive Writers' Association's literature to radio and to the Bombay commercial film industry (Gopal, *Literary Radicalism in India*, 2005, 123–24). Abbas also traveled extensively throughout the United States, writing both fiction and journalistic pieces about the place of American race politics in thinking through questions of decolonization and revolutionary action in India. As is evident in his autobiographical writings, Abbas was particularly interested in the relationship between institutions of caste in India and ideologies of race in the United States, and, further, the logics of heredity that lock both of these ideological structures into place. For Abbas, the politics of antiracist struggle and socialist activism figured prominently in his vision of the global struggle against empire and fascism. Above all, Abbas is perhaps most famous for his neorealist film collaborations between the Bombay popular film industry and the state sponsored film industry of Russia in the 1950s and '60s.

While Abbas found international success working in the Bombay film industry, he is not known for his literature. In fact, despite the fact that Abbas was a prolific writer of social realist fiction, his literary experiments in English have been characterized as awkward, clichéd, and overly didactic. Gopal describes Abbas's fiction in English as "stylistically flawed and dogged by inelegant and didactic political diatribes" (*Literary Radicalism in India*, 128). My interest in Abbas's literary experiments, however, is in how the often clichéd and didactic style of Abbas's social realist novel is opened up by his cinematic aesthetics in his visceral portrayals. More precisely, my interest lies in how his peculiar aesthetic hybrid of a popular melodramatic film aesthetic and socialist realist literary one is mobilized in the moments when Abbas attempts to render the transformations of consciousness of his revolutionary subject. Thus, while the social realist novel I examine in this chapter has received nearly no scholarly attention or literary interest, I recuperate Abbas's novel not only to mine its visceral logics but for how its visceral emplotments move against the grain of the nationalist (and "national realist") framing of the text (Mufti, 183). As Lisa Lowe writes, attention to the literary form of liberal genres, as well as their "narrative contradictions and contesting voices, suggests methods for reading subjugated histories" (47). Similarly, I am interested in the formal "tensions and inconsistencies" that arise within this postcolonial genre of liberation and national freedom, the narrative forms and historical emplotments of what David Scott terms the "modern longing for complete revolution" (6).

Abbas's novel *Inquilab* (Revolution), which provides the focus for this chapter, was written in English in 1955 and quickly translated into numerous Slavic languages in the Soviet Union. Abbas aligned his literature with an emerging group of Indian authors writing in English and experimenting with social realism, most notably Mulk Raj Anand—"the harbinger of social realism in India" in Abbas's own words ("Social Realism and Change," 147). *Inquilab* follows the development of an eight-year-old boy, Anwar Ali, whose transition into adolescence is charted against a now-mythologized national narrative of India's struggle for independence. Key historical events within popular national narratives, such as the Jallianwallah Bagh Massacre and the Gandhian protests, are narrated through Anwar's experience. In fact, Anwar is positioned as an eyewitness to these large-scale historical events, whether dodging bullets from British soldiers, discussing politics with figures like Gandhi and Nehru, or listening in on informal gossip circles at his neighbor's home or in college dormitory rooms, where the politics of these events are being debated. The novel tells this story of the nation through Anwar's eyes as he claims and redefines a budding masculnity as a new national subject. Like all of Abbas's most famous filmic plotlines, the story of *Inquilab* utilizes the figure of the "bastard" (*haramzaada*) in order to dismantle the logics of heredity that structure ideologies of class, caste, and religion in the postindependence moments in India.

As the plot of *Inquilab* unfolds through an elaborate Bollywood-style series of twists and turns, we find out that while Anwar (and the reader) have been led to believe that he is the son of Akbar Ali, a Muslim businessman, he turns out to be the illegitimate child of Akbar's Hindu business partner and a local courtesan. The strategic naming of Anwar as a haramzaada, or bastard, in the novel becomes pivotal to its critique of the familial fantasies that come to structure sensibilities of national belonging. Furthermore, the illegitimacy of Anwar's birth yokes together the "communal" logics of the family with the religious antagonisms that threatened the unity of the nation at this critical historical juncture. The utopian ending of Abbas's *Inquilab* positions the very possibility of radical new citizen subjectivities within the illegitimate body of Anwar, as he is able to transcend the gendered logics of paternity and heredity, as well as of religious identity, that threaten the new nation.

The narrative arc of *Inquilab* is plotted through a sequence of historical events through which the nationalist movement gains momentum. The emergence of the Indian nation is staged through a series of internal transformations that Anwar undergoes in the course of his politicization, one that leads him to become an active participant in the struggle for national independence. As *Inquilab* charts the buildup and eventual triumph of the nationalist resistance movement in India, the novel tracks the mounting fervor of the nation and its capacity to mobilize and manipulate mass affect. Abbas strains to captures in a social realist mode, the collective yearning and desire that is depicted as eventually bringing the nation into being. For example, Anwar's first experience of participating in the resistance movement centers on the emotional intensity he experiences among the sea of people gathered around him and echoing the revolutionary call:

> For the first time Anwar tasted the thrill of uttering those magic words—*Inquilab Zindabad* [Long live the revolution]—that seemed to stir everyone in the crowd to the very core of his being. Lost in the crowd, a drop in the ocean of humanity, merging his individuality in the mass, compelled by collective emotions, Anwar felt a strange transformation within him. (Abbas, *Inquilab*, 83)

The emotional transformation that Anwar undergoes in this moment is impelled from the power of the masses chanting in unison. This scene recalls Anderson's articulation of the "the experience of simultaneity" that emerges from the collective chanting of the Pledge of Allegiance or the singing of patriotic songs, which concretizes the "imagined community" as "people wholly unknown to each other" feel that they inhabit the same homogeneous temporal moment (149).[1] Within Abbas's renderings of these mass protests, the power of the collective voice of the crowd appears to act as a narcotic of sorts. "The very repetition of the two words," the narrator tells us, "seemed to act as a stimulant" (*Inquilab*, 37). What is it about these collective chants that produces this experience of simultaneity? What is it about the repetition of the revolutionary call that brings about such an intensity of collective emotion, Abbas seems to ask, and what is the nature of this peculiar *stimulant*?

The following discussion centers on two key scenes of emotive transformation that take place within the novel's revolutionary teleology: one of nationalist emotion and one of religious spirituality, where Abbas's cinematic aesthetic emerges. For in a novel that upholds a staunchly secular Marxist view of nationalism, it is noteworthy that it turns to a scene of Islamic spiritualism to represent the "emotional complex" of the emergent nation. Writing in the devastating moments when eruptions of communal violence, battled on the grounds of religious difference, rapidly followed Indian national independence, Abbas's stagings of the triumph of nationalist emotion also bring us a set of questions surrounding the relationship between nationalist and religious emotion. Thus, probing the visceral aesthetics of this novel, which is also to probe its "political unconscious," in the words of Fredric Jameson, I reveal a latent preoccupation of the novel with the very possibility of a secular modernity in postcolonial South Asia.

What I seek to explore in this chapter is a set of eruptive moments in Abbas's novel in which the more clichéd, didactic style of his social realist writing fuses with his cinematic aesthetic in an attempt to chart the internal transformation of his protagonist. Throughout the novel's depiction of Anwar's development, Abbas continues to return to this scene of the resistance movement: this sea of bodies chanting the revolutionary call in unison. The momentum of the scene is located in the collective voice of the crowd and the sonic properties of the "magic words" *Inquilab Zindabad* (*Inquilab*, 37). The narrative attempts to capture the distinct melodic pattern of this collective voice, its cadence and its rhythm and, further, its capacity to choreograph the crowd's emotions. The power of this scene derives from the experience of simultaneity, as Anwar turns to see his own emotional state mirrored in that of his friend:

> Like a big tidal wave ... Inquilab Zindabad, long live the revolution ... it reached a crescendo and faded into silence.... He did not even know the full meaning of the word except vaguely that it meant radical change. But somehow the cry made him burn with fierce excitement, the hair on his body seemed to be pulled out of their roots, there was a rush of blood to his face and his head reeled as it had once reeled when he had got a sunstroke. He looked at Ratan and his friend seemed to be experiencing a similar emotional impact. (Abbas, *Inquilab*, 37)

Abbas mobilizes a form of biological realism to render the emotional transformation that Anwar undergoes in this moment, one that centers on the materiality of embodied experience. The passage focuses on Anwar's physiological reactions in search of capturing the emotive impact of these collective waves of sound and feeling. From the excitation at the hair follicles to the rushes of blood and reeling of the head, the power of this "stimulant" is rendered through its capacity to awaken and animate the body—indeed, to *agitate* the body at various levels of perception.

It is the ear of our protagonist that we inhabit in this moment of political agitation: the place not only of sound, but of balance and stability. The mysterious stimulant of the crowd renders our protagonist dizzy and reeling. The power of the sun here is not drawing on its allegorical function of illumination and enlightenment, of clarity in thought and perception. Rather it is describing an experience of radical disorientation and confusion. Throughout *Inquilab*, these moments of political awakening are rendered through tropes of radical instability, dizziness, and disorientation. The potentiality of Abbas's revolutionary subject is thus located within a complete disruption of the body's perceptive capacities—a complete overhaul of the senses.

Within this somatic rendering of our protagonist's experience, the exhilaration and disorientation that characterizes the scene of protest also comes to mark the critical shifts in consciousness throughout the novel, from the excitement of Anwar's first experience on a train to the euphoria of his first sexual experience. For example, the novel depicts Anwar's first experience on a train as a small child and the exhilaration of disorientation when "the train station is running away'" (Abbas, *Inquilab* 20). Abbas writes, "The mere fact that he was traveling in a fast-moving train made the blood tingle in his veins. He felt like clapping his hands for joy, he wanted to shout, jump, and dance!" (*Inquilab*, 21). This thrill and exhilaration is again rendered through the physiological responses of the body—a kind of somatic awakening. The feel of the train's forward movement—indeed, progressive momentum—comes to anticipate Anwar's experience of the rising momentum of the nationalist movement.

These corporeal stagings, scenes of political agitations, characterized by disorientation and exhilaration (rather than the more modernist representations of interiority that I explore in later chapters, for example), can most usefully be theorized for our purposes, I argue, as the experience of ecstasy through which our revolutionary subject emerges in *Inquilab*. As the film critic Linda Williams reminds us, while contemporary meanings of "ecstasy" are associated with sexual excitement, the more classical meaning of the Greek word is akin to states of insanity and bewilderment (4). Thus, head reeling and vision blurred, immersed in the repetitive chants of the crowd echoing the revolutionary call "Inquilab Zindabad," our agitated subject in this scene is found among the masses lost in a moment of nationalist ecstasy. What interests Williams about ecstasy, and a whole palette of ecstatic affects, is the peculiar feature of its contagion. Williams seeks to examine the strangely infectious phenomenon of viewing another body convulsing in hysterical tears, from sexual pleasure, or terror, in her exploration of the "bodily hysteria" of ecstasy (4), although in what perhaps seems an unlikely parallel, we find that Abbas's melodramatic stagings of the nationalist movement surface a similar preoccupation with the contagious dimensions of nationalist fervor and the euphoria of the rallying masses. I argue that Williams's astute psychoanalytic insight into ecstatic film genres may help us probe the visceral contours of this experience of nationalist simultaneity, its peculiar "stimulant" so critical to the history of radical political thought out of which this novel emerges.

In her stunning essay "Film Bodies: Gender, Genre, and Excess," Williams interrogates the spectatorial politics of a series of melodramatic film genres that are classified by their displays of ecstatic or emotive excess. These melodramatic genres are exemplified for Williams by the horror film, the pornographic film, and the sentimental "weepie," whose excessive displays of emotion, sex, or violence feature the spectacle of "the body 'beside itself' with sexual pleasure, fear and terror, or overpowering sadness" (4). What is critical about Williams's discussion of these displays of emotive excess is what she locates as their strange mimetic impact on the spectator: "the perception that the body of the spectator is caught up in an almost involuntary mimicry of the emotion or sensation of the body on the screen" (4). This involuntary mimicry, characteristic of what Williams theorizes as the ecstatic spectacle, along with its peculiar dynamic of emotive transfer, remains critical to my readings of Abbas's political "agitations."

In his renderings of Anwar's emotive transformation in moments of nationalist euphoria, Abbas's realist prose is inflected by the use of a discernibly cinematic aesthetic that draws on melodramatic conventions of the Bombay film industry. Abbas attempts to mimic a series of film and camera techniques within the novel to capture the heightened euphoria of these scenes of anticolonial resistance. For example, he stages moments of radical disorientation and instability through the melodramatic film effect of a room rapidly revolving and the visual field rendered increasingly out of focus. Yet what I highlight in the following reading is how the novel draws the spectator into the "frame" to interrogate the impact of the ecstatic spectacle on the spectator. In the next section, I trace these scenes of euphoria through their dynamics of contagion and mimicry to interrogate the parallels being drawn between the moments of nationalist ecstasy with one particular scene of religious ecstasy, so seemingly antithetical to the Marxist secular vision of liberation.

Religious Ecstasy

In a collection of essays reflecting on the world of Bombay cinema in the 1950s, Abbas writes about his own, unique career: "Human destiny in its social setting has been my special preoccupation. Whether doing my weekly column, writing short stories and novels, scripting screenplays for other producers, or writing, directing, and producing my own films, I have been involved with the themes of social transformation and social justice" (*Mad, Mad, Mad World of Indian Films*, 63). What destiny has to do with social transformation for Abbas becomes evident when we turn to the fate of his story's characters. The protagonists of Abbas's narratives, whether in his literature, plays, or films, are figures whose marginalization in society stems from the circumstances of their births. Abbas's subaltern subjects are thus produced out of social logics of filiation and reproduction: the orphan, the prostitute, and, most prominent, the "bastard" (*haramzaada*) are the central figures of his stories. As Abbas writes in his autobiography, "All my life I have been an upholder of social environment, and an opponent of heredity, as the decisive factor in determining the character and destiny of man—or woman" (*I Am Not an Island*, 21). Abbas's figures of social illegitimacy, unhinged from nationalist logics of the family, come to represent the promise of political transformation within his postcolonial imaginings. In this sense, Abbas's artistic engagements with colonial affect and transformative feeling are concentrated in the narrative "destinies" of his characters.

As unveiled in the didactic conclusion of the novel:

> Could it be that he who by birth was neither a Hindu nor wholly a Muslim or, rather, who was both, an oddly symbolic Son of India, was in a peculiarly advantageous position to understand both communities and to work for the synthesis that was already symbolized in his person, while the memory of his mother would ever be there to identify him with the unfortunate, the underprivileged, and the oppressed? (Abbas, *Inquilab*, 342).

Published in the historical moment when the triumph of national independence was swiftly replaced by eruptions of communal violence, *Inquilab* resolves the problem of communal antagonism on the level of plot through this critical reworking of the familial fantasy of the nation.

Early in the novel, when Anwar joins his father on a trip to Panipat, they wander into an old mausoleum. There they encounter a group of people enraptured in the collective performance of a *qawaali*, a performance of Sufi devotional music. The practice of qawaali is characterized by the singing of the Sufi poetic form, which expresses the longing of man for the divine. The performance is described as a mass of bodies lost in the euphoria of religious emotion: "Eyes were closed and everyone was lost in the surging waves of emotion that seemed to flow out of the Sufistic poetry" (Abbas, *Inquilab*, 25). The narration portrays the scene through a pseudoethnographic voice, depicting the religious spectacle and the profound emotional impact of the scene on the young Anwar as he stands aside and watches.

The qawaali is described as a group of two dozen people seated in a circle as one sings Persian verses while the others "ke[ep] time" by clapping and singing the refrain in a chorus. Suddenly, the performance picks up in intensity and tempo: "Like rising tidal waves, the tempo of the singing was getting faster and faster, the clapping became more frantic and heads rolled from side to side, keeping time with the tempestuous melody" (Abbas, *Inquilab*, 24). The mounting tempo and the momentum of the music, generated in and through this synchronized mass, recalls the immanent time of the nation to come. This immanent time further echoes the revolutionary chanting of "Inquilab Zindabad" through the repetition and undulating cadences of the collective singing, as well as the emotive crescendos it seems to orchestrate in the mass of bodies. The "tempestuous" melody comes to register the emotional volatility of these accruing and mounting energies of the collective. The parallel drawn between the emotionalism of the nationalist rally and this spiritual scene, in fact, is inscribed within the time of yearning—a mounting temporality, growing in intensity, that organizes scenes of both nationalist and religious emotion.

I would argue that Abbas turns to this Sufi expression of longing to explore what he terms the "emotional complex" of Indian nationalism. Within this scene of religiosity, however, as the music suddenly accelerates and the singing and clapping become increasingly vigorous, the climax renders a single body that falls out of sync—out of *time* with the collective. The progressing movement of the synchronized mass surging forward is suddenly stalled in the quivering muscles of a singular male body. Anwar witnesses this strange progression:

> Anwar saw a man in the centre of the crowd open his eyes and stare vacantly. For a moment this man was silent, ominously silent and motionless in the midst of the emotional storm that raged around him. Then he was

caught by a sudden frenzy, his whole body quivered and moved, beating time to the song which by now reached a weird and frightening crescendo, faster and faster, louder and louder. The man's hands rose in the air and as if clutching an unseen rope, he raised himself and started to dance, wildly, ecstatically, tearing his clothes and pulling his hair, completely unselfconscious and unrestrained, oblivious but some mysterious inner urge that demanded expression in this wild manner. (Abbas, *Inquilab*, 25)

In staging this display, the ethnographic gaze of the scene echoes familiar orientalist tropes of the primitive, superstitious, and hyperemotive body caught in terrifying spasms of hysteria. The lyric patterns that invoke the trance-like emotionalism of the qawaali singers thus seem to cross some vital portal, tipping over into a complete bodily possession. What begins as steady and rhythmic repetitions accelerates into the hysterical spasms of an individuated body who falls out of time. The agitated subject of this scene brings us to a vital threshold between a stimulant that moves a body to action and an excessive excitation that, paradoxically, renders the body immobile.

Caught in a sudden religious frenzy, moving—or, rather, being moved—in the absence of his own volition, the novel brings to focus a conundrum surrounding the bodily agency of the politically agitated subject. However, that it does so on the grounds of religious euphoria is what is of interest here, because this scene of spiritualism and religiosity is rendered as an orientalist spectacle through the display of the ecstatic body. The Orientalized and primitivized body of this scene is an ecstatic body crossing over from an accelerating tempo of the forward or progressive momentum, inscribed within the time of yearning, to a moment caught or stalled in what Ngai terms a state of "suspended agency" (1). Ngai writes of the African American body made comic spectacle, of the hyperanimated and agitated black body that converts "a way of moving others to political action ('agitation')" into "the passive state of being moved or vocalized by others" in the context of (32). Similarly, Abbas's renderings of the ecstatic body, frenzied and hysterical, deprived of bodily agency, thus may at first glance seem to warn against the excessive emotionality of this spiritual practice, for the progressive tempo and momentum of the scene, the historical teleology enacted by the progressive novel form itself, is stalled and suspended in the quivering muscles of the single body that falls out of time. However, such an interpretation is complicated by what follows, when the spectacle is framed by the gaze of the spectator.

Following the qawaali performance, we "pan out" from the scene of religious ecstasy to the way in which it activates and animates Anwar's own body. Consistent with the novel's coding of revolutionary transformation, the emotive impact is represented through the excitement at the level of the body and the disorientation at the level of Anwar's perceptive capacities. This reaction is further charted in the very visceral cavities of our agitated subject:

> For several minutes, Anwar was speechless; so great had the effect of this spectacle been on him. His pulse beat faster, his mind was in a whirl and, as the song stopped, *he felt a gnawing emptiness in his bowels*. (Abbas, *Inquilab*, 25, emphasis added)

Abbas thus stages this religious spectacle in view of the agitated spectator, bringing Williams's insights on the "involuntary mimicry" of the ecstatic spectacle in the body of the spectator to the fore (L. Williams, 4). Here I probe the infectious dimensions of this scene of religious euphoria that is made salient in this detail, quite literally the visceral impact on our agitated spectator, for, when the performance ends, the silence is depicted as an aching emptiness, a yearning, as a time of longing that remains lodged in the bowels of our protagonist.

Williams characterizes the nature of ecstasy, or "the body beside itself with sexual pleasure, fear and terror, or overpowering sadness," as premised on the peculiar affective excess that manifests in the convulsive body logic of the affect: "the spectacle of a body caught in the grip of intense sensation or emotion ... [whose] ecstatic excesses could be said to share a quality of uncontrollable convulsion or spasm" (4). In other words, what strings together three very different states of pleasure, terror, and sadness as ecstatic film genres for Williams (the pornographic film, the horror film, and the sentimental "weepie") is the physiological response: the mimetic transfer between spectacle and spectator. Bringing Williams's insight surrounding the involuntary mimicry of ecstasy to the fore, we may understand this uncontrollable convulsion in the qawaali scene as bringing to question the politics of bodily agency for the agitated subject (here the religious subject, and later the political, national, communal subject). The ambiguity surrounding the agency of the agitated subject is further embroiled in the infectious dimensions of this ecstatic spectacle as its modality of emotive transfer. In other words, these convulsive logics of contagion are foregrounded as the very vehicle of political agitation, synching the bodies of the masses into the "simultaneity" of the nation.

A profound ambiguity underwrites the representational politics of Abbas's novel that interests me for the way it hovers around its visceral aesthetics as it is tracks the scene of nationalist ecstasy to come. Within the novel's development, this scene of religious ecstasy becomes a kind of staging ground or rehearsal for what is to arrive on the stage of national history. In this sense, the form of nationalist "simultaneity" celebrated in the novel as the moment that brings about India's independence is also premised on the contagion explored in this scene of religiosity—a visceral manipulation and mimicry specific to the affect of ecstasy. On the one hand, as the agitation of the ecstatic body crosses over to hysteria, the body is lodged within a state of suspended agency, which seems to warn against the excessive emotionality of the religiosity being staged. And yet in turning to the emotive transfer that takes place between spectacle and spectator, the corporeal cues of exhilaration and disorientation anticipate the revolutionary transformations that are celebrated in the scenes of nationalist resistance. In further probing this ambivalence, I turn to the filial logics of the novel, so critically tethered to the novel's critique of the "communal" antagonisms historically taking hold of the national imaginary at the time of the novel's publication.

Within the broader narrative trajectory of *Inquilab*, as Anwar struggles to find his place in a social order that is in the midst of a transformation and rebirth, a recurrent focus remains on Anwar's budding sense of masculinity. One of the most concentrated sites of this exploration is staged through Anwar's relationship with his father. Anwar's development is mapped in and against the political and more orthodox religious ideologies of his father, tracking the shifts in views of these two generations of men as their ideas and political stances continually converge and diverge. The novel tracks the marked divergence in Anwar's emotional responses with those of his "austere and puritanical father" (Abbas, 1977b, 8). As the narrator explains, "His father disliked all active demonstrations of joy, sorrow, or excitement," and thus Anwar learns these lessons of masculine affect from an early age: "Anwar had learnt never to weep aloud even when he was hurt by a severe fall, never to laugh too loudly even at the best jokes of Hakim Bedil, never to display excitement even when the tailor brought his gleaming golden sherwani for Eid" (*Inquilab*, 21). How the protagonist eventually disrupts these repressive codes of masculinity provides the impetus of the bildungsroman form, making inextricable the emergence of new masculine subjectivities and the project of the new national social order. For it is precisely on the grounds of a nationalist structure of feeling, a heightened nationalist emotionalism, that the nation is imagined to be willed into being in the novel.

Anwar's response to the spiritual spectacle of the qawaali occurs in sharp contrast to the reaction it invokes in his father. Whereas Anwar is unmistakably moved and exhilarated by the qawaali performance, as the rhythm of his own pulse begins to beat in time with the bodies of the singers, Anwar's father is "annoyed, ashamed, almost humiliated," for "he did not like this wild emotional exhibitionism" (25). Abbas stages the father's anger—indeed, *agitation*—at this excessive emotional display in contradistinction to his son's excitement. The novel highlights the divergent gut reactions engendered by this spectacle of ecstasy for these two generations of Muslim men in India. Anwar and his father are both agitated by the religious spectacle, but the nature of this agitation critically differs. Whereas Anwar is exhilarated by the contagious elements of the qawaali, his father is angered, shamed, and made anxious by such an unrestrained exhibition of ecstatic excess. As Williams ultimately argues, what may relegate the ecstatic film genres to their culturally "low" status is that we, as spectators, may feel "too *viscerally manipulated* by the text in specifically gendered ways" (5). We may read the father's response as an angered reaction to the way in which he is manipulated, to the "involuntary mimicry" of his own body that is taking place. It is through this affective divergence of son from father that a progressive masculinity is coded in the novel.

Hence, in this scene of religious ecstasy, the divergence in visceral reactions between these two men marks a key transformative moment in Anwar's development. The visceral education that Anwar gains here disrupts the generational reproduction of masculinity that is premised on emotional repression. In other words, the spectatorial dynamic of the qawaali performance depicts a mode of affective transfer that is not based on a logic of heredity or a passing down of a form of masculinity from father to son. The revolutionary potential is located in the visceral mode of transfer specific to the contagious dynamics of ecstasy, for the spectacle makes available a new emotive terrain that undoes the visceral lessons of masculinity imparted by the father. This, I argue, is precisely what enables the possibility of a budding new national consciousness in the novel, one, indeed, through which Anwar will claim a new form of masculinity that is not mired by the repression of emotions from which he suffers. By bringing the spectatorial responses of father and son into this scene, I would further argue, the novel privileges this *affiliative* transfer of ecstasy and its visceral transmission over a filial one, to borrow from Edward Said, which critically alters the political "destiny" of our protagonist and paves the way for radically new structures of feeling (*The World, the Text, and the Critic*, 23).

How, then, do we read this scene of religious ecstasy as it emerges within the novel's trajectory of Anwar's ascendance of national consciousness? Do we read the spirituality of the qawaali scene as one that prepares Anwar's body for the national feelings to come? Or are these misdirected energies—"reactionary" forces, in the words of the Progressive Writers—mass opiates more akin to Fanon's famous argument about the false consciousness of spiritual practices and superstition in *The Wretched of the Earth*?

What is at stake in Abbas's depictions of nationalist ecstasy is the question of violence, the question of being "moved" to violence, which remains at the heart of Abbas's aesthetics of agitation, as it motivates the divergent plights of the novel's political agitators (both violent and nonviolent paths to revolution). Focusing on the question of nationalist affect within this novel, in which the spectatorial aesthetics emerge in search of the ecstatic terrain of the national, we find that the visceral logics of the novel thwarts an easy celebration of the nationalist frame of the book. While I turn to Abbas's forgotten novel, *Inquilab*, for the vision of decolonization that it expresses, my interest in mining the aesthetic ambivalences and contradictions housed in the visceral lies in rendering legible its political unconscious. I further argue that the visceral aesthetics of *Inquilab* provide the concentrated site of the historical contradictions inherent in the project of secular nationalism in South Asia, sublimating what Aamir Mufti terms the "crisis" of the minoritization of the Muslim in India, as I discuss in the next section. In pursuit of these questions, I return one final time to the scene of nationalist ecstasy with which we began to probe the politics of ecstasy for the agitated subject of Abbas's *Inquilab*. Here we move from the ecstatic terrain of longing and yearning to the ecstasy of terror, previewed in the explosive climax of the Sufi qawaali.

Ecstatic Terror

As I have argued, the transformative potential of ecstasy organizes the key revolutionary moments of *Inquilab*. The climactic moment of the novel, however, is portrayed as one of the most avidly memorialized events in Indian national historiography—popularly known as the Jallianwallah Bagh Massacre—in which colonial officials famously opened fire on a crowd of unarmed Indian nationalist protestors. The revolutionary climax of *Inquilab* is Anwar's encounter with the spectacular nature of colonial violence in the face of the national resistance, as Anwar witnesses the horrific display of violence exercised against the mounting resistance movement in India. Anwar's experience of this devastating moment is charted in marked contrast to that of his best friend, Ratan, who witnesses the murder of his own father on this day. However, while the trauma of the event remains etched in Anwar's memory and motivates him to take up a nonviolent political stance, Ratan is moved to take up violence as a freedom fighter. The place of violence within the resistance movement becomes a central question of the novel. As the two friends continue to meet and debate throughout the novel, we follow the divergence in how this spectacle of violence produces two very different kinds of political activists—indeed, two very different forms of political "agitators."

While *Inquilab* takes a largely nonviolent stance on nationalist resistance, I argue that the ecstatic representations of the potential national subject carries a poignant resonance with Fanon's anticolonial writings in *The Wretched of the Earth*. In his famous chapter "Concerning Violence," Fanon theorizes the colonized subjects' rituals of "ecstatic" dance and possession as vital forms of emotional release. I quote at length from his discussion to draw out the remarkable parallels in the visceral grammars of Fanon and Abbas:

> In the colonial world, the emotional sensitivity of the native is kept on the surface of the skin like an open sore which flinches from the caustic agent; and the psyche shrinks back, obliterates itself and finds outlet in muscular demonstrations which have caused certain very wise men to say that the native is a hysterical type.... [W]e see the native's emotional sensibility exhausting itself in dances which are more or less ecstatic. This is why the colonial world should take into consideration the phenomena of the dance and of possession. The native's relaxation takes precisely the

form of a muscular orgy in which the most acute aggressivity and the most impelling violence are canalized, transformed, and conjured away..., for in reality your purpose in coming together is to allow the accumulated libido, the hampered aggressivity, to dissolve as in a volcanic eruption. (57)

As Fanon argues in this passage, the rituals of dance and possession are what keep the colonized subject complicit with the colonial order. For these mounting energies, the "hampered aggressivity" that is diffused and released through communal practices of possession, should instead be, as Fanon argues, mobilized against the colonial order. If it is not possession and dance that "canalize" this aggression, according to Fanon, it would be explosions of tribal warfare.

Fanon's argument is that these inevitable explosions of aggression can instead be transformed and released through revolutionary violence. As theorized in great detail in the previous chapter, the emotive energies of the colonized subject, his revolutionary rage and indignation, are lodged within the "tensed muscles" of the colonized body:

> The native's muscles are always tensed.... That impulse to take the settler's place implies a tonicity of muscles the whole time; and in fact we know that in certain emotional conditions the presence of an obstacle accentuates the tendency towards motion. (*The Wretched of the Earth*, 53)

Fanon thus locates the ecstatic dances of the "native" as an energetic release from the muscular "tension" of the colonized and potentially revolutionary subject.

Like Fanon, Abbas imagines the emotive life of the revolutionary subject through this accruing energy and its inevitable release, which also finds an outlet through the physicality of ecstatic spiritual practices. These emotions are imagined as exploding through the agitated musculature of the body, through its convulsive catharsis. What Abbas calls the "emotional complex" of the emergent nation, whether in the context of the mass protest or of the qawaali, is depicted through the anticipatory time of yearning, the collective momentum of its frustrated desire, these same accumulating and accelerating energetic forces. For Abbas, however, it is the critical threshold of this volatile energetic that seems to be of primary concern within the aesthetics of agitation.

Within such a logic of accumulating and accelerating energies, the explosive climax is inevitable. Fanon theorizes that there will be a cathartic release one way or another. For Abbas, when the qawaali reaches its hysterical climax, the accumulated energy of the assembly is rapidly diffused, and the once-frenzied body goes limp like an evacuated vessel, deprived of the energy that had animated it seconds before: "And then the song died on the lips of the singer, the waves of emotion receded.... And then deprived of the emotional support of the song, his knees sagged and he collapsed to the ground" (*Inquilab*, 25). The form of nationalist ecstasy in *Inquilab*, its structure of feeling, is also no exception to this visceral logic: there is an inevitable climax, an explosion. This energetic arc, in fact, structures each of the novels I study in this book. The inevitable explosion takes the form of the Jallianwallah Bagh Massacre, the eruption of colonial violence on the colonized. In this scene of violence, what we find to be the ecstasy of religious rapture in the qawaali is instead an ecstatic terror that renders Anwar's body immobilized, quite literally convulsing in "shock."

Depicting one of the most passionately remembered historical events within Indian nationalist narratives of independence, Abbas's dramatic staging of the Jallianwallah Bagh Massacre is represented as a key moment in the politicization of Anwar and the impetus for a budding nationalist consciousness. The novel portrays with great melodramatic flair both Anwar's experience of the mass protests that precede the British attack and its escalation into the massacre as colonial military soldiers are ordered to open fire without warning on the unarmed gathering. Anwar's initial reaction to the mass resistance movement at Jallianwallah Bagh is to identify the mass fervor with the exhilaration of the qawaali: "It was an experience such as the *qaawali* at Panipat, only it was a very different kind of qawaali. And the emotional fervor had produced none of the mystical aroma of a tomb but rather the frenzy of the battle field" (Abbas, *Inquilab*, 37). The scene begins with the masses chanting the revolutionary call when, suddenly, the British begin encroaching on the gathering, eventually opening fire on the unarmed crowd. The trajectory of this scene at Jallianwallah Bagh mirrors the progression of the ecstatic body in the scene of the qawaali, as it follows the excitation of Anwar's body in the mounting exhilaration of the crowd, when it suddenly crosses over and accelerates—in fact, explodes—into the bloody scene of the massacre:

A few yards from them someone was moaning aloud and, raising his head a little, Anwar saw that it was Nandoo, the hotel servant. Evidently he had been shot through the abdomen, for *he clutched his stomach every time there was a spasm of convulsions.* Once he managed to turn his head a little, and holding his stomach with both hands, spat out—blood! *Anwar's own stomach turned* at the sight of blood, thick, reddish-black blood as it spurted out of Nandoo's mouth and then as he lay back exhausted, it oozed out in a thin trickle....

Everywhere there was blood. Anwar's head reeled, *his bowels contracted within him, he wanted to vomit but could not.* He laid his head on the ground and saw the sky revolving and the stars dancing. (Abbas, 1977b, 40–42, emphasis added)

Attempting to capture the emotive impact of the scene through Anwar's horrified gaze, Nandoo's murder is spectacularized: caught in spasms as his body seizes, blood oozing from the mouth. What I want to foreground, however, is the mirroring that occurs between Nandoo as horrific spectacle and Anwar as terrified spectator, or the involuntary mimicry of the ecstatic excess. As Anwar witnesses Nandoo clutch his stomach in painful convulsions, Anwar's own stomach "turns," bowels "contracting" at the sight. The scene is thus driven here by Anwar's gut reactions, as his own body seems to mime Nandoo's convulsions. The spectacle of the body caught in spasms sets off Anwar's own contractions.

The melodramatic depiction of this scene of violence and trauma features a redeployment of the somatic vocabularies of the qawaali scene, the excessive excitation and accompanying "spasms of convulsion," as well as the accompanying experience of bewilderment, dizziness, and disorientation, the epistemological overhaul that mark these ecstatic moments for their revolutionary potential. But here it is an ecstatic fear or terror rather than the prolonged desire of religious or nationalist longing that motivates the violent climax of this scene of political protest. Suggestively, Abbas attempts to integrate into this scene a number of the filmic techniques that Williams contends define horror as an ecstatic body genre: "horror's display of ecstatic violence and terror" through the use of the tortured body, marked, again, by uncontrollable convulsions or spasms, the body trembling in fear or terror, but also "the accompanying presence of fluids," here the trickle of blood, that marks these ecstatic genres as excessive. All of these films, we remember, are premised on a certain excessive sensory excitement that induces in the spectator an involuntary mimetic shock to the body. These are genres, Williams tells us, that are "designed to give the body a jolt." This is particularly interesting given that this is arguably the moment of political agitation that initiates the protagonist into a radical political consciousness.

By the end of the scene, Anwar's head is reeling, and he is left in a state of shock, both in the sense that the affect conveys the violent disturbance in the emotions and as it refers to a muscular spasm as a result of an "overstimulation" of nerves, as the physiological reaction to an electric current passing through the body or, perhaps most appropriate to our discussion, defined medically as "a violent agitation."[2] The scene ends with Anwar's suspended visceral desire: "He wanted to vomit but could not" (Abbas, *Inquilab*, 42). Inscribed within this anticipatory temporality of the nation, the time of yearning, this thwarted desire is once again lodged within the viscera of our agitated political subject. Like Fanon's nausea or his thwarted desire for an explosive laughter discussed in the previous chapter, Anwar's nausea here is inscribed within a suspended state, a frustrated desire for an explosive release, a trope I will return to throughout this study. This is the space that Williams terms the "anticipatory temporality of the fantasy spaces"—a figure that underwrites the visceral throughout the imaginaries of this study—as it is mapped onto what Dipesh Chakrabarty terms the "waiting room of history" (8).

In depicting this moment in *Inquilab*, Abbas uses the heightened cinematic mode to convey Anwar's experience of ecstatic shock. The visual frame lingers in slow motion on the buildup and anticipation of the violent events to come: "The series of events that followed, swift and incredible, remained sharply etched on Anwar's memory for years to come. As he stood, frozen to the spot, he watched everything as in a dream. He was too shocked even to experience fear, even to realize the horrible significance of what was happening around him" (Abbas, *Inquilab*, 37). In a resonant parallel, within his published memoirs Abbas writes about his own process of politicization:

> At the age of nineteen I did experience an emotional shock which did many things to me—it sharpened my perception of happiness and sorrow, it made me revolt against conventional values and codes of morality, it challenged my imagination, and it aroused my latent powers of self-expression.... It made me a skeptic, an agnostic, a socialist..., an ally of all causes that

were devoted to the building of new values in a new society.... But inside me, that last moment of emotion congealed, it did not die, it became fixed like a moving picture that suddenly freezes. (*I Am Not an Island*, 7)

Abbas's inquiries into the "emotional complex" of nationalist fervor, as Abbas puts it, is thus faithfully underwritten by these principles of the convulsive energetic of ecstasy, which powerfully "moves" the body to action and the mind to an ascendance of political consciousness. However, whether spiritual or secular, within the visceral aesthetics of this novel this energetic also seems to stall in the convulsing muscles of the agitated subject. The hysterical and frenzied conclusion of the scene of religious ecstasy is here taken to its violent conclusion in the scene of national protest. The frenzied subject of the qawaali, who tips over into complete hysteria and a loss of emotive control, may thus be read as one that foreshadows the eruption of violence that becomes the (inevitable) conclusion of the nationalist euphoria when it crosses the vital threshold. Such a logic of inevitability, which is so central to the visceral, as we will see across the chapters of this book, is built into the affect of ecstasy in Abbas's novel.

My argument throughout this chapter has been that *Inquilab*'s scene of religious and patriotic emotion is brought into critical interrogation and relationality on the grounds of nationalist ecstasy. Reading the scene of the qawaali as one that anticipates the Jallianwallah Bagh Massacre allows us to focus Abbas's preoccupation with the excessive energetic potential of longing and ecstasy through the figure of the agitated political subject of the novel. In a text that seeks to celebrate and commemorate a now popularized narrative of India's struggle for independence, what Abbas terms the "emotional complex" born out of the collective yearning of the nation, I argue that embedded within the aesthetics of agitation is a fundamental ambivalence directed toward the very nature of the emotive "stimulant" under interrogation: the ecstasy of longing and its imminent promise of national belonging. This ambivalence becomes deeply symptomatic of an anxiety surrounding the agency of the politically agitated subject that threatens to cross over the threshold where being "moved" becomes paradoxically immobilizing. Even as the novel privileges the emotive shock as one that impels the revolutionary subject to national consciousness, we may also mine in the aesthetic unconscious of this scene of visceral mimicry a profound distrust of the structure of longing and the precipice where national euphoria explodes into (religious) violence. I read the specter of communal violence in the novel as sublimated through a nationalist imaginary, where the colonizer is the only agent of gruesome violence, even as the novel is written during the moments in which the Indian nation descends into civil war.

I would argue that such a reading does not relegate Islamic spiritualism to the realm of false consciousness, or to what the Progressives called "reaction." Rather, sublimated in the parallel drawn between the scenes of religious and national euphoria is the anxiety surrounding the nationalist vision of secularism, constituted by what Mufti theorizes as the "minoritization" of the Muslim in India. Even as Abbas remained a committed Marxist and secularist throughout his career, his agitated bodies reveal a profound grappling with the place of Islam and spiritual experience—and, more precisely, what the place of the Muslim is in the production of the modern Indian national subject.[3]

Reading the scene of the qawaali back through the rhythmic chanting of the nationalist call to revolution, if there is a sense in which the spiritual may have a place in the emotional complex of the revolutionary subject, it is in the emotive power of this mass "stimulant." The novel, in fact, articulates this tension in depicting the emotive—and, indeed, poetic—power of Anwar's Islamic education. Early in the novel, Abbas writes:

> More than anything [Anwar] *had been moved* by Musaddas-e-Hali—the inspiring epic of Islam's rise and fall.... The nine-year-old boy knew nothing about the technicalities of poetry; he did not even understand the historical allusions, but the rhythm and flow of Hali's immortal words swept along on a wave of emotion. As he recited the stanzas, he experienced the same uplifting feeling of joy and power that he used to feel when reciting verses from the Quran. (Abbas, *Inquilab*, 57)

The emotive power of this cultural history of an Indo-Islamic lifeworld under the threat of erasure is not depicted here as false consciousness or reactionary literature. Rather, it is positioned as exemplary of revolutionary poetry—indeed, of progressive writing: "Out of it is born a vague sense of the urgency of change, a desire for dispelling the gloom of ignorance by the lamps of learning, which too, was just as the poet had undoubtedly planned" (Abbas, *Inquilab*, 57). In fact, I would argue that in his staging of the qawaali in anticipation of the scenes of nationalist fervor, the novel also invites us into a line of questioning surrounding the very possibility of a secular nationalist sensibility emerging in the South Asian context. Is this embodied archive of religious experience, the novel seems to ask of us, embedded in the emotional complex of the nation, lodged in the somatic unconscious, in the muscle memory of the modern Indian subject?

Given Abbas's success as a Bombay Cinema filmmaker, it is perhaps not surprising that the heightened melodramatic dynamic of the ecstatic spectacle emerges in the aesthetics of *Inquilab* as the mode through which the novel explores the possibilities and pitfalls of the visceral transmission of political feeling. The goal of progressive literature and art during the era of decolonization in India was to "move" the emergent national audience to political action and nationalist consciousness. However, that this affective (and aesthetic) transmission is accomplished through the structure of contagion, through a dynamic of mimicry, confronts us with the involuntary nature of our visceral reflexes. We are thus confronted with the difficulty that the visceral poses in thinking through the agency of the potential national citizen. In other words, that this dynamic of political transfer entails a state of being "viscerally manipulated," I argue, provides the site of the subterranean anxieties and ambiguities expressed toward the agitated affects of the text when we read the novel against the grain.

2. Irritation

In the final scene of the anticolonial Indian author and activist Mulk Raj Anand's most celebrated novel, *Untouchable*, a certain revolutionary imagining of an independent India is projected through the voice of the poet, standing in a crowd gathered at one of Gandhi's public speeches. "We can feel new feelings," the poet declares. "We can learn to be aware with a new awareness. We can envisage the possibility of creating new races from the latent heat in our dark brown bodies" (153). What is so remarkable about this articulation of decolonization, years before India would gain independence, is its imagining of a human collective whose very ways of feeling could be a site of radical transformation. The poet declares that it is our impalpable bodily registers, what we obscurely refer to as a racialized awareness, that can be a site of radical relearning. From within this taut historical moment of anticipation, Anand's poetic doubling of verbs as their objects—feeling new feelings, being aware with a new awareness—unsettles the tautology of these experiential concepts and opens them up to an imagining of what it could mean to inhabit a human sensibility that is not yet perceptible. Within this articulation of revolution, the transformational energy and potentiality of this moment rises, a latent heat, from within the racialized sensations of the colonized body.

This chapter brings into focus the revolutionary promise of the visceral within the internationalist imaginary I chart in this book: that which makes possible the transformation of feeling and consciousness. Returning to the concerns that frame this study of decolonization, I ask what it would mean to feel new feelings when one's complicity with the colonial regime of thought has become naturalized in the automatized reflexes of the body. In this chapter and the chapters that follow, I explore some of the more experimental aesthetic engagements with the poetics of revolutionary feeling, centering the complex relationship between the materiality and metaphor of bodily life critical to theorizing the visceral. Taking the question of political anger as a case study, the materialist inquiries of this chapter focus on the possibilities of revolutionary rage in impelling a revolutionary consciousness. The poetics of "irritation" that characterize the imagined revolutionary subject of this chapter mobilize the double meaning of the term at the surface and depths of the colonized body, conjugating the tactility of embodied experience with the internal engine of a political anger.[1]

Here I engage the questions of the visceral surrounding the possibilities of transformative emotion through Anand's distinctive corporeal preoccupations as he was writing in the anticipatory moments of India's decolonization and emergent nationhood. The chapter examines his materialist engagement with the sensory and emotive life of the subaltern subjects of India, which provided the staging ground for his vision of a nationalist transformation. Invoking a mild abrasion of the skin, as well as a mild or undeveloped anger, "irritation" mobilizes the sensation of the skin, the site of both racial and caste oppression for Anand's subaltern subject, with the internal engine of a revolutionary rage, the latent heat of the revolutionary subject of India. Thus, this chapter moves from the muscular logics of political "agitation" in chapter 1 to the epidermal logics of "irritation," focusing on a very different set of emotive energetics through which the possibilities of nationalist liberation are imagined.

Anand is perhaps most famous for his pioneering role in the development of the Indian English novel, a literary tradition that has been made increasingly visible internationally by contemporary South Asian diaspora writers such as Salman Rushdie, Arundhati Roy, Anita Desai, Jhumpa Lahiri, and Amitav Ghosh, to name just a few. While Anand's literary and political education included an apprenticeship with the revered Urdu poet Iqbal and an extended stay in Gandhi's ashram, he was also a central figure in the Afro-Asian Writers Association and deeply influenced by his intimate albeit ambivalent ties with the British modernists of the Bloomsbury Group.[2]

Foregrounding Anand's role as a founding member of the Progressive Writers' Association (PWA), I turn to his manifestos, lectures, letters, and political writings, through which I read his most celebrated novel, *Untouchable*. My reading of *Untouchable* theorizes the visceral contours of complicity as they emerge in Anand's poetics of touch and feeling. I conclude the chapter with a reading of a lesser known experimental novella of Anand's, published a few years later, titled *Lament on the Death of a Master of Arts*. I read *Lament* for how it reworks the revolutionary trajectory of *Untouchable* when the protagonist is a middle-class, Muslim, male subject. More precisely, I read *Lament* as an energetic inversion of the progressive novel form exemplified in *Untouchable*, where the novel charts the ascension of consciousness in and through the decay and demise of the body rather than through the energetic arousals and awakenings of affect and sensation. This inverted form, what I explore as the novel of "evisceration" in chapter 4, explores the structures of feeling that emerge out of the "minoritization" of the Muslim in Indian national life, residing in the ever-expanding gap between sensation (the raw experiential energies of affect) and the sense-making mechanisms of nationalism, the emotive genres made available by an emergent (Hindu) nationalism (Mufti, 2).

Experiments in Touch as Feeling

Published in 1935 with the help of Leonard and Virginia Woolf and with a preface written by E. M. Forster, Anand's *Untouchable* attempts to stage the radical transformation of a subaltern protagonist as he emerges onto the scene of the nascent national body. Within the novel, we follow the protagonist through the events and the mundane routine of a single day; the tactility of the novel's prose emerges out of Anand's attempt not only to translate into an English literary medium the injustices of caste oppression and colonialism in India but, further, to render the consciousness produced out of its lived experience. *Untouchable* has gained critical acclaim for its sensory depictions and psychological explorations of the casteized protagonist. Jessica Berman writes, drawing on Leela Gandhi, "The novel's triumph rests in the combination of its representation of the complexity of its untouchable hero Bakha's inner thoughts and emotions and 'its prose [that] subtly picks up the dense corporeality and tactility of

Bakha's existence'" (149). As Toral Gajarawal writes about the novel, "The affective realm of casteism is one major contribution of [Anand's] modernist lens on the caste question" (80).

The novel has also been widely and for some time critiqued for its attempts to speak for the subaltern "other" in a condescending Gandhian idiom of caste, as well as for the problems inherent in representing caste within the Marxian frame of the Progressive Writers.[3] As Snehal Shingavi writes, it is "fairly indisputable [that] Anand's attempt to capture the authentic untouchable ends up reproducing the ideological baggage of the upper-caste view of lower castes" (54).[4] In fact, Ramnarayan Rawat and K. Satyanarayana's recent *Dalit Studies Reader* cites this novel as a key culprit in perpetuating the romanticized Gandhian "scavenger" figure (9). However, other recent scholarly interest in the novel also challenges earlier scholarly tendencies to read it as an earnest representation of caste experience, in either celebration or critique. The novel has been most productively read for its rich aesthetic insights into the problematics of Indian national politics and the project of literary progressivism out of which it emerged.[5]

To what extent we can even read this novel to be about caste at all, then, animates much of recent scholarship on *Untouchable* and remains an unresolved representational question embedded in the self-reflexivity of the novel's tactile aesthetics. I propose that we read Anand's experiments in the touch of the "untouchable" subject through the lens of the visceral and the somatic vitality of skin, for a visceral reading of this novel circumvents debates on the relative political "success" or "failure" of the novel and restores the aesthetic and political nuance and complexity of its revolutionary imaginings (as well as its failings). It is how the touch of our historical protagonist in the novel, at the interface of the body and the world, comes to be read as "feeling" that I seek to interrogate in the context of its emancipatory politics—how it is, in other words, that the body's surface comes to narrate its emotional depths.

The narrative gaze of *Untouchable* oscillates between the biological and psychic life of its protagonists as it orbits the eighteen-year-old body of a young boy named Bakha who is born into the untouchable caste. More specifically, the narrative is dispensed through a peculiar movement between Bakha's inner thought movements and the somatic minutiae of his body. I argue that we can locate the visceral inquiries of Anand's prose in these narrative oscillations, a technique that stages a materialist exploration of the interiorities of Bakha's characters. Anand's visceral poetics thus traffic between the realms of "feeling" and consciousness. As we will see, the possibilities of the subaltern's transformation are rendered via modernist experiments in character interiorities in combination with the kinds of biological realism we witnessed in chapter 1 in the writings of Khwaja Ahmad Abbas, who was a friend and comrade of Anand's within the progressive artistic movements in India.

Aamir Mufti argues that Anand's *Untouchable* exemplifies what he calls the "national realist" novel form, as the social realist novel is transplanted to the colony in India.[6] The arc of *Untouchable* represents the development of the protagonist from an animal-like existence, trapped by the shackles of his caste, into the "higher" consciousness of the national citizen subject. As Mufti argues, *Untouchable* attempts to "narrate the conditions of possibility of the passage from this limited state of existence to the universal consciousness of the citizen subject" (184). The novel traces the coming of age of its protagonist against the coming of age of the nation, as the ascendance of the subaltern consciousness functions allegorically in depicting the radicalization of the emergent nation. As Baer puts it, "all body and little mind, for most of the novel Bakha is the figure of a sleeping giant. He signifies a massive physical potentiality constrained by the cruel workings of a millennially ancient caste system.... Bakha is the figure of a class, of a power, as yet unconscious to itself, struggling with its own unfocused sense of injustice" (586–87). What interests me for the purposes of this study is that Bakha's ascendance of consciousness in the novel, his journey from an intellectual "darkness" to enlightenment, is mapped onto the temporal trajectory of a plot that moves from night to day, what Anand articulates as the transformation "from raw nature into life" (Anand, *Untouchable*, 21). Indeed, Anand's early descriptions of our protagonist portray him as little more than a physical organism combating the elements of his natural environment.

The novel opens, for example, with the following materialist description of Bakha's battle with the cold of the night:

> He felt that his bones were stiff and his flesh numb with the cold.... A hot liquid trickled down from the corners of his eyes. One of his nostrils seemed to be blocked and he sniffed the air, trying to adjust his breathing to the congested climate of the corner where his face was turned. His throat too seemed to have been caught, for as he inhaled the air it seemed to irritate his trachea uncomfortably. He began to swallow air in order to

relieve his nose and his throat. But when a breath of air pierced the cavity which was clogged the other became impenetrable. (Anand, *Untouchable*, 14)

What I want to focus on in these early scenes is how Anand's modernist experimentation with character interiority emerges in conjunction with a peculiar biological realism or naturalism, such that a Bloomsbury-style stream of consciousness is largely replaced by the flows of the body's somatic functions. The interpenetrability of this unbounded body to its environment within these early—and, indeed, "primitive"—stages in the novel depict the movement of natural elements (air, fluid, heat, and cold) moving in and out of the organism and the environment. More precisely, though, the corporeal drama staged in this scene is that of pressure and (frustrated) release, brought on by the "irritant" in the trachea.

While the densely embodied depiction here narrates Bakha's condition through the body's logics of touch—the numbness of his flesh, the insensitivity of his skin, and the immobility of his body—the emphasis is on the orifices of the body. As we orbit the anatomical minutiae of our protagonist, we linger at the sites where, in Mikhail Bakhtin's words, the body opens up to the world: its orifices, apertures, and convexities (317). Bakha's body is a grotesque body in Bakhtin's sense of the word. Anand's fictive bodies throughout his novels are both receiving and releasing bodies, as his novels are saturated with abject figures of excrement, sweat, urine, vomit, and mucus—the sites where, in Bakhtin's words, the body exceeds itself. *Untouchable* thus renders a topography of the abject body under colonialism through its openings to the world: its automated logics of register, release, receiving, and perceiving. As we further explore, to take seriously Anand's corporeal poetics, this play with the psychological and biological interiors of the subaltern subject, is to open up a critical site of his engagement with "progressive" writing, for this engagement with the experiential receptors and perceptual networks of the subaltern subject ultimately reveals his investment in these sites as the gateways of consciousness.

Within the narrative trajectory of *Untouchable*, Bakha's ascendance of consciousness from intellectual darkness to enlightenment is mapped onto the teleology of the novel that moves from night to day. What is peculiar about this trajectory is that the novel not only traces the temporal logic of the day but also its concomitant thermal logic rising within Bakha's body as the extreme cold and darkness of the night transforms into the scorching heat of the day. In other words, while Anand draws on a day-in-the-life structure, largely indebted to the modernist forms of Bloomsbury writers such as James Joyce and Virginia Woolf, this structure of contingency emerges in tension with the social realist, or national realist, teleology of the novel.[7] As I chart, the formal dimensions of this single-day structure become tied up with the social realist teleology of the novel through the visceral logics of our revolutionary subject, which, as I have been arguing, consistently provides the engine of an emergent national consciousness.

Much of the recent scholarship on Anand's fiction centers on how the generic codes of realism and modernism are deployed and reworked within it. As Gajarawala writes, for authors writing in the colony in the 1930s "the newness of the novel, the presence of indigenous forms of narrative, social, and political radicalism, and various types of experimentalism meant that realism and modernism often functioned side by side and sentence by sentence" (72). Or, as Ben Conisbee Baer succinctly puts it, realism and modernism in Anand's fiction "hybridize at both ends" (582). The visceral, as we will see, emerges through this peculiar conjugation of modernism and realism in the Anand's writing, hovering at a variety of intersections between the materiality and metaphor of bodily life as these generic codes of realism and modernism are transplanted into the colony.

Bakha's caste alienation is represented in the novel as a critical disconnect between the automatized actions of his body and the movements of his consciousness. Anand configures the disconnect between Bakha's sensations and the sense-making mechanisms of his consciousness as the result of the violent subjection of caste humiliation. V. Geetha defines the key role of humiliation in caste alienation as a process through which the Dalit body is forced to bear witness "against itself" through iterative acts of humiliation (97). Scenes of humiliation surrounding water usage and food taboos, clothing, and the association with refuse and death saturate the novel—"an evil that is stunning in its banality" in the words of Gopal Guru (9). Geetha further writes of caste alienation:

> Untouchability is a form of extreme alienation where the labourer ... is dissociated not only from the products of her own creation, but also from her own labouring body ... , for according to the stunning circular logic of the caste order, the untouchable's labour, her vocation, by simply being of her body and being, is doomed to irrelevance. This body in which the untouchable lives but does not inhabit is her prison house.... [F]orced to

live out of a body that is its own ruin, the Dalit suffers a state of permanent dissociation. (97)

Dalit scholars and activists have long understood the critical role of affect in the ritualized humiliation of caste and gender oppression India, as well as its imbrication in the forms of racial humiliation constitutive of the colonial order. Guru's foundational study on humiliation continues to incite critical debates on what we might call the visceral logics of caste and gender humiliation, a critical vantage point from which to understand the social reordering of Indian public and private life under postcolonial modernity.[8] While I align myself with critics such as Snehal Shingavi who argue that Anand's experiments of interiority are mostly to be read as projections of middle-class colonial humiliation onto scenes of caste humiliation, such that "caste chauvinism only becomes legible through the radical intellectual's "understanding of his own racialized body" (55), this is not to say that Anand's tactile poetics have nothing to contribute to debates on caste alienation, particularly through the lens of Geetha's reworking of alienation.[9]

In *Untouchable*, caste alienation is represented as a critical disconnect between raw sensation and the sense-making capacities of emotion and consciousness, rendered through an aesthetics of skin that carries interesting resonances with, as well as key divergences from, the "epidermalization" theorized by Frantz Fanon. In one of the opening scenes of *Untouchable*, the narrator tracks Bakha's rising body heat in the morning against the rising temperature of the day as he engages in the strenuous labor of his work. In dwelling on one particular task, which entails the shoveling of refuse into a furnace, the description focuses on Bakha's sensations of heat intensified by the fire: "He worked unconsciously. This forgetfulness or emptiness persisted in him over long periods. It was a sort of *insensitivity* created in him by the kind of work he had to do, a *tough skin* which must shield against all the most awful *sensations*.... The blood in Bakha's veins *tingled* with the heat as he stood before it" (Anand, *Untouchable*, 20, emphasis added). While the omniscient gaze moves between the somatic and psychic planes of Bakha's body, the language remains at the register of the skin. Within the depiction of the mundane labor and daily condition of the casteized subject, Bakha's mental and emotive state is likened to the callusing of skin, while it is a tingling sensation that vaguely registers the heat of the fire. These depictions of Bakha's consciousness as unfeeling and unresponsive are set against the stimulation at the level of his tactile reception. Bakha's emotive callousness and psychic insensitivity are further positioned in sharp contrast to the intensely affective personification of the fire that causes the sensations of his skin: "Quickly [the fire] flared up, suddenly illuminating the furnace ... an angry consuming power ..." (Anand, *Untouchable*, 20). The fire that stimulates the body's nerves is itself personified by an intense anger, a flaring temper, a dynamic and consuming force, but also a force that brings with it the power of illumination. What are we to make of this strange emotive displacement that makes salient an awakening of the somatic life of Bakha's body, even as his psychic life remains numb and unresponsive?

It is a very tactile encounter, the physical contact of a slap to Bakha's face, an assault on the untouchable surface of his skin, that catalyzes the moment of his transformation of consciousness in the novel. Before returning to this scene of tactile displacements, as Bakha shovels refuse into the fire, I argue, it is critical to examine the modalities of felt experience. As Anand writes of this staging in his 1972 lecture at Karnatak University, "Through the crisis of a slap on his face for touching a Brahmin, he changed his view of life itself and became aware of his dignity as a human being. This was an inward change, a revolution" (Anand, *Roots and Flowers*, 28). This "revolution" is set in motion in the novel by a traumatic encounter in the marketplace, where Bakha accidentally bumps into a Brahmin man. Having already been touched by the untouchable, the Brahmin decides to retaliate by slapping Bakha in the face hard enough to knock him to the floor: "The tonga-wallah heard a sharp, clear slap through the air.... [Bakha] stood aghast. Then his whole countenance lit with fire and his hands were no more joined.... [H]orror, rage, indignation swept over his frame (Anand, *Untouchable*, 50). Bakha's radical transformation in this moment is thus represented as the habituated reaction of shame and humility is replaced by a sudden eruption of anger. While Bakha's reactions of shame and humility are internalized manifestations of his complicity with his social subjugation, his explosion of anger is a visceral manifestation of a budding comprehension of the injustice of his situation.

Following the slap, Bakha's anger continues to build, metaphorized as the rising heat of a burning fire as he begins to connect the traumatic memories of his past abuses to the larger religious and ideological system from which he suffers: "There was a smoldering rage in his soul. His feelings would rise like spurts of smoke from a half-smothered fire, in fitful, unbalanced jerks when the recollection of some abuse or rebuke he had suffered kindled a spark in the ashes of remorse inside him" (Anand, *Untouchable*, 51). The slap is thus depicted as a somatic awakening, a violent stimulation of tactile feelings that is transmitted and translated into new emotive ones.

This transmission of tactile feeling to the stimulation of emotional feelings brings on a critical stream of self-questioning for Bakha, depicted through an intriguing blend of biological realism and Bloomsbury modernism: "'Why was all this?' he asked himself in the soundless speech of cells receiving and transmitting emotions, which was his usual way of communicating with himself" (Anand, *Untouchable*, 51). The violent awakening that registers at the levels of both surface and interior of the subaltern subject is thus rendered as the engine for a budding self-consciousness and self-interrogation, staged through the synaptic connections and relays of the body's somatic response. This transformation of emotions is inextricably wired to Bakha's intellectual awakening, as this scene initiates a lengthy stream of consciousness that eventually leads to the moment in which Bakha comes to intellectually grasp the source of his suffering.

Aesthetically, this moment is marked by a sudden shift in the metaphors of heat to those of light: "'For them I am a sweeper, sweeper—untouchable! Untouchable! Untouchable! That's the word! Untouchable! I am an Untouchable!' Like a ray of light shooting through the darkness, the recognition of his position, the significance of his lot dawned upon him. It illuminated the inner chambers of his mind. Everything that had happened to him traced its course up to this light and got the answer.... It was all explicable now" (Anand, *Untouchable*, 53). While these tropes of illumination are familiar articulations of intellectual enlightenment, what is significant here is that the illumination, the moment of a modernist epiphany, is revised through the thermal logic of the novel: the visual metaphors of light are crucially anticipated by the tactile metaphors of heat.[10] As we have seen, Anand invokes a common idiomatic mode of representing the emotion of anger through metaphors of fire, so that while the visual metaphor of light represents Bakha's epistemological transformation, it is the tactile metaphor of heat that represents his emotive transformation.

The thermal logic of the day is thus corporealized, in a sense, within the body logic of the novel's revolutionary arc, and it is the blazing of Bakha's anger that propels the radicalization of his perception. The social realist arc of the novel is charted through the heat of anger, the sensory and somatic transformation that brings about an emotive and intellectual one.

What is so interesting about this climax is that Bakha's budding anger is configured as a revolutionary impulse precisely because of its capacity to re-hinge the synaptic disjunctures between the sensations of his body and the sense-making matrices of his conscious awareness. In other words, the visceral response of anger is a revolutionary energetic for the casteized subject of the novel precisely for its capacity to reorder the sensory and cognitive registers of the body such that Bakha comes alive to his own tactility—through which a transformation of consciousness is posited as a possibility.

Dwelling in these seemingly marginal, densely tactile and sensory moments within the novel reveals the visceral emplotments of the social realist arc that moves through the sensory and emotive interface between the habits of mind and automated reflexes of the body. Every shift in consciousness is inextricably tethered to a concomitant shift in the visceral states of the body (and here the energetic life and vitality of skin and touch). This is a transformation that involves the relay and relation between what Parama Roy terms the conjugation of physiological and epistemological registers of the body—a "re-somatizing" of the subject. This reconstitution of the casteized and colonized subject becomes key, I argue, to the revolutionary vision of the novel. What is so remarkable about this rendering is the way in which the visceral response of the untouchable subject emerges as a revolutionary catalyst precisely for its capacity to rehinge and reorder the sensorial and intellectual registers of the body.

Despite *Untouchable*'s utopian trajectory, the novel ends without resolution, concluding with the arrival at a public gathering of Mahatma Gandhi, who at some moments inspires and excites Bakha by his speech and at others confounds and troubles him. As Ulka Anjaria writes, "The novel ends on a note of ambivalence, as it is not clear to what extent [Bakha] has been inspired by Gandhi's support of the eradication of untouchability and to what extent it has merely reinforced his despair" (68).[11] While *Untouchable* concludes rather ambivalently, as Bakha's interior focalization merges with a cacophony of voices and opinions emerging from the crowd of Gandhi's public gathering, there is one particular voice that seems to remain with Bakha. It is the voice of the poet standing in the crowd: "We can feel new feelings. We can learn to be aware with a new awareness. We can envisage the possibility of creating new races from the latent heat in our dark brown bodies" (Anand, *Untouchable*, 153). This "latent heat" that rises within the body of our protagonist throughout the trajectory of this novel is thus staged in the moment of the slap as the righteous anger of the revolutionary subject; his epiphany is represented as a new way of "seeing" enabled by the feeling of new feelings.

It is with this understanding of the emotive and tactile valences of feeling at play in this staging of *Untouchable*'s internal revolution that we can further make sense, I argue, of the epidermal drama with which I began. If we return to the tingling sensation that vaguely registers in Bakha's body as he shovels refuse into the furnace, we find that the fire (which, as we remember, is personified as angry) reappears in the revolutionary moment of the slap as a metaphor for Bakha's anger—the anger that will catalyze the moment of his illumination. In other words, through this chiasmatic reorganization of literal and metaphorical registers, the fire and its metaphorical anger of the earlier scene becomes Bakha's literal anger, metaphorized by the fire in the moment of his illumination. This emotive transformation is thus paralleled by a fascinating aesthetic transformation as we witness a semantic splintering of the very emotive idiom of anger under interrogation. Within this narrative progression we can understand the vague tingling sensation against the fire of the furnace as an anticipatory staging of the violent slap, the sting, he will experience in the marketplace.

What is intriguing about this anticipatory staging is that this tactile detail, this tingling, is echoed in a number of scenes in the opening of the novel. A series of mild epidermal stimulations—tingling, prickling, stinging sensations that are weak yet unmistakable registers of irritation and abrasion at the surface of the skin—serve as premature threshold moments in the narrative's development. One of the most explicit foreshadowings of Bakha's eventual revolution begins as an extended depiction of his tactile sensitivity to the afternoon sun. Like the figure of the fire that mobilizes its imbricated properties of light and heat, the sun acts as a central trope within the narrative of *Untouchable*, structuring the temporal logic of the day's narration, as well as the enlightenment of the protagonist. In a scene in which Bakha breaks from his day to seek the warmth of the afternoon sun, the narrative focuses on the sensations of the heat as it permeates and penetrates his skin's surface. The omniscient gaze moves between the surfaces of Bakha's hands, which register the heat of the sun, and the pupils of his eyes, which attempt to take in the sun's light: "He wanted to warm his flesh; he wanted the warmth to get behind the scales of the dry powdery surface that had formed on his fingers.... He lifted his face to the sun, open-eyed for a moment, then with the pupils of his eyes half closed, half open. It seemed to give him a thrill, a queer sensation which spread on the surface of his flesh where the tincture of warmth penetrated the numbed skin" (Anand, *Untouchable*, 33). The tactility of this depiction centers on Bakha's desire for the feeling of the warmth on his body and, more specifically, his desire for the feeling to "penetrate" the numbed skin of his body and the calloused surface of his fingers. As we know, Bakha's sensory register of the sun's heat in this scene will be transformed symbolically into the heat of his revolutionary emotions. The scene thus stages Bakha's desire to awaken the modalities of his "felt" experiences—a desire that is realized through the trajectory of the narrative. In an attempt to draw the warmth from inside of his body and to make his skin more penetrable to the sun's rays, Bakha instinctively begins to create friction on the surface of his face with his own hands to bring heat and energy from within the body: "Instinctively he rubbed his face in order to make it warm enough to take in the rays of the sun, to open out its pores. A couple brisk rubs and he felt the blood in his cheeks rising to the high bones" (Anand, *Untouchable*, 33). The scene thus depicts Bakha's yearning for the sun not simply as a passive desire but as a desire that motivates the active stimulation of his own somatic logics.

It is one such minor epidermal detail in particular that occurs early in the novel, however, that more fully opens up the logic of Bakha's skin. In this early scene, the rhythmic portrayal of Bakha's daily routine is suddenly interrupted by a focus on the feeling of his woolen sleeve against his face as he wipes perspiration off his forehead: "Its woolen texture felt nice and sharp against his skin, but left an irritating warmth behind. It was a pleasant irritation, however, and he went ahead with the renewed vigour that discomfort sometimes gives to the body" (Anand, *Untouchable*, 17). Residing within the slippages between the emotive and tactile valences of "feeling," irritation, in the words of Sianne Ngai, connotes "a conspicuously weak or inadequate form of anger, as well as an affect that bears an unusually close relationship to the body's surfaces or skin" (35). In this sense, this scene of irritation anticipates the explosion of anger that brings about the moment of illumination in both the tactile sting of the slap and the anger that catalyzes Bakha's transformation of consciousness. The novel thus charts the evolution of the protagonist into the consciousness of the national subject through a critical shift that moves, to invoke Anand's own phrase, from the palpable to the "impalpable feelings" of his untouchable body.

This movement between the tactile and emotive valences of feeling, however, invokes a conflation that exists in our everyday speech, for it is not uncommon to speak of feeling numb or irritated or to describe someone as hot-tempered or callous. What interests me, rather, is the politics of this particular poetics of touch and feeling, how the surface of the body comes to stand in for its depths, as Anand renders the transformational potential of his protagonist through the sensations of the skin. Probing the epidermal logic at play here, the etymology of the verb "to irritate" invokes the energetic logic that drives the novel's form: "to excite an organ to some characteristic action: as motion, contraction, or impulse, by the application of a stimulus," or simply, "to stimulate to vital action." Within these threshold moments of the novel, then, the epidermal logics of Bakha's irritations reveal a fundamental concern with the nature of progressive feeling—the feelings that will incite and excite the subaltern body to "vital action." These tactile stagings represent the transformative possibilities of these feelings: the very possibility of feeling new feelings. The poetics of touch in these anticipatory moments thus reveal Anand's investment in the question of what stimulates and moves the body, and, by allegorical extension, the national body, into political action. This narrative indulgence in the somatic properties of Bakha's palpable feelings thus serves as the site through which his impalpable ones are not only anticipated, but theorized.

The poetics of Bakha's tactile dramas, in fact, return us to Anand's own thought experiments surrounding the politics of feeling at the heart of what constituted progressive literature. In his drafting of the PWA manifesto, this investment in the transformative potential of feeling, in fact, lies at the core of his very definition of the collective's use of the term "progressive": "All that arouses in us the critical spirit, which examines institutions and customs in the light of reason, which helps us to act, to organize ourselves, to transform, we accept as progressive" (Anand, "Amended Manifesto," 20). For, as we will find in his theoretical meditations on the "intensity" of literary realization, it is the transformative potential of the vital energies of human emotion and experience that remains at the core of Anand's notion of progressivism, staged within the embodied life of his fictional protagonist.

The corporeal poetics within Anand's fiction thus provide a critical lens into the ways in which the author imagines the very consciousness he sought to transform. The visceral reflex of the untouchable subject is invested with revolutionary potential in *Untouchable* precisely for its capacities to reorder and reconstitute the sensory registers of the body that provide the pathway to an "ascendance" of consciousness. In tracking Anand's experiments in character interiority, we find that the progressive novel form and its national realist trajectory are fundamentally structured by the visceral conditions of the revolutionary subject. That is, the developmental arc of the novel draws on the visceral logics of its protagonist's body. Conceived through emerging scientific epistemologies of the time, from psychoanalysis to thermodynamics, the visceral eruptions of Anand's novels are imagined as critical energetics that vitalize the subaltern body to an "ascendance" of political consciousness. As we find throughout this book, the question of what would define literature and art as progressive in a decolonizing India—not only for Anand, but also for the diverse array of political visionaries that constituted the Marxist political movements in India—brings to focus their dynamic aesthetic grappling with revolutionary feeling and the revolution *of* feelings.

The Dialectic of Feeling: On Progressive Writing

Throughout Anand's published essays and public lectures on the nature of progressive writing, the force, or "intensity," through which a literary work is able to communicate the realms of what he refers to as felt experience and awareness remains a central concern. In a public lecture he delivered in 1939 to the newly formed PWA, these experiential realms appear at the center of his theories on progressive literature: "Writing is not only great when it is proletarian or bourgeois, but when it is an intense enough realization of experience through those creative forces the exact nature of which has not yet been defined by psychological science" (Anand, "On the Progressive Writers Movement," 5). In the next section, I pursue these questions surrounding the affective dimensions of "progressive" writing by turning to a novel Anand wrote a few years after *Untouchable*: *Lament on the Death of a Master of Arts* (1938). By honing Anand's visceral aesthetics, I read *Lament* as a reworking of the revolutionary trajectory of *Untouchable*. What interests me about the later novel is that—in centering on a middle-class, Muslim, male protagonist instead of the subaltern—the novelistic form of the "lament" reverses the affective structure of the progressive novel form of *Untouchable*. For, while *Untouchable* charts an ascendance of consciousness through the energetic animation and activation of the sensory and emotive registers of the protagonist, as Bakha awakens to a new sense of tactility and bodily life, *Lament* charts an ascendance of consciousness through the slow decay and deterioration of the sensory relays of the Muslim protagonist—an energetic inversion that I theorize in chapter 4 as the novel of "evisceration."

Anand described *Lament* as a "long short story," an extended Whitman ballad that he wrote on a sea voyage "under the influence of" Federico García Lorca's *Lament for the Death of a Bullfighter* (Anand and Cowasjee, 109). In a letter he wrote to his friend and critic Saros Cowasjee, Anand complained that, while his novel *Lament on the Death of a Master of Arts* was one of the "intensest, if not the best" contributions to the PWA, academics had largely overlooked it because of their "ignorance of felt experience in a novel" (Anand and Cowasjee, 109). How one measures the so-called intensity of the progressive work, I argue, opens up a generative set of questions surrounding the relationship between the consciousness of both the reader and the writer of the progressive novel. In light of Anand's visceral aesthetics, it is worth probing this notion of literary realization, for exploring the conceptual coordinates through which Anand reflects on his own process of writing, the transmission of feelings he seeks to enact between the readerly and writerly consciousness, proves particularly instructive in unlocking the polemics of progressivism in his fiction. When one traces the reflections on Anand's creative process documented in personal letters and essays throughout his lengthy career, what becomes evident is that his notion of realization invokes a process of transmission in which the author becomes a kind of conduit between the reader and the lived energies of the subaltern figures of his fiction. Anand once described this process as a kind of possession through which he expresses the depth of the emotional lives, the "impalpable feelings," of his characters (Anand and Cowasjee, 124).[12]

In another letter Anand wrote to Cowasjee, he relates an anecdote that describes his motivation for writing his novel *The Road*. Anand tells Cowasjee that while he was visiting Haryana, he was shocked to find that the caste Hindus would not touch the stones being carried by untouchables for building a road there and that "the outcastes not only in South India, but in the mixed north[,] were still consigned to the limbo of oblivion" (Anand and Cowasjee, 124). Anand reports that he brought this to the attention of Jawaharlal Nehru, but Nehru did not believe him. In fact, Anand relates, Nehru was angered by Anand's report. In response to Nehru's reaction Anand writes,

I said I would prove it to him by showing it to him in the "enchanted mirror." I, therefore, pursued the mirror game, at various levels of consciousness of the people, *concave and convex*, involved in the drama of the road. You will notice that, technically, it is not a straight narrative, but diversified by breaking through the obvious planes to the impalpable feelings of the characters involved.... I, therefore, tried to achieve awareness of the insulted and injured, by transcending the first "amazement" through the dialectic of feeling. (Anand and Cowasjee, 124–25, emphasis added)

Anand's response to Nehru's disbelief is thus not to take Nehru to Haryana to show him the situation with his own eyes. What is assumed is that Nehru would not be able to see the situation, even if he witnessed it himself. It is, in fact, only through the manipulation and distortion of Anand's literary reflection—through the "enchanted mirror"—that Nehru would actually be able to "see" the injustices of this situation. Anand insists that it is what can be seen only through distortion, what cannot be seen through transparency, that will bring about justice for the casteized subjects of Haryana. The moment of "awareness," then—for Anand's reader, the moment of a privileged aesthetic seeing—is impelled by a certain kind of emotive transmission, which Anand refers to as "the dialectic of feeling."

Anand often described his process of writing as an evacuation of the author's self, as he writes in a letter to Atma Ram: "There is achieved a glow, a flow and a current of vital communication which may not only give a certain glimmering to the writer, but also reveal some candescence to the reader" (Anand and Ram, 633). Anand's "realization" is often conceptualized and, in fact, visualized through optic metaphors of electricity and the transfers of illuminative energies, as he describes this transformation of both the writerly and readerly consciousness through flows of energy and vital "currents" that result in a "a moment of candescence." The climactic moment in *Untouchable*, in fact, recalls Anand's own formulations of literary "realization" as a transmission of feeling—a "dialectic of feeling" that brings about the illuminated moment to the reader. It is this transfer of emotive energy in literature, when it is "intense enough," that enables an intellectual transformation for the reader, or what Anand calls the moment of illumination, a term borrowed from the French poet Arthur Rimbaud (Anand and Cowasjee, 114). In fact, Anand describes the act of transmission in his 1939 lecture to the PWA through this visual metaphor: "At the best one can only attempt to ... fix one's gaze in the hypnotic trance, the aesthetic vision of an illuminated moment and increase one's understanding and enjoyment of life" (Anand, "On the Progressive Writers Movement," 5).

It is in this context that we may come to understand that when Anand describes *Lament* in his letter to Cowasjee as one of the "intensest, if not best" contributions to the PWA, the metric of intensity measures the text's transmission of feeling. The progressive possibility of transforming a collective consciousness for Anand is the object of his narrative stagings, as well as the very transformation he attempts to actualize in the consciousness of his readers. In turning to Anand's fiction, my focus remains on how these underlying preoccupations with the emotive contours of progressive writing surface within the visceral aesthetics of Anand's fiction. That is, it is how Anand's fiction self-reflexively theorizes this transformation and transmission of affect that he seeks to enact in his reader that I further explore, for what appears as rather undeveloped and elusive, mired in the discourse of secular rationalism within the language of Anand's political writings surrounding the place of emotion in the transformation of consciousness, finds creative expression within the "impalpable feelings" of his fiction.[13]

The story of *Lament on the Death of a Master of Arts* revolves around a central protagonist, Nur, who has been suffering from a debilitating and undiagnosable illness for five months, rendering him bedridden in the final days before his death. In the novel, Anand replaces the subaltern protagonist with a middle-class Muslim subject. Just as the protagonist of *Lament* is physically immobilized by the disease that consumes his body, the narrative is spatially constrained to the singular bedroom in which Nur lies. The movements of plot within the short story are almost entirely contained within his movements of thought and consciousness. Through the use of dense sensory character focalization, the novel travels among Nur's states of lucid consciousness, or fevered hallucinations, and dives into obsession, dreams, nightmares, daydreams, fantasies, and memories, while the boundaries among these states are perpetually unclear.

As Nur's body deteriorates and his condition worsens, a range of painful memories rises to the surface. Nur is forced to reflect on his deep sense of shame surrounding his poverty; his inability to live up to his father's expectations; the emptiness of his arranged marriage; and his mistreatment of his wife and child and his inability to provide for them. Moving among Nur's psychic and emotive states as he charts these traumatic memories, the narrative gaze simultaneously orbits the biological life of Nur's failing body. As in Anand's *Untouchable*, the reader is thus led through narrative oscillations that travel between the surfaces and depths of Nur's anatomy and the movements of his thoughts and consciousness, mapping his psychological trauma onto the degeneration of his body. As we will see, it is across this layered cartography of the unconscious and conscious that Anand interrogates the visceral logics and political meanings of his suffering.

Throughout the narrative of *Lament*, an exploration of how the colonized subject is disciplined through logics of shame and fear is staged through the figures of his father, his schoolmaster, and his mullah. These disciplinary figures, who often blend together and morph into one another in Nur's dreams, function metonymically in the narrative to critique the repressive logics of the family, the colonial education system, and religious institutions. In one such moment, we drift into a traumatic childhood memory surrounding Nur's early schooling. Anand renders these memories through a stream of consciousness that traces the conditioned pathways of Nur's thoughts and their movements through chains of associations. These memories, however, are narrativized not simply through a sequence of thoughts and events but, further, through the surfaces and sites of his body in depicting his experience of nausea:

> Far off from this dawn, remote, half-forgotten, ages before now, before the high school and college, there was a queer impatience, in the feel of early mornings, the fear of being late at school, the violent nausea in the belly even as he had gulped hot tea and swallowed mouthfuls of fried *parathas* dipped in mutton gravy.... As he had hurried on his way to school, the dizzy vision of the Master's perpendicular rod had blotted out space and time, while the clothes stuck to the flesh in the clammy heat and perspiration of summer mornings. (Anand, *Lament*, 14)

Nur's anxious recollections here are rendered to us through various sites of bodily reception: the feeling of nausea in the belly moving to the tastes and the temperatures of tea and *parathas* on the tongue, the site that anticipates the presence of vomit; then the feeling of the texture of his damp clothing clinging to his flesh, the site that anticipates the beatings of the schoolmaster with the weapon that he dizzily envisions. Moving between these sensory sites, the narrative logic of this memory traces the intricate orchestration of the body's emotive logics. In the very narrativization of this memory, Anand thus exposes the machinations of fear that operate through their capacity to condition not only the habitual pathways of Nur's thoughts but also the involuntary somatic functions of his body.

As Nur's sense of fear is thus depicted as conditioned through the automatization of his corporeal reflexes, we also find that his panic emerges out of the contradictions of colonial time, caught in the incongruity of the temporal logics of his Islamic and British educations. Nur's memory of his "queer impatience" and the panic of his anticipation reveal the way in which his experience of terror and shame operate through the temporal logics of colonial modernity: "His grandmother had no sense of time and did not start cooking his meal until she had said her prayers.... He had begged his father to buy him a watch, one of those nice shiny watches with a chain, which he could carry in the pocket of his waistcoat to school, as all the other boys had watches and wouldn't show them to him except from a distance, affecting to be superior sahibs like Mercado Sahib, the Headmaster" (Anand, *Lament*, 14). As Anand exposes the sense of time in this passage as a profoundly visceral logic of the body, we see that the fear that Nur experiences is rooted in a deep sense of belatedness as he is caught in the disjuncture between these two temporalities. Thus, in the very subtleties of how Nur narrates his memories to himself, Anand interrogates the visceral channels of his colonial desires. Indeed, Nur's desire for the pocket watch, what he refers to as "his attempt to be happy and fashionable," exposes his sense of both time and taste as functions of time and mechanisms of corporeal control (Anand, *Lament*, 14). Nur's fetishization of the pocket watch reveals how his experience of temporality simultaneously structures the logics of his desire.

Anand's experimentation in character interiority, as we have seen in *Untouchable*, moves between Nur's stream of consciousness and the sensory receptors and surfaces of his body, interrogating how the colonized subject registers social experience. This oscillation of the narrative gaze, I argue, reveals a key representational preoccupation of Anand's with the discipline of the colonized subject. In other words, the choreography of the biological and cognitive networks within Anand's prose interrogates the interrelation of these spheres as concentrated nodes of ideological reception and register. As we witness in the memory of Nur's schooling, Anand renders the sensory registers of the body as somatic sites of discipline and pedagogy.

One of the most jarring aspects of Anand's corporeal prose is his use of an exceedingly technical biological vocabulary amid a modernist sensory poetics through which the discipline of the colonized body is depicted. In one of our very first introductions to Nur, for example, the narrative gaze scans the ailing physiognomy of his body through the systematized language of pseudomedical discourse. We are thrust into an anatomical inventory of Nur's physiology, from dilated nostrils to eyeballs bulging from their sockets, from flushed cheeks to aching spine, cracking ribs, and irregular heartbeats, even as the cause of Nur's illness and suffering evades the diagnostic promise of the language (Anand, *Lament*, 9). As the body of our protagonist is scientifically systematized, an existentialist stream of consciousness emerges in tension with a peculiar turn to a kind of biological realism.

As we scan the various biological interiors of Nur's ailing body in the opening of the novel, however, it is at the eye of our subject that the narrative lingers: "the hard ribs and collar bone which seemed to crack as they rose out of his transparent flesh.... [T]he clear forehead which sighted with cool composure each anxious thought in his fevered brain.... The tender eyes that bent their light now inwards, now outwards" (Anand, *Lament*, 9). Invoking his discussion of the concave mirror, Anand draws attention to the rhythmic bending of the eye's light, reminding us as we scan the interiors of Nur's mind and body that it is always through a manipulation of light, and its distortion, that we can see. Despite the precision of the symptoms within the biological lexicon deployed and the apparent "transparency" of the flesh and "clarity" of the forehead through which we read Nur's thoughts, the scientific discourse is unable to fulfill its promise: to name and cure the sickness from which Nur suffers. This preoccupation with the optic register of our protagonist emerges throughout the narrative of *Lament*. In a momentary pause, for example, as Nur glances at the looking glass and assorted glass bangles on the bookshelf, drawing attention to the curvatures of these glass objects, the prose invokes the tension between the transparency and distortion of these objects that we find at the core of much of Anand's play with interiority and omniscience (Anand, *Lament*, 20). As with the biological gaze that focalizes the convexity of Nur's eye, the reader is caught in a number of moments in which what we see in the novel has an uncanny reflection back on the distortions, or the visceral logics, through which we see it in the first place.

As Nur moves back and forth throughout the narrative of *Lament* between a desire for death and the will to live, his stream of consciousness is continually disrupted by waves of nausea. As a Sartrean trope of existential crises within the narrative, this figure of nausea, as an involuntary and psychosomatic reaction of the body, also becomes a focalized site of Nur's fundamental struggle with his inability to control the reflexes of his body. Repeatedly throughout the story Nur suffers momentary lapses in which he feels he is about to vomit as these waves of nausea enact his battle with the betrayal and retaliation of his failing body. The figure of nausea thus depicts a critical disconnect between Nur's will and his capacity to command his physical body. This visceral trope that pervades the narrative, I argue, stages the technologies of social subjection as a violent automatization of the body through which hegemonic logics are sustained through self-infliction. Nausea, in this novel, is the concentrated site through which this problematic is hashed out on the terrain of the visceral.

As the story of *Lament* opens, in fact, we find our protagonist in an intense battle to gain control over his involuntary reactions and reflexes. The narrative begins with our protagonist suffering through the verbal abuses of his father, who reproaches him for his illness and for draining his money through medical bills, when Nur suddenly experiences a wave of nausea. Nur reluctantly rises to consciousness when he is jolted awake by his father, and the narrator tells us, "His eyes opened against his will" (Anand, *Lament*, 8). Our introduction to Nur is thus framed by this apparent disjuncture between his will and his capacity to control the reflexes of his body. The narration then shifts from the verbal abuse of Nur's father to an intensely phenomenological account of the fear his father invokes within him: "He quavered, struggling to throw off the spell of fear which his father cast on him" (Anand, *Lament*, 8). As Nur attempts to interrupt the fear his father provokes and reroute his emotive reaction, the narration locates its somatic manifestations in the muscles of Nur's lips, the sound of footsteps resounding in his ears, the warmth in his limbs, and the feeling of bile in his mouth:

> He twisted his lips as waves of resentment warmed his heavy, sleepy limbs. "No, I don't want to live," he said.... "I wish I were dead." As soon as he said it he wanted to stifle the thought: his father's footsteps were out of reach of his ears now.... But he felt an involuntary bile in his mouth as though he wanted to be sick with disgust. (Anand, *Lament*, 8)

As Nur attempts to interrupt his morbid desires, the narrator travels through these perceptual receptors of Nur's physiology to reveal their links with the logic of his thoughts. In this staging of Nur's experience of fear, the novel depicts a drama of control over both the somatic and psychological realms of his body.

What is of interest to me about Anand's depiction of nausea, however, is its peculiar coupling of the involuntary and the desired. As Anand describes Nur's wave of nausea in this scene—"He felt an *involuntary* bile in his mouth as though he *wanted* to be sick with disgust" (emphasis added)—he invokes a tension inherent in the biological figure itself: nausea is an involuntary reaction of the body that is characterized by the frustrated desire for release. What is striking in this passage, however, is that the desire for release in this moment is embedded in a conditional phrase: it was "*as though* he wanted to be sick with disgust" (emphasis added).[14] Hence, as we move from the sensory reception of bile in Nur's mouth, we encounter a marked linguistic resistance in this phrasing to precisely pin down its corresponding emotion. The interruption that this conditional phrase inserts into our movement from Nur's sensation of bile to its affective register destabilizes the semiotics of Nur's body so that the sensation of bile and what it signals through its register of feeling is shifted to what it *should* signal and what that signal should be. Anand's language thus codes Nur's wanting to be "sick with disgust" as a desire to make his body readable *as* sick with disgust; to symptomize his sickness as a function of his disgust. As Nur confides in his friend near the end of the narrative, "There is a bile in my mouth and a sickness in the stomach—as though the world sickens me" (Anand, *Lament*, 32). Nur's verbal articulation of his symptom is again marked by this grammatical interruption, by the punctuated gap of the hyphen that amplifies the disjuncture between his sensation and that of which it is symptomatic. Nausea, as an intensified site of Nur's corporeal struggle, then, stages not simply the synaptic disjuncture between his will and the neurological impulses of his body but, further, the disjuncture between the sensorial logic of bile in his mouth and what it *should mean* to him.

What is fascinating about the corporeal poetics of *Lament* is that this semantic gap we see in Anand's depiction of nausea, between Nur's sensations and how he is to make sense of them, is present in nearly all of the descriptions of Nur's failing body. As the narrative gaze dips into the physiological minutiae of Nur's body, it is almost always interrupted by a linguistic resistance, an "as though" or an "as if," that unhinges the body's sensation from the semiotics of his feelings. The failure and betrayal of Nur's body, then, is not simply of his will and his capacity to translate a desire into a physiological act but of the very readability of his body. As Nur's undiagnosable illness continues to intensify, the synaptic as well as the semiotic connections and pathways of his body disintegrate. Nur continually turns to his failing body for answers as to how to get well, but he is met with increasing corporeal defiance: "There was no answer from the depths of his body which now seemed stretched in a morbid self-questioning. His heavy heart beat out a refrain: "I must get well, I must get well,' *as if* it were still drugged with its obstinate belief in existence. And there was a quickening at the back of his head *as though* of defiance" (Anand, *Lament*, 21, emphasis added). Nur thus continues to mine his ailing body for meaning, desperately seeking to understand his sickness to become well again. Yet what is amplified in this semantic gap is that, as Nur searches his body for answers, he is increasingly imprisoned by both the corporeal betrayal of his will and his body's semiotic defiance.

As we have seen amplified in the heightened visceral figure of nausea, the linguistic refusals of Anand's corporeal depictions continually rupture the semiotics of Nur's failing body. It is from within this rupture that we encounter a critical gap between what his body logics mean and what they *should* mean to him. However, I argue that it is precisely this disjuncture of the *should mean* that opens up the terrain of what they *could* mean. In other words, it is Nur's corporeal failures of readability—his body's refusals to adhere to a legible semiotic logic—that open up the terrain of "experience" to the possibility of a radical relearning. As Anand describes the story of *Lament* in his letter to Cowasjee, "In it, the man who was aware of the despair in life generally in the beginning, begins to be conscious of his own despair" (Anand and Cowasjee, 107). I argue that Anand charts this ascendance of consciousness through the synaptic and semantic breakdown of Nur's somatic logics, for as his biological functions continue to disobey, through the melancholic development of the *Lament*, he reaches greater levels of understanding surrounding his own misery and trauma, as well as the social structures that have imprisoned him. It is therefore in the very breakdown of Nur's body, *its* betrayal and defiance, and the widening gap between his sensations and the sense-making properties of thought and consciousness toward the end of the novel—the synaptic and semiotic breakdown with which *Untouchable* conversely begins—that we can locate the transformative potential latent in his failing body.[15] While for Bakha the visceral logics of irritation catalyze the body coming alive to its modalities of touch and "feeling"—the "lower" sensations of tactility driving its semantic links with "higher" order emotions and thoughts, which make the ascendance of a revolutionary consciousness possible—it is exactly the inverse in *Lament*. It is precisely in Nur's bodily failure, in its semantic betrayal and refusals of intelligibility and meaning, that I locate the possibility of a critical visceral unlearning—that is, new ways of seeing enabled by the feeling of new feelings.

3. Compulsion

This chapter is a visceral exploration into how the female body—its erotic curvatures and grotesque protuberances, sticky and viscous textures and fluids—becomes the focal object of violent subjection by both colonial and anticolonial nationalist regimes of discipline. In light of a remarkable pair of leading Muslim feminist activists and authors, Ismat Chughtai and Rashid Jahan, this chapter opens up the ongoing legacies of sexual violence in the postcolonial subcontinent by exploring the visceral nature of the threat of women's sexuality and desire through a figure that I call the erotics of disgust. While in the previous chapters the visceral stimulants of political rage and nationalist emotion are invested with the potential to impel the colonial subject into various states of consciousness and political action, disgust in this chapter emerges as an unruly energetic, posing a particular kind of conundrum in thinking the feminist politics of progressive feeling. The feminist phenomenology of disgust in this study is theorized through its relationship with its dialectical other, desire, and thus through its energetic forces of repulsion and attraction. The chapter offers a feminist critique of the traditional phenomenology of disgust by centering the codes of erotic texture produced out of histories of colonial hygiene and bourgeois sexual discipline in late colonial India.

It is through the femme figure of craving—a figure for the interanimation of desire with disgust—that the instability and unruliness of the visceral energetic in this chapter is centered for both its role in violent disciplinary regimes, as well as for its potentiality for subversion.

The question of how the gendered and racialized body is "moved" in this chapter centers the role of texture in craving. More precisely, it raises the question of how texture animates and activates bodily appetites, both sexual and gastronomic, through the compulsive figure of craving. It is how the very materiality of the female body becomes the heightened object of the violent moral regimes of disgust and corporeal control in late colonial India that provide the historical frame of this study. The phenomenology of texture forces us to contend with disgust's relationship to desire and, in so doing, with how texture animates the imbricated relationship between colonial appetites and aversions. In her book *Touching Feeling*, Eve Sedgwick proposes that to "perceive texture is always, immediately, and de facto to be immersed in a field of active narrative hypothesizing"—to ask "what could I do with it, what is it like? Or how does it impinge on me?" (13). My interest in textures in this study derives from the way they *move* the body, what the body is moved to do, and how the body is moved to want. This chapter thus complicates the trajectory of the previous chapters by underscoring the dialectic of attraction and repulsion that underwrites the visceral energetic. However, it is also from within the push and pull of the dialectic that these feminist writers locate the possibility of progressive feeling in the very affects harnessed by violent disciplinary regimes of colonial taste.

Rashid Jahan, feminist activist and author, and her student Ismat Chughtai were part of a new, prominent, and young internationalist generation of Muslim Marxist intellectuals and anticolonial activist authors who wrote and published widely throughout India from the 1930s through the 1950s. While the Marxist political movements in India were dedicated to the role of art and literature in transforming the emergent national consciousness, Jahan and Chughtai intervened in these political debates through an interrogation of the female body that structured the very imaginaries of "progressivism" and postcolonial modernity. Jahan's and Chughtai's unique literary styles bear the mark of Russian and European literary influences, and, most notably, the influence of Sigmund Freud. Chughtai is acknowledged for being the first to write in *begumati zuban*, the distinctly feminized Urdu dialect of middle-class Muslim women, as she reworked the generic codes of social realism through a feminist lens sharply attuned to the sensory minutiae of everyday life (Gopal, *Literary Radicalism in India*, 157). By exploring the materialist poetics of their prose, I show how this pair of feminists relentlessly interrogated the violent disciplining of the female body that structured discourses of progress and modernity in late colonial India at the brink of nationhood. In tracking their feminist investments in the dialectic of desire and disgust, I center the places where colonial and nationalist regimes of obscenity give way to female erotic desire, as Chughtai and Jahan exposed and challenged the masculinist assumptions of their male comrades.

Obscene Textures

Jahan's activism was wide-ranging. As a doctor trained in Western gynecology, she offered women's health care in low-caste and impoverished communities; educated women in reproductive health and marriage rape in sweepers' colonies; held adult education classes; ran her own gynecological medical practice; participated in trade union rallies and protest marches; wrote articles for her political magazine, *Chingari*; and wrote and orchestrated political street theater.[1] Jahan was an accomplished journalist, a short-story writer, and a playwright. She wrote and directed her own theater and radio plays and adapted the stories of Chekhov, Gorky, James Joyce, and Premchand for radio. Jahan was also one of the few women to join the Communist Party of India in the 1930s; she, in fact, chose to be buried in Moscow, where she had spent her final days, with her epitaph reading, "Communist. Doctor. Writer" (Jalil, ix).

Infamously, Jahan was the sole woman among a group of Urdu writers who in 1933 published an incendiary collection of short stories titled *Angarey* (Burning Coals, or Embers), which staged a Marxist and feminist critique of both Islamic orthodoxy and the colonial government in India. The publication created such a backlash in Muslim communities that the colonial government banned it and had all copies burned. The publication of *Angarey*, however, gave birth to the generation of Muslim Marxist intellectuals and anticolonial activist authors writing and publishing in India from the 1930s to the 1950s. As Priyamavada Gopal writes, "Jahan became an icon of the literary radicalism of *Angarey* itself, decried by some and celebrated by others," and it was from this position that Jahan "would find herself thinking about articulating a critique of colonialism without conceding ground to patriarchy and traditionalists within her community"

(*Literary Radicalism in India*, 42). Testifying to the enduring controversy of Jahan's legacy, in 2004 Alighar Muslim University banned a proposed observance of Rashid Jahan's centenary, fearing it would provoke political "agitation."

What little has been written on Rashid Jahan's fiction centers on her remarkable short story "Woh" (That One), which depicts an encounter between a young female teacher and a prostitute in a clinic who suffers from a venereal disease. Jahan centers "That One" on the gendered subaltern figure of the prostitute, a common aesthetic object of Marxist social realist literature in South Asia during this era. A young middle-class woman, newly graduated from college and working at a women's school, narrates the story; she represents a semiautobiographical Jahan, who was a part of a generation of middle-class Muslim women trained in Western gynecology by the British colonial government.[2] As Rakshanda Jalil writes, "The action in 'Woh' takes place in a newly-opened space, a public space, where women from different social classes meet, an encounter that was inconceivable even a decade earlier" (92). One day, the narrator encounters a woman who, she finds out, is a prostitute and who comes to the clinic for treatment. The prostitute's face is so disfigured as a result of venereal disease that the others working in the clinic recoil in disgust when they see her; they refuse to touch the chair she sits on and repeatedly curse her repulsive and depraved presence:

> I first met her at the hospital.... She had come there for treatment.... Seeing her the other women turned away. Even the doctor's eyes strained shut in disgust. I felt repulsed too, but somehow managed to look straight at her and smile. She smiled back, or at least I thought she tried to—it was difficult to tell.... [S]he had no nose. Two raw, gaping holes stood in its place. She had also lost one of her eyes. To see with the one she had to crane her neck around. (Jahan, "Woh," 119)

Jahan adds another grotesque detail: "often the two raw holes in her face were running" (119).

Later, this nameless, faceless woman, referred to by the others in disgust as "that one" (*woh*), finds the narrator at her workplace, a women's school. When that one arrives, the narrator holds back her revulsion and offers her a seat. That one presents the narrator with a flower. The narrator again holds back her disgust at the mere touch of the flower and tucks it behind her ear. Her revulsion arises not only from the disfigured woman's appearance, but also from the prospect of touch—the fear of proximity and "pollution." A daily ritual begins: that one visits the narrator at the school, says nothing, and presents her with a flower, which the narrator tucks behind her ear. Gopal astutely reads these ritual encounters as "an inverted romance with [the narrator's] own emotional existence at the centre.... There is only a hint of irony here as the narrative draws on the high sentimental rhetoric of the 'afsana' or romantic short story that was especially popular with a female readership" (44). This ritual unfolds a peculiar set of recursive intimate gestures in their daily encounters, which recalls Lauren Berlant's provocative meditation on intimacy: "To intimate is to communicate with the sparest of signs and gestures.... But intimacy also involves an aspiration for a narrative about something shared, a story about both oneself and others that will turn out in a particular way" ("Intimacy," 281). And yet, despite these aspirations for a shared story that could "turn out" a different way, the prostitute's daily visits bring the narrator to a state of panic. The women who work at the narrator's school become increasingly agitated and indignant regarding that one's debauched presence at the school and begin to ridicule and condemn the narrator. The unrelenting presence of the subaltern figure in the story thrusts the narrator into a stream of self-reflection and speculation:

> I felt awkward and humiliated, I was being made into an object of humiliation in school. Still, whenever she placed a flower before me, I would tuck it into my hair and her face would once again crease into that horrifying smile. Why does she stare at me like this? Who is she? What has she been? Where did she come from? How has she become like this? (Jahan, "Woh," 121)

The privileged gaze here is inverted; the entire scenario is somehow turned inside out. "There she sat, just gazing at me with that crooked eye and that ghastly noseless face," the narrator declares, "*Sometimes I thought I saw her eye fill*. What was passing through her mind?" (Jahan, "Woh," 120, emphasis added).

Highlighted over and over again in the grotesque imagery of the subaltern figure is that we quite literally *see* her insides but have no access to her interiority. This frustrates the narrator, as the opacity of the prostitute's face makes impossible the project of feminist empathy and at the same time grants an unwanted access to the nameless woman's biological interior. In the place of a psychic or emotional interiority we are offered this raw topography of the unbounded woman's body: its horrific Bakhtinian openings to the world. The woman's bodily fluids run and fill and ooze, untethered, as it were, to the emotive reflexes that they index. The narrator can only speculate that she sees the prostitute's eye "fill," as she is looking to read this somatic reflex as a gateway into the woman's emotive state or consciousness. Yet all we are presented with is raw viscera, lacking the body semiotics that would allow us to interpret them—all soma, no psyche.

The story thus stages a crisis of interiority and proximity with the feminist object of Marxist representation. With the erosion of the subaltern subject's face, Jahan denies any idealized revolutionary feminist inter-face between the narrator and this patient. Rather than centering on the prostitute's struggle, which would align with the social realist protocols of the era, Jahan centers the narrative crisis on the young and naïvely idealistic teacher struggling to find compassion amid her revulsion for the nameless, faceless prostitute. As Priyamvada Gopal astutely argues, the story ought to be read as a reflection and auto-critique surrounding the failure or limits of empathy and women's solidarity, as well as the failed project of recuperating the subaltern more broadly: "The liberal—and Gandhian—fiction of reciprocity and mutual understanding across class boundaries within the emergent nation is one that the narrative participates in even as it recognizes its impossibility under the circumstances" (Gopal, *Literary Radicalism in India*, 46). Such a critique echoes Gayatri Spivak's famous intervention into the Marxist projects of recuperating the agency of the subaltern, one that redefines the subaltern not as an identity but as the very cusp or "limit of representation," in the words of David Lloyd.[3] The figure of the subaltern in these scenarios of forced intimacy comes into view as a predicament that calls for an ethics of progressive readings and practices of feminist solidarity that are "attentive to the aporetic structure of 'knowing' in the encounter with the other," in the words of Rosalind Morris (9).

Framed by an ironic self-criticism of the narrator's own naïve aspirations as feminist activist and reformer, the story thus centers on her unlearning of her privilege and political optimism. What does it mean, however, that we are forced to "read" the female subaltern subject, not simply through her effacement and her opacity,[4] but through her grotesque disfigurement—the hollow cavities of her face and the viscous fluids running out from the unspeakable depths of her body down its grotesque surface? Indeed, against any easy experience of empathy or even pity for the subaltern, the reader becomes implicated in a theater of revulsion.

Here I seek to foreground the fear of intimacy that is invoked by the bodily fluids amplified in Jahan's story, as well as the deep anxieties set into action by the aversive reflex of disgust—one that is provoked by the unbounded body of the prostitute in these modernizing spaces as India decolonizes. This becomes particularly heightened in a fascinating way at the end of the short story. "That One" concludes with the nameless woman blowing her nose and wiping her fingers on the wall, both amplifying the revulsion already associated with the liquids of her interiors, oozing, running out of her face, and pushing the underlying threat of violence over the threshold. Suggestively, it is the sweeper woman who works in the school who loses control and begins senselessly beating the woman: "You bastard, you whore, who do you think you are? Yesterday you were loitering at the street corner, and today as your flesh falls rotting apart, you parade here like a lady!" (121). A fascinating relationship or slippage occurs here between the nameless woman's grotesque *physical* appearance (the disgusting presence of her mucus on the wall being the very last straw) on the one hand, and her *social* moral depravity as a "whore" on the other ("today as your flesh falls rotting apart, you parade here like a lady!"). The threat posed by this leaking and oozing body, I argue, is the site of political critique.

This begs us to inquire into the nature of this disgust, this knee-jerk aversion, to which we become witness and perhaps also experience. What exactly is it about the mucus on the wall that incites the sweeper woman's seemingly uncontrollable moment of physical aggression toward the prostitute? I suggest that a series of unbearable intimacies and proximities, both real and imagined, are at play here, to which we must draw our attention. I propose that this visceral logic of disgust—the involuntary emotive response that sets the sweeper woman upon the unbounded body of the prostitute—invokes a series of metonymic logics that traffic between the physical and moral reflexes of disgust on the terrain of postcolonial appetites and aversions. The disgust directed at the nameless woman's physicality—the oozing orifices, the gaping holes—comes to stand in for a moral disgust directed toward her life of prostitution. The disgust further rests on the viscous textures leaking out of the face of that one—unspeakable sexual textures and fluids that invoke both the prostitute's social depravity and exploitation, her sex "work." The disgust operates through both vision and touch. "'We should observe purdah from that vile creature,' one fat old teacher said acidly," the narrator tells us; and, similarly, "No-body would sit in the chair she used. I don't blame them. It wasn't their fault.

She looked so revolting. I couldn't bring myself to touch the chair either" (Jahan, "Woh," 119–20).

This revulsion becomes the heightened affective idiom through which the scenario of forced intimacy with the subaltern emerges in "That One." Here, I am reading Jahan's provocative yet sparse short story through the aesthetics of her student Ismat Chughtai. Chughtai's signature sensory prose is saturated with these kinds of depictions of the unspeakable textures of the female body. Chughtai, however, invokes these metonymic logics of female bodily texture in the colonial context, its stickiness and viscosity, and, as I argue in the following sections, takes it to its erotic conclusions.

While Jahan's and Chughtai's inquiries into the polarized affects of desire and disgust are undoubtedly inflected by their interest in the work of Sigmund Freud and are thus ripe for psychoanalytic exploration, I argue that their aesthetic preoccupation with these affects also profoundly resonates with the writings of the German phenomenological theorist Aurel Kolnai, who diverged from Freudian theories of disgust as a repression of sexual desire. Kolnai, instead, repeatedly returned to a preoccupation with disgust's internal paradox—what he calls "a certain invitation hidden in disgust ... a certain macabre allure" (42). In an attempt to distinguish disgust from other aversive emotions such as fear, Kolnai argued that whereas disgust is an aversive emotion—a protective bodily reflex designed to inhibit our contact with danger or threat—fear is an emotion that causes us to immediately flee from the dangerous object in front of us. Disgust paradoxically causes us to dwell on the material and sensory aspects of the object that disgusts us. According to Kolnai, this is what lends disgust its peculiar magnetism even as it is an aversive reflex. It is this sensory quality of disgust, then, that causes one to "almost savor its object at the same time it is revolted by it" (Korsmeyer and Smith, 9).

I argue that it is precisely this material quality of the disgusting and, further, the sensory pull of the disgusting—its "internal paradox"—that is brought under magnification in the affective amplifications of Chughtai's prose. As we will see, disgust, as an evaluative and aversive reflex of moral conditioning, cannot be fully understood without attending to the paradoxical structure of desire embedded within in it. The next section traces Chughtai's densely phenomenological explorations of these figures of desire and disgust in her short stories "The Mole" and "The Quilt," before turning to the work of Kolnai in conjunction with Chughtai's novel *The Crooked Line*. Here I mine the interrelations of desire and disgust as the concentrated site of both gender discipline and liberation in a decolonizing India.

The Erotics of the Disgusting

Ismat Chughtai is perhaps best known for the obscenity charges brought against her by the colonial government in the 1940s for the erotic content of her literature. In 1942, Chughtai was tried for obscenity by the colonial courts for the specifically homoerotic depictions within her literature. As Chughtai recounts, she was acquitted because the prosecution could never point to actual words that were considered obscene. The target for the obscenity charge was her most famous short story, "Lihaaf" (The Quilt), which narrates a young girl's encounter with the erotic relationship of a middle-class Muslim woman and her female servant. As Gopal notes, "The lawyer's argument worked because 'The Quilt' in fact makes no explicit reference to either sexual activity, or indeed, to lesbian relationships. Yet the story contains some of the most suggestive and sensual representations of homoeroticism in modern Indian fiction" (*Literary Radicalism in India*, 65). My inquiry into the visceral logic of disgust in this section centers on Chughtai's unique amplification of sensory language, which, I argue, managed to evade and critique the colonial censorship codes that demanded that the female body remain unspeakable in a moment, at the brink of an emergent nationhood, that it was precisely women's sexuality and the symbolic valences of the female body that provided one of the densest sites of contestation.

In a collection of Chughtai's memoirs and "reminiscences," I came across an essay titled "The Lihaaf Trial." However, to my surprise, the essay contained very little about the famous obscenity trial. Instead, it centers on the adventures of Chughtai in Lahore, where she was summoned for the trial; she uses the event as an occasion to gallivant around town with her husband, the progressive writer Shahid Latif, and her friend, the progressive writer Saadat Hasan Manto, who was also being tried for obscenity at the time. In the middle of the essay, Chughtai recalls that the three of them were wandering around Lahore when they ended up following their noses to a hotel that was selling hotdogs and hamburgers. As Chughtai recounts, "'Hamburgers contain ham, which is the meat of the pig, but we can eat hot dogs,' Shahid suggested. So like good Muslims we kept our religious faith intact, and ate hot dogs" (Chughtai and Naqvi, 138). However, as Chughtai writes, some days later they discovered that that they were in fact wrong about the meat they had consumed that day:

> We discovered that the white race is very crafty. Hamburgers don't have ham and hot dogs contain pork sausage! Even though it had been two days since we had eaten those hot dogs, Shahid suddenly began to feel nauseous. Then a Maulwi Sahib issued a fatwa that [if] you eat pork by mistake it's not a sin, and only then did Shahid cease to be sick. But when Shahid and Manto got very drunk in the evening they came to the joint decision that hamburgers are not at all safe and hot dogs are better on all accounts. The argument threatened to take on a rather dangerous turn, and finally it was decided that for the time being we should abstain from eating both.... So tikkas are the best, we decided. (Chughtai and Naqvi, 138)

With characteristic humor and irony, Chughtai pokes fun at the fickleness of her husband's religious sensibility. I wondered, however, what this strange anecdote was doing in an essay supposedly about her obscenity trial. It was by attending to Chughtai's sensory poetics that I became acquainted with the codes in which she speaks. In an essay about the obscenity for which she was being prosecuted, Chughtai foregrounded the story about the fickleness of the moral disgust of her husband, a bout of religious nausea that arrived only after he discovered what he had consumed. In my search for Chughtai's experience of the obscenity trial, she led me to the aesthetics of disgust in her own writing. It is with these clues in hand that I now turn to her semiautobiographical novel to pursue this issue of disgust in relation to the erotics of her prose.

Ismat Chughtai's "The Quilt" has gained substantial critical attention as a powerful counternarrative to both Indian colonial and anticolonial national narratives that are predicated on the heteronormative regulation of the female body and women's sexuality. Indeed, the story's depiction of women's sexual pleasure and homoerotic desire disrupts bourgeois constructions of the chaste, asexual Indian woman that remain central to the modernizing project of Indian nationalism. Published in 1941, "The Quilt" is set within the home of a wealthy landowner and his wife, Begum Jan. Moving through the gender-segregated spaces of the home, the story depicts Begum Jan as both confined within the home and entirely neglected by her husband. While the story is narrated through the retrospective voice of an adult remembering her stay at the Begum's house as a young girl, "The Quilt" centers on Begum Jan's erotic relationship, which takes place beneath the quilt of her bed with her female servant, Rabbo, who "came to her rescue just as she was starting to go under" (8).

Chughtai's strategic play with the narrative gaze and the visual field of her stories remains central to the amplification of sensory detail in her prose. She uses a formal technique that dispenses her narrative through a kind of cinematic camera eye, which becomes central to her strategic manipulation of what gets seen and what remains outside the optic frame.[5] It is, thus, what we are able to glimpse through the "chinks in the drawing-room doors," and what we are able to make out from the shadows cast on the bedroom walls, that this story is told (Chughtai, "Lihaaf," 8).[6] As Gayatri Gopinath has argued, it is precisely through this optic play that the story's erotic arrangements heighten alternative sensory realms of sound, smell, and sensation that exceed the realm of the visual and refuse to make the sexual configurations of the text explicit on the planes of either what we can see or what we can say.[7]

In a scene in which the narrator remembers how she is woken up in the middle of the night by peculiar noises coming from Begum Jan's bed, we witness the child struggling to make sense of what is happening: "Begum Jan's quilt was shaking vigorously, as if an elephant was struggling beneath it.... I heard Rabbo sobbing. Then there were sounds of a cat slobbering in a saucer" (Chughtai, "Lihaaf," 13). While the sexuality and homoeroticism for which Chughtai was legally tried as obscene evades the optic field of the narrative through the opacity of the quilt, where we find the sexual energy rendered most explicitly is through the heightened auditory medium of the narrative. Throughout the telling of the story, these sounds saturate Chughtai's prose, as we find that in the second night the narrator is again awakened by these noises: "smack, gush, slobber—someone was enjoying a feast!" ("Lihaaf," 13). Homoerotic sexual pleasure is conveyed through these textured sounds of the female body. These sounds of sexual pleasure come to echo a set of visuals surrounding Begum Jan's body, as well, as the narrator continually describes her through a fixation on the texture of her bodily surfaces: "The most amazing and attractive part of her face were her lips.... Her skin was fair and moist.... [W]henever she exposed her ankles..., I stole a glance at their rounded smoothness.... [H]er hands were large and moist, her waist smooth" (Chughtai, "Lihaaf," 10). Rendering Begum Jan through the fragments of her body, the narrative gaze not only describes the slipperiness of her surfaces but also lingers on the curved contours. As Geeta Patel writes, Begum Jan's "body and face engage the child's budding sexual attention. The latter is evoked, created, and gendered in exquisitely textured detail as simultaneously male and female: "Sometimes her face became transformed under my adoring gaze, as if it were the face of a young boy" (142). Rabbo is similarly described through these slippery and protruding textures: "a tight little paunch and full lips, slightly swollen, which were always moist" (Chughtai, "Lihaaf," 11). The erotics of the story here are conveyed through these narrative fixations on the slippery protrusions of the female body's surfaces and the viscous fluids that mark her sexual desire.

These textured sounds and visual fragments, as we will see, function metonymically in Chughtai's writings to represent what is to remain unspeakable and contained within the gendered logics of bourgeois respectability within both colonial and postcolonial nationalist narratives. And yet these are precisely the sites where women's sexuality and homoerotic pleasure ooze out of the boundaries of the optic field. As Gopinath has compellingly argued, Chughtai's sensory prose pushes against the representational capacities of language itself while interrogating the optic as well as the discursive as sites of discipline and national ideology production.[8]

One fascinating dimension of these textured depictions of the female body is that in "The Quilt" they are delivered through a dense affective screen that oscillates between the desire of the remembering narrator, on the one hand, and her nausea, on the other. One of the most prevalent coded idioms through which Chughtai articulates women's sexual desire throughout her writings is that of hunger and bodily appetites. The narrator's own memory of Begum Jan is at times mediated by feelings of this intense hunger for her and thus triangulates the scene of homoeroticism, and yet in other moments the narrator's recollection is laced with feelings of nausea.[9] In one such moment, the narrator recalls how Begum Jan invites her to lie down with her: "I wanted to run away from her but she held me closer.... I felt gripped by an unknown terror.... I started feeling nauseated against her warm body" (Chughtai, "Lihaaf," 16). In contrast to the desire that mediates her memory of Begum Jan in particular moments of her narrative, her feelings in this scene are suddenly inverted, and her depiction of Begum Jan's sexual "hunger" is countered with her feelings of nausea and disgust.

Furthermore, in the midst of the child narrator's feelings of nausea brought on by Begum Jan's advances, the child's mind suddenly and unexpectedly darts to her lessons of hygiene. "I thought of my school hygiene," she recalls, to her own bewilderment. "Very confused thinking"

(Chughtai, "Lihaaf," 15). The narrator's involuntary association with the moral disciplinary regimes of hygiene and filth in this moment of female intimacy with Begum Jan depicts the modes through which gender conditioning manifests in the reflexes of the body that structure the habits of her mind, as she unconsciously equates homoerotic sexual desire with impurity and filthiness and, thus, repugnance. While these scenes of disgust in "The Quilt" certainly depict homophobic sensibilities evoked by the scene of same-sex desire, I would also argue that what these visceral *oscillations* of the child foreground is a critical tug-of-war between the heteronormative gendered logics that have conditioned the narrator's bodily complicity with ideologies of women's chastity, on the one hand, and her unruly bodily impulses that refuse to comply, on the other. While this encounter between Begum Jan and the narrator is staged through these figures of attraction and repulsion, the narrator's own movements between desire and disgust, fascination and fear, refract the homoerotic energies of the story through phobic and philic visceral reflexes. What is of particular interest here is that the desire and the disgust of the narrator are consolidated through her experiences, or even imagined experiences, of touch and bodily texture.

    I argue that this textural inquiry into the unspeakable desires of women's sexuality, staged through this push and pull on the terrain of taste and appetite, emerges as a critical aesthetic preoccupation of both Jahan's and Chughtai's sensory prose. For example, returning briefly to the short story "The Mole," discussed in the introduction, the power struggle between the bourgeois male artist and his female subject, mapped onto a scene of aesthetic struggle, comes to center on a particular point on the girl's body that the artist cannot seem to capture: a fleshy and protuberant mole, for which the story is titled, located somewhere "below her neck." As the artist's frustration intensifies throughout the short story, it is not simply the color or shade he cannot seem to get right but the distinct *texture* of the mole that comes under scrutiny. It is the fleshiness, the roundedness, and the protuberance of this mark on her body that is increasingly magnified in the story as the object not only of artistic frustration but of sexual frustration and desire for the girl he cannot seem to repress.[10] The story's aesthetic play with the failed mimetic project of the artist is consolidated symbolically through the trope of this mole as a metaphor for what lies in that unspeakable region "below her neck."

    In thus amplifying the visual medium of the artist's palette, the colors, the patterns, the lines, and the shapes on his canvas become the idiom through which the story represents the psychosexual landscapes of the repressed male artist and, further, of the production of discourses of bourgeois respectability that remained central to colonial and nationalist discourses. Furthermore, the brazen protuberance and fleshiness of the mole as depicted through the artist's gaze comes to aestheticize the very affects it incites within the short story:

> That fleshy, protuberant mole. To Chaudhry it seemed that the mole had struck his chest with a thud, like a flying bullet.... His eyes plunged at the black, fleshy mole like hungry vultures and ... ohh.... As if transformed into a black stone by his revulsion, the mole crashed against his forehead. (Chughtai, "Til," 120)

Attending to the textured metaphors of Chaudhry's desire, the protuberance of the mole in the language of the story is further imagined as not simply obtrusive, but dangerous and aggressive. Through these (phallic) sensory descriptions of piercing and penetration, the mole not only functions as a metonymic representation of her sexuality. It further represents the violent threat her sexuality poses to Chaudhry.

In *Touching Feeling*, Sedgwick, drawing on Renu Bora, writes that to "perceive texture is always, immediately, and de facto to be immersed in a field of active narrative hypothesizing"—to ask "what could I do with it, what is it like? Or how does it impinge on me?" (13). Chaudhry's desire for Rani is depicted through a kind of tug-of-war, a push and pull between the textured object and subject of the artistic gaze, for as Chaudhry's eyes "plunge" at the mole, the mole is described as thrusting itself back upon him. As his gaze is imagined as thrusting toward the textured object, it is then the object, imagined as a flying bullet, that comes plunging back. Chaudhry's intense feelings of sexual desire suddenly flip into a sensation of revulsion—echoing the oscillations we witness in "The Quilt." It is this feeling of revulsion that then "transforms" the directionality of the "narrative hypothesizing"—what turns the question from "what I would like to do to it" to the threat here of "how does it impinge on me?" Tracking these paired affects of revulsion and attraction, I turn to Chughtai's experiments in the novel to further interrogate these aesthetic inquiries into desire and disgust as the sites through which the sexual logics of bourgeois respectability and obscenity are conditioned in the gendered body, but also where they go awry.

The Crooked Line (*Tehri Lakir*), published in 1944, is a semiautobiographical novel that charts the development of the middle-class Muslim protagonist, Shamshad, from the moment of her birth through adulthood, ending with her pregnancy against the tumultuous social transformations of the transitional phase of late colonial India. As Gopal notes, Shamshad comes of age while the Indian nation comes into existence, between 1920 and 1943, and Chughtai plots her transition from gendered colonial subject to gendered national citizen subject (*Literary Radicalism in India*, 68). The novel also depicts Chughtai's participation in the anticolonial movements of the time through a feminist lens attentive to the gender dynamics and contradictions of the Progressive Writers' Movement. Like many of the realist novels by her comrades in the Progressive Writers' Association, *The Crooked Line* maps the protagonist's coming of age against the nascent nation's coming of age. However, Chughtai rejects the notion that social realist literature must center on the plight of the peasant and proletariat and is, in fact, critical of romanticization of the laborer, choosing instead to draw on her own experiences. She wrote, "When the policy of the Party rigidly concluded that Progressive literature is only that which is written about the peasant and the labourer, I disagreed. I cannot know and empathize with the peasant class as closely as I can feel the pain of the middle and lower class. And I have never written on hearsay" (quoted in Gopal, *Literary Radicalism in India*, 69). Patel writes, "As a participant in a Marxist movement that relentlessly promoted social realism and an attendant belief in the 'real' as a simple, visible given, Chughtai was in a constant negotiation with realism as a literary ideology.... For her the real was as much an ideologically coded production as any other and one that cycled back into colonial representation of what constituted the subcontinent, its real native inhabitants, and the projected nation-state" (143).

Gopal further notes that, as Chughtai draws on personal and sensory experience, the emphasis in the novel is on "how subjects are produced," on the multiple "intersecting and conflicting frameworks and narratives" through which colonial, national, religious, filial, class, and gendered disciplinary institutions are at play in producing modern middle-class Muslim femininities, and on the "civilizing process at the heart of Indian modernity" (*Literary Radicalism in India*, 72–74).[11] In one of the earliest scenes of discipline in the novel, Chughtai depicts attempts by Shamshad's older sister, Manjhu, to teach Shamshad the Urdu alphabet. This scene is characterized by Shamshad's frustration with what she understands as the nonsensical relationships between the letters and images of the alphabet book:

> "Here ... *alif* for *anar*." "What? *Alif* isn't *anar*, *anar* is in a firecracker ... phrr, phrr. Right?"
>
> "Silly! Look here, this is alif, alif for anar ... say alif." "Say alif."
>
> "No this is how you say it ... *alif*!" "I don't want to say it, first tell me what is this...." [A]*lif* for *anar*? Hunh! How could that be? This round, pitcher-shaped *anar*, with no red shooting sparks, nothing? So useless! (Chughtai, *The Crooked Line*, 11)

Chughtai thus renders this cognitive phase in which the logics of language and discourse have not yet been naturalized for the little girl. As the scene continues, however, the narration takes a peculiar momentary detour from her lesson in the semiotics of language to the perceptual semiotics of Shamshad's body. As the narrator describes the reading lesson, Chughtai's prose suddenly zooms in on a set of strange sensations that Shamshad experiences as she watches her older sister sew the pages of the alphabet book with which she is teaching her to read:

> Watching the teeth of the machine go *"kat, kat"* over the paper, [Shamshad] experienced a somewhat pleasurable, tingling sensation in her teeth; she rubbed a finger over her teeth and felt a strange current streaming through her body. (*The Crooked Line*, 10)

This scene of pedagogy is thus disrupted by the magnification of sensory minutiae: the hard, rhythmic sound of the *"kat kat"* as the needle pounds across the page and the tingling sensation Shamshad experiences in her teeth.

As Shamshad's sense of frustration continues to mount throughout her reading lesson, the sensory descriptions, again, disrupt the narration of the scene: "She examined the book closely to distract herself and her eyes fell on the marks made by the sewing machine. Her teeth began to tingle again. She tugged at the piece of thread at one end of the seam and, like sutures on a wound, the stitches unraveled neatly all the way to the end of the seam. It felt good, as if she were hastily skipping down a staircase" (Chughtai, *The Crooked Line*, 11). Everything, here, from the tingling in Shamshad's teeth to the kinesthetic description of the momentum and exhilaration that she experiences in tugging the thread of the seam, reveals the representational energy invested in not simply the *feel* of this experience, but the pleasure of it. Within the context of the novel, we can really understand Shamshad's excitement and exhilaration elicited from the rhythmic, penetrative motion of the machine's needle as not merely a sensory awakening, recalling the protagonists of Abbas' and Anand's novels, but a coded sexual one.

What interests me about Chughtai's portrayal of this primal scene of language in the novel is that, as Manjhu attempts to interpellate Shamshad into the symbolic and semiotic order of social discourse, it is the girl's budding sexual urges and the destructive impulses that accompany them that rupture the narration. In other words, the destructive—or, rather, deconstructive—urges of the female child, aimed pointedly at the linguistic text(ile), accompany the little girl's sexual impulses and sensations. By mapping the visceral logics of Shamshad's body onto this scene of pedagogy—one that centers on the very logics of language itself—Chughtai configures the girl's unruly sexual urges as not simply a corporeal rebellion against the civilizing regimes through which she is being socialized but, further, as a threat to the very binding of the semiotic order into which she is being disciplined. Like those of her protagonist, who is reveling in the disintegration of the arbitrary "suturing" of symbols and sounds, Chughtai's own literary engagements with the unspeakability of women's sexuality and desire in the novel emerge from the linguistic sites where discourse itself is unraveling at its very seams.

Throughout the early chapters of *The Crooked Line*, Chughtai lays out a feminine cartography of urges, impulses, and instinctual desires and drives. What happens to them as Shamshad matures provides the pulse of the novel. The novel opens with a portrayal of the protagonist from the moment of her birth through her development into early infancy, rendered through a dense concentration of sensory detail and through the depiction of the baby's infantile dreams. Within the earliest stages, both the sensoriality of Chughtai's signature prose and the affective terrain foregrounded in her renderings of the baby's dreams center on Shamshad's intense attachment to her teenage wet nurse, Unna. In one particular scene, narrated through the sensory experiences of Shamshad as a baby in this prelinguistic phase of infancy, Shamshad falls asleep and begins dreaming. As the dream is depicted, Chughtai portrays Shamshad's deep attachment to the wet nurse through a hunger for her body; however, in a strange moment of inversion, we find that this infantile dreamscape suddenly flips to a scene of nightmarish terror:

> On a pile of thatching grass, fleshy and ripe like a mango, was her soft, warm Unna. She cooed and burrowed herself into the rounded softness, her lips moving, the veins in her throat throbbing as if she were gulping

> great quantities of milk. *She gagged*. And when she reached out her chubby hands a monster pushed her away, and grabbing Unna, wrestled her down. She screeched fiercely. . . , her childish eyes dazed by the revolting scene before her. (*The Crooked Line*, 3, emphasis added)

What is made salient through the idiom of hunger here is that, as the scene inverts from fantasy to nightmare, the narrative focus remains on the organs of ingestion. In one moment, the baby is insatiably gulping down breast milk, and in the next, she is gagging. The somatic inversion of this moment from appetite to aversion that we have now seen in both "The Quilt" and "The Mole" registers here through the digestive and aversive reflexes of Shamshad's throat. We discover in the novel that what brings on this moment of terror and revulsion is the child's witnessing of lovemaking between Unna and her lover. The scene of terror emerges from the infant's perception of the sexual act as a scene of aggression toward Unna. In the staging of the gag reflex at this phase of the infant's development, Chughtai depicts the biological function of the disgust reflex as an intuitive and instinctual defense mechanism in the face of what the baby perceives as danger. As we will see, Chughtai traces the development of this visceral affect of disgust throughout Shamshad's development in the novel as this innate reflex is shaped by the social disciplinary mechanisms of colonial and anticolonial nationalist institutions.

Chughtai's critique of the violent disciplining of women's bodies that is sanctioned by the modern discourses of hygiene we witness in "The Quilt" is provocatively developed in *The Crooked Line*. Furthermore, the psychological tug-of-war that we witness in "The Quilt" between the child's teachings of hygiene and the appetites of her body is developed into one of the most peculiar and haunting phases in *The Crooked Line*: our protagonist enters a stage in which objects that should be disgusting—mud, filth, excrement, secretions—become, for Shamshad, objects of an insatiable and obsessive craving.

The novel centers the unruliness of Shamshad's desires in an early phase of her development, where Chughtai describes her rigorous daily cleaning routines:

> Manjhu dressed her up, gave her strict orders that she was not allowed one hair to get out of place or else she'd be dead, but she was powerless; she had no control over her restless legs.... [A]s soon as Manjhu's back was turned, she slipped out of the house, and reappeared in the evening looking like a

mad bitch who had just finished tossing about in an earthen platter filled with sludge. (*The Crooked Line*, 5)

This phase is characterized by Shamshad's insatiable desire not only to immerse her body in the mud, to be consumed by the mud, but, further, to consume the mud. Although Shamshad is punished daily with physical beatings for her filthiness and promises that she will never go near the dirt again, she finds herself, as if possessed, uncontrollably drawn to the mud. Her cravings are characterized by this kind of bodily disconnect, a refusal of the body to comply with the will. Not only is this disconnect characterized by an inability to control her urgent desires, but, furthermore, the very behavior they engender are characterized as hopelessly recursive, occurring repeatedly every day, and at the same time. Shamshad's bodily rebellion against the disciplinary regimes surrounding cleanliness and hygiene could thus be described as not only involuntary but compulsive.

Shamshad's compulsive cravings depict a disorder of the very mechanism of disgust that she stages in her infancy: the aversive reflex of disgust that is designed to protect the body from contact with threat or danger, in this instance, seems to backfire. In a kind of inverse of the disorder often associated with involuntary and ritualized cleaning routines (now popularly termed obsessive-compulsive disorder), Shamshad's compulsive behavior hurls her into the very substances that pose the threat of danger and impurity to her body. This perversion of "taste" that plagues Shamshad, in fact, eventually leads her in the story to contract ringworms that nearly kill her, an episode depicted as a phantom pregnancy: "Like pregnant women, they relished the aroma of mud.... In time they began to resemble women who are pregnant" (Chughtai, *The Crooked Line*, 7). Attending again to the sensory detail of Chughtai's prose, what is brought into focus is not only how involuntary and irresistible the experience of her cravings is, but how sensual the magnetic pull of these disgusting objects are for Shamshad:

> The red mud in the fields and the whispering sand on the edge of the pond tantalized her, the moist, fragrant grass in the stables pursued her with open arms, the dirty, foul-smelling chicken coop drew her to itself as if it were a bride's flowery bed. She forgot everything. The pledge she had made repeatedly to her conscience.... Her struggle to turn away from these evil splendors left her exhausted. They continued to beckon her and finally, like a kite cut off from its cord, she fell into the pit of sin, an act for which she paid with daily suffering and pain. (*The Crooked Line*, 6)

What becomes salient in this description of Shamshad's impulses is not only the intensity of the sensory experience—the red of the mud, the whispering of the sand, the moisture and fragrance of the grass—but how sexualized the language is: the "tantalizing" of the sand, the grass "pursuing her with open arms," and the equation of the smelly chicken coop with the "bride's flowery bed." What we find in this stage of Shamshad's development is not the oscillation between desire and disgust, hunger and nausea, that we witnessed earlier. Here, instead, the very terrain of the disgusting is densely eroticized. In other words, while we found the subjects of Chughtai's short stories "The Quilt" and "The Mole" caught within the prohibitive bourgeois logics that police the appetites of their bodies, even as the body continues to revolt, within this moment in *The Crooked Line* we find these two affects strangely embedded within the logic of the other. To further probe this, I turn to the writings of the German phenomenologist Aurel Kolnai, who was preoccupied with the imbrication of desire in disgust, what Kolnai theorized as disgust's internal paradox, its "hidden invitation." Within this scene of discipline, I argue, what Chughtai's aesthetic indulgence in the materiality and sensuality of Shamshad's compulsive craving for mud opens up for interrogation is the erotics of the disgusting.

In an attempt to distinguish disgust from fear, Kolnai argued that disgust is an aversive emotion designed to inhibit our contact with danger or threat. What distinguishes disgust from fear is that fear causes us to flee immediately from the dangerous object in front of us, while disgust causes us to dwell on the material and sensory aspects of the object that disgusts us. Thus, in an attempt to distinguish disgust from fear, Kolnai argued that disgust "is more aesthetically determined than is fear" in that it causes us to "focus on the quality of the object as presented to our senses" (9). As Chughtai's prose lingers in what Kolnai identifies as the aesthetic quality of the disgusting, we find her narrative investment, yet again, in the distinct textural detail of the experience—what Kolnai identifies as the sensory materiality of the disgusting object that lends it its peculiar magnetism. It is precisely this material quality of the disgusting and, further, the sensory pull of the disgusting—its "internal paradox"—that is brought under magnification in the affective amplifications of Chughtai's prose. Chughtai reveals that disgust, as an evaluative and aversive reflex of moral conditioning, cannot be fully understood without attending to the paradoxical structure of desire embedded within in it. To draw out the textural quality of Chughtai's prose describing Shamshad's return home, "looking like a mad dog who had just finished tossing about in an earthen platter filled with sludge," I quote at length here:

> The once billowing frock resembled a dead rat's skin, its surface decorated with a shower of fine dust, her hair, eyes, and face would be blanketed with a thick layer of dust, her nostrils so densely packed with snot and muck they reminded one of doors walled in with cement. Plastered over everything was a covering comprised of secretions and seeds from mangoes, guavas, berries, or whatever fruit happened to be in season.... [S]he was covered with spittle and blood ... , round silky balls of mud.... She wished she could take all of the world's mud and collect it under her tongue, mix it with her spittle and then let the viscous curds glide down her throat. (*The Crooked Line*, 5)

As Chughtai indulges in the materially abject nature of Shamshad's cravings, what we find amplified in her writing is not only the intensity of the draw of the disgusting but the distinct textures of the objects of her irrepressible desire: the stickiness, the gooeyness, the sliminess, and the viscosity of the mud and secretions covering her body, generated by her body, and gliding down the digestive tracts of her body. Furthermore, through the textural terrain of the "gross" and "gooey" Chughtai magnifies the intimacy of her bodily contact with the disgusting. We recognize these textural details that echo the viscous textures that saturate the aural and visual depictions of "The Quilt" as metonymic extensions of women's sexual desire and pleasure.

What Kolnai theorizes as the central feature of disgust is the proximity and bodily intimacy of the disgusting object, for it is the threat of contact with the toxic or dangerous substance that triggers the aversive response. Kolnai writes, "The principal feature of the disgusting [is its] somehow obtrusive clinging to the subject" (41). Recalling the mucus smeared on the wall in Jahan's "That One," of repeated interest in Chughtai's textural depictions is the dense, adhesive quality of the disgusting: the surface of the dress "blanketed" with a layer of dirt; the mucus and dirt so densely "walling up" the inside of the nostrils like cement; the saliva, blood, and secretions of fruit "covering" and "plastering" the child's body. As Kolnai proceeds to meditate on this feature of intimacy inherent in the threat of the disgusting, he writes:

> One particular aspect of proximity constitutes the character of disgust[:] ... its will to be near, its non-self-containedness, or, as I would rather put it, its shameless and unrestrained forcing itself upon us.... The disgusting object grins and smirks and stinks menacingly at us. (41)

What is critical, then, in light of Kolnai's writings, is that Chughtai's aesthetic indulgence in the dense clinginess of the mud characterizes the disgusting as a corporeal sensibility that is decoded, through the conditioned registers of the body, not simply through a logic of excess, but through a logic of bodily threat. Kolnai's articulation of disgust as predicated on proximity and intimacy personifies the disgusting as both uncontained and aggressive, and thus shameless and threatening. However, I want to push Kolnai's articulation a bit further through Chughtai's aesthetics of the disgusting, for what Chughtai's aesthetics invite us to see within Kolnai's personification of disgust is how these sensory properties of the disgusting—these tactile, textural properties of sensory excess—seem so seamlessly to slide into a social discourse of moral excess. Put another way, Chughtai's poetics track how a sensory logic of excess translates into a discourse of shame.[12]

It is precisely this metonymic translation through the semiotics of the bodies—the translation of a tactile register of a texture into a discourse of shame—that Chughtai's prose works to estrange in this scene of compulsive cravings: how a sensory logic becomes encoded as a moral logic; how a texture becomes shameless, registering as threat. Chughtai's prose thus exposes the social technologies through which the materiality of a woman's body, as well as her sexual desires, gets marked as excessive, and therefore disgusting, and therefore erotic (and therefore disgusting)—or, in other words, what marks the woman's body and her desires as obscene.

What is so critical about Chughtai's work with these sensory registers is its interrogation of this legal and social discourse of obscenity not simply as some ideological figment of a collective imaginary surrounding what cannot be seen or said in public but, rather, as an ideology that is naturalized in these involuntary aversive reflexes and appetites of the body. It is this manipulation and conditioning of this reflex of disgust—and, more precisely, the prohibited erotics in the disgusting—that is brought under interrogation as a concentrated site of gendered and classed discipline within Chughtai's sensory aesthetics at this critical transitional juncture in India's history. In this sense, Chughtai dismantles the legal discourse of obscenity as a constructed moral ideology of the state but, more important, as a deeply gendered visceral logic, for it is the seduction of the visceral that is at stake, laying bare the emotive modes through which ideologies are naturalized in the automatized reflexes of the body and must therefore provide the site of its transformation.

Chughtai locates the promise of decolonization in the push and pull of disgust and desire, where the vitality of the somatic response refuses to comply with the will. Compulsion, as the visceral logic of the female Muslim subject of decolonization, presents us with a crises of the reflex. The unruliness of her appetites under colonial and nationalist regimes of subjection becomes the site of Chughtai's feminist inquiry into both power and resistance. In fact, the revolutionary potentiality of the visceral reflex in this chapter is a function of the volatility and unpredictability of its energetic activity. These scenes of erotic disgust, in other words, expose the possibilities of decolonization, the transformation of a colonized consciousness, as inextricable from the disruptive and nonnormative forms of gender and sexuality, precisely because this is where appetites and somatic reflexes misbehave—*where these affective energies go awry.*

Decolonization for Chughtai, the liberation of a colonized consciousness, is always contingent on the radical reconstitution of the female body and her desires, precisely because gender provided the grounds of colonial subjection through corporeal refashioning. Visceral regimes of gender (re)fashioning in "taste" and sensibility are produced out of, and therefore inextricable from, colonial and postcolonial regimes of racialization. Chughtai's textured aesthetics emerge from their sustained preoccupation with gendered processes of affective and sensory discipline, through which racialized habits of thought and feeling sediment in gendered sensibility and comportment, and thus provide the site of their revolutionary undoing. The erotics of disgust in Chughtai's writings impel a gendered reordering of the sensorial and affective nodes of the racialized body, a reordering that includes the disorganization of the metaphorical and material registers of the body.

Like her protagonist in *The Crooked Line*, tugging at the stitches of her book of letters and reveling in the disintegration of the arbitrary suturing of symbols and sounds, we find that Chughtai's own literary engagements with the unspeakability of women's sexuality and desire emerge from the aesthetic sites where discourse itself is unraveling at its very seams. Chughtai's visceral logics reveal an important parallel with Mulk Raj

Anand's aesthetics of (e)visceration in *Lament*, where the possibilities of "feeling new feelings" are located in the disintegration and disordering of the sensory and semantic ordering of the subject. Like Anand, for Chughtai it is where the binding, to invoke the deconstructive image of the alphabet book, is coming undone—between sensation and language—that the discursive frameworks through which affective energy becomes intelligible through colonial and national frameworks. This, in other words, is where the promise of visceral unlearning is held. Chughtai's somato-poetics thus conjure a vision of decolonization and feminist emancipation not simply as a transformation of social consciousness but as an emotive revolution that would be predicated on the possibility, to borrow Jennifer Fleissner's articulation, of making the female body *mean* differently (278).

4. Evisceration

In a lecture delivered at the first All-India Progressive Writers' Association (PWA) meeting in 1936, Ahmed Ali attends to the question of progressive literature through a discussion of progressive art, which quickly turns to a theory of emotions. Progressive art for Ali is defined by the emotional activity it elicits in its audience. "Emotion is of two kinds," he begins. While one "has its source in dreams; the other is rooted in life" ("A Progressive View of Art," 68). One kind of emotion is "dynamic and generates in us an energy which leads to action," while the other "exists for its own sake" (Ali, "A Progressive View of Art," 68). Ali thus characterizes reactionary emotion this way:

> [It is] conducive only to dreams, inanity, reaction (because it tries to arrest the forces which work in every society). It is wholly static and lifeless, for which we have no use today, for which there is no use of any time. At best it is sentimental, whose adherents start weeping over a dead ass as if the ass were their brother, as one finds in some Georgian English poetry. If a community encourages such artists, it encourages opium-eaters who take their daily dose of the narcotic and try to pluck the stars from the heaven. ("A Progressive View of Art," 68)

Echoing the PWA manifesto, Ali defines progressivism here through its opposition to what the movement termed reactionary, which are imagined to impede the progress of society. Reactionary emotions within Ali's portrayal of progressive art are articulated as lifeless and lacking vitality, static even, opiatic, and, "at best," sentimental. Progressive emotion is imagined as dynamic and as generating energy—emotions that "lead to action." As Ali proceeds on the question of what constitutes progressive art, he states that art "acts by imparting to us powerful emotion[,] thus leading to action, by which I mean mental and emotional activity—stimulation of a Progressive type, which leads us along the lines of the highest consciousness" ("A Progressive View of Art," 68).

Echoing this articulation of art and emotion, the novels I have thus far examined display a series of visceral reflexes that energize and move the body to political action and toward an enlightened national consciousness. These visceral eruptions propel the engine of the national teleology of the progressive novel. In contrast to the visceral affects examined thus far, Ali's novels are saturated with the affects of mourning, grief, nostalgia, melancholy, and lamentation—a completely different palette of emotions from the ones that are thought to impel the body into action. The emotions of Ali's novels are, in fact, depleted of the momentum and cathartic energy deemed necessary for revolutionary transformation. The nostalgic and sentimental structures of Ali's novels are wholly antithetical, then, to the progressive emotions that he champions in his lecture. Instead, the aesthetic energy of his novels is directed toward the emotions he critiques as reactionary: the "lifeless" and opiatic forces of sentimental emotions, those that are said to threaten the "progressive" forces of society. How, then, are we to read Ali's decision to write a progressive novel saturated with what he would call counterprogressive emotions?

In the first three chapters of this book I traced a visceral preoccupation specific to each oeuvre to probe each author's thought experiments surrounding the affective dimensions of decolonization. This chapter rethinks the visceral logics of decolonization through the fiction of founding member, Ahmed Ali, read contrapuntally with respect to the previous chapters. This chapter is about the erasure of the visceral, a flattening of affect, a hollowing out of feeling as staged in the literature of Ahmed Ali. Unsettling the nationalist teleology that structures the progressive novel form, Ali's novels, like Anand's *Lament*, perform a complex rewriting and inversion of this progressive structure of time and feeling when centering the figure of the Muslim subject, such that his novels follow a temporality of decay and demise. Ali's experiments in modernism and the social realist novel thus attempt to stage a very different revolutionary trajectory as they shift the emotive landscape from progressive to "reactionary" feelings. Ali's experiments in social realism rework the historical frame from the utopian vision of an emergent nation to a nostalgic rendering of the fall of the Mughal Empire and the rise of colonial rule in India. In so doing, Ali moves the narrative thematic of the realist novel to focalize a burgeoning affective structure of a Muslim minoritization and a separatist imaginary of cultural nostalgia in a decolonizing India—one that Ali depicts *as* reactionary. Such an erasure of the visceral becomes the modality through which the "crises" of the potential Muslim citizen subject of India, to draw on Aamir Mufti, are brought to view. I propose we read this erasure as the representational mode of a Muslim minoritization, as an aesthetics of evisceration, holding in tension its critical double valence: to both disembowel and deprive of essential meaning or vital content.

Ahmed Ali and the Search for Emotion

With Mulk Raj Anand, Ahmed Ali was a founding member of the Progressive Writers' Movement and a central, albeit contentious, figure within the political and aesthetic debates of the PWA.[1] Ali had famously heated disagreements with members of the PWA over what he felt was an overly rigid view of socialism and its mandates for progressive literature, leading to an eventual falling out with the group a few years after its inception.[2] Ali is perhaps best known for his internationally acclaimed novel *Twilight in Delhi*, published in English by Hogarth Press in 1940, a text that was praised by E. M. Forster for its portrait of the decay and demise of Indo-Islamic culture in India and of the rise of British colonial rule at the cusp of the independence movement (Padamsee, 29). Ali's decision to write what is read as a nostalgic rendering of a great Indo-Muslim past in *Twilight in Delhi*, which thus fuels a separatist or retributive politics, combined with his decision to translate the Quran, prompted the Progressive Writers to label him a cultural "reactionary."

As we will examine, Ali's novels must be understood as a deeply self-aware and critical exploration of the emotive landscape of what he and the Progressives deemed reactionary. As Ulka Anjaria argues,

> The rich affective significance of Delhi's history and its implications for Muslim South Asia—especially when seen from the vantage point of 1940—is part of the palpable emotional experience recorded in the novel, and for this reason it is overwhelmingly read as lyrical and nostalgic.... Yet such a view does not account for the pervasive logic of performance that underlies the novel.... It is not that *Twilight* never takes seriously the nostalgia expressed by the characters within it or conveyed extradiegetically in the narrative of historical decline. Rather, Ali presents nostalgia itself as performance. (107)

In this chapter, I build on Anjaria's incisive reading of *Twilight in Delhi*, which foregrounds the logics of performance in the novel to reveal how nostalgia itself is rendered performatively, *as* text, among a variety of "individual, historical, and political performances" (107).

Twilight in Delhi depicts the slow disintegration of a middle-class Muslim family against the decline of Indo-Islamic life and the Mughal Empire in India, foregrounding a series of key historical events that take place in Delhi—namely, the Sepoy Mutiny, the 1857 rebellion that resulted in the exile of Muslims from Delhi; as well as the coronation of King George V, which marked the end of Mughal rule. It is largely through the melancholic description of the urban landscapes and city ruins of Delhi that saturate the text that the nostalgia is rendered. The cityscapes and memorialized ruins in the novel function as the historical palimpsests and repositories of a lost history and culture of Muslim India—a nostalgic depiction that does represent this cultural past with great reverence but cannot be taken fully at face value.

Like Anjaria, Alex Padamsee intervenes in critical interpretations of *Twilight* as a purely nostalgic text by foregrounding the novel's complex temporal dislocations within an emergent Urdu literary modernity. Padamsee adeptly locates *Twilight in Delhi* within a key historical juncture at a moment of transition between Urdu and Indo-English literary cultures and thus reveals how Ali's novel comes to reference and resignify an Urdu literary tradition of mourning and exile in India:

> The rebellion of 1857 and its physical devastation of the Delhi Muslim community occasioned the first extended prose act of literary mourning in Urdu.... Muhammed Husain Azad's *Ab-e-Hayat* (*Water of Life*, 1880), which effectively set in place a paradigm of decay that remained predominant throughout 20th century Urdu criticism. (30)

Azad's extended poetic depiction of five ages of Urdu cultural degeneration, as Padamsee argues, engendered a proliferation of Urdu novels in the 1930s that revolved around this "teleology of loss" and "portrait of extinction" (30). Thus, in response to critics who view Ali's novel as purely aligned with this literary tradition of cultural mourning, Padamsee argues that *Twilight in Delhi* "must be seen as a troubled and disruptive site of mediation on this literary and cultural imaginary of loss and mourning" (30).

Ali's novels must be read as writing within and responding to—indeed, performing—this cultural imaginary of an Indo-Islamic nostalgia to critically render its structure of feeling *as* reactionary. In fact, this chapter returns us to the central thematic concern of *Inquilab* and Khwaja Ahmad Abbas's deeply ambiguous relationship to the structure of longing so central to the anticipation and revolutionary hope of the postcolonial nation. However, as opposed to *Inquilab*, *Twilight in Delhi* it is not a longing for a utopic future that fuels the novel's representation of nationalism. Rather, it longs for an imagined past and reverses the directionality of the nationalist longing with which we began. What is of interest to me is that Ali stages this narrative of loss and nostalgia not only as one that arrests the teleology of history, but also as one that renders an increasing attenuation of emotional "depth." By the end of Ali's novels, his characters are left physically immobilized, psychologically alienated, and emotionally numb, searching for emotional connections and, quite literally, searching for emotion. Reactionary emotions, for the Muslim figures of Ali's world, I argue, are eviscerating ones.

I turn briefly to a discussion of *Twilight in Delhi*, Ali's most famous novel, before examining in greater depth a lesser-known postpartition novel he wrote nearly twenty years later, *Ocean of Night*, for how it reworks the novelistic structures of *Twilight*. Like *Twilight in Delhi*, *Ocean of Night* depicts the demise of an Indo-Islamic lifeworld by entwining parallel plotlines that center on the diminishing emotional lives of two generations of Muslim men in India. This thematic is depicted in *Twilight* through the characters' troubled and failed marriages. However, in *Ocean of Night* the romance plot shifts from the traditional confines of husband and wife to a set of romantic affairs with female figures that opposes such a domestic gendered framework—the figure of the courtesan, or *tavaif*. Shifting the nostalgic thematic from a spatial logic of the urban city in *Twilight* to the figure of the courtesan, a figure, as Mufti has argued, that symbolizes the high-culture literary world of an elite Muslim past under erasure, I argue that *Ocean of Night* surfaces a preoccupation embedded within the nostalgia performed in *Twilight in Delhi*: the search for emotion—or, more precisely, emotive *form*—for the Muslim subject of India within the increasingly alienating affective matrix of the modern Indian nation.

Like Ismat Chughtai, Ali disagreed with many of the Progressives over the proper subject of the social realist novel. In *The Prison House*, a compilation of some of his short stories published in 1985, Ali appends a fascinating essay that seeks not only to explain his position in relationship to the Progressive Writers' Movement, but also to set the record straight regarding the history of the movement published from Sajjad Zaheer's perspective.[3] In the essay, Ali explains that he opposed "the view that only proletarian literature could alone be considered progressive.... I held that progress or progressivism could not be narrowed down or confined to Communist channels, and that it applied equally to the middle-classes and literature produced by them, of which all of us, were members" (*The Prison House*, 162). He rejected the proletariat figure as the protagonists of his novels and instead chose to focus on the lives of middle-class Muslim characters with whom he was intimately familiar. Not only did Ali refuse the subaltern as the proper subject of his progressive novel, but he split the protagonist, mapping the trajectories of a father and son pairing, and their generational tensions, across the tumultuous transition in late colonial India. The coming-of-age narrative of the son is grafted onto and cut across by the father's narrative of aging and decline, which structures the dominant temporality of the novel: the teleology of loss and "extinction" of Muslim life in India.

Against this trajectory of decline, *Twilight in Delhi* maps the historical transition from the fall of Mughal rule to colonial rule through the generational tensions of Mir Nihal and his son, Asghar. Predictably, the generational tension is staged initially through this opposition of tradition and modernity, embodied by these two male figures. The tension is also staged through a preoccupation with their divergent masculine forms. As in the father-son relationship of Abbas's *Inquilab*, Mir Nihal is initially characterized by his stoic, masculine repression of emotion, while Asghar is depicted as almost hyperemotional, unable to control his emotions, as well as overly sentimental and romantic. While the father, Mir Nihal, is depicted as tethered to Islamic traditions and the patriarchal orthodoxy of the past, his son has longings for his future that are initially described as romantic.

The story thus traces two opposing narrative teleologies embodied by these two male figures: the father's narrative of aging, embedded within the teleology of decline and degeneration, on the one hand, and the son's coming-of-age narrative, which at first glance seems to take up the progressive teleology of the new nation, on the other. At the novel's opening, the progressive energy of the narrative appears to be encased in Asghar's emotions. His coming-of-age story is seemingly impelled forward by his restless, future-oriented longings and desires, while his father, Mir Nihal, is more and more dragged down by his frustration with the new era and his ever-intensifying nostalgia and lamentation for the past.

The drama of the opening of the novel centers on the fact that Asghar has fallen in love with a woman of a lower class, against his father's approval. The ideological tension between the two generations is depicted through the struggle over the form of marriage and patriarchy. Struggling to break from the orthodoxies of the father, Asghar's emotions seem to represent the progressive mode embodied in his longing for the change of the future, further emblemized by this romantic desire for the woman of his "dreams." Asghar's plot thus performs the genre of the modern romance, the marriage plot, so central to the Indian novel form, and it is this heterosexual romance that becomes the site of the novel's allegorical inquiries: how this love in marriage is to map onto a love for the nation, an affective arrangement enacted through the semiotic of woman as nation.

I argue that in performing a variety of sentimental genres in *Twilight in Delhi*, Ali heightens the feeling of time—through its passing and in its anticipation—but, conversely, brings to focus the genres' underlying temporal structures, the historical *time* of these feelings, a central preoccupation of the visceral throughout this book (and one that I take up in the following chapter). The difference between the two developmental emotive genres at play within *Twilight in Delhi*—the progressive feelings of the son and the nostalgia of the father—emerges from the temporalities that structure them, both immanent and belated. The novel reveals how their opposing historical temporalities are further productive of their divergent generic forms and the teleologies that underwrite their forms of sentimentality and interpolate nationalist subjects. In other words, Ali performs these genres to interrogate the emotive forms that structure them and how they come to organize sensibilities of national belonging and postcolonial modernity.

The opening of the novel indicates the hope and future potential of Asghar's romantic desires. For example, Asghar's longings are indicated by the "quickening" of blood coursing through his veins—a common trope of the Progressive Writers that represents the energy of progressive transformation. Because of these emotive and corporeal cues, the reader's sympathies are engineered to lie with Asghar and his desire for the woman his father disapproves of. However, how the story comes to unfold is rather unexpected, for even as the father eventually loses the battle over his son's marriage and Asghar is finally able to marry the woman of his dreams, Asghar loses interest in his new wife soon after the marriage, and the couple find themselves increasingly alienated, from both each other and themselves, and miserable within the prison of their new domestic life. The novel stages a critique of the bourgeois family as Asghar's "progressive" narrative suddenly reverses into a narrative decline. In fact, the son's narrative then begins to parallel and sync up with the father's so that the two story lines begin to mirror each other.

As the progressive novel form comes to parallel the temporality of decline, an emotive structure that fuels the retributive and separatist ideology of Pakistani nationalism, *Twilight* invites a set of questions about their parallels and how they come to structure opposing sensibilities of masculine desire. What the novel seems to open up here, I argue, are questions about the politics of these structures of *longing*: how one structure of an impassioned longing for the future comes to mirror the lamentation of a longing for the past, rendering a critical view of both of these organizations of desire and their attending logics of national belonging.

While Anand's *Untouchable* presents us with a paradigmatic example of the progressive novel form, Ali's *Twilight* invokes its nationalist trajectory, only to subvert and rework its coordinates of time and feeling, its *visceral* logics. *Twilight* opens with a meditation on the oppressive and volatile heat of the city. Delhi is depicted as "wrapped in a restless slumber, breathing heavily as the heat becomes oppressive or shoots through the body like pain. The smell from the flowers dies smothered by the heat.... heat exudes from the walls and the earth, and the gutters give out a damp stink" (Ali, *Twilight in Delhi*, 3). As the narrative unfolds, the heat of the city seems to rise to intolerable heights. The novel describes the heat of one particular day as so terrible that "fires broke out"; "tempers rose and from all around came the loud voices of women quarreling, husbands beating their wives, mothers their children, and there seemed no rest for man." The narrator remarks that it had not been this unbearably hot since the 1857 "Mutiny" (Ali, *Twilight in Delhi*, 66). While the narrative of transformation of Anand's

Untouchable is ushered in through the revolutionary energy of a "latent" heat within its protagonist, charting a righteous rage that would stimulate and ennervate the body to new feelings and new forms of awareness, this emotive and energetic force in Ali's *Twilight* is both invoked and critically revised. The generative heat that is imagined as a progressive force in *Untouchable* is reconfigured as an oppressive and volatile force within *Twilight*, drawing out the violent and explosive dimensions of its energetic potentiality.

Twilight's energetic logics are further inscribed in the novel's temporality of decay and extinction. As the emotive landscape performs an elegy of nostalgia and mourning for the past, what begins in the restless and volatile heat of the city, exploding in bouts of rage and violence, ends in a state of extreme stasis, frozen into a state of petrification. By the end of the novel, the physical body of the father, Mir Nihal, degenerates into literal paralysis, much like the protagonist, Nur, of Anand's *Lament*. The volatility of the energetic in the *Twilight* thus foregrounds the two extremes of the emotive stimulant: on one end of the spectrum, the body is violently and viscerally moved into a series of destructive eruptions, and on the other, the body loses the capacity to move altogether. On one end, the stimulant leads to an explosive violence, and on the other, it degenerates into a complete immobility and paralysis. Even the emotions of the characters themselves begin to harden and empty: the father grows more and more indifferent and calloused; the son's past idealism and fervor evaporate as he joins the emotive ranks of his father; the women become numb from grief and a lifetime of mistreatment. As Anjaria writes about the novel's representation of nostalgia, emotions are reduced to "iterable gestures" staged through "tropes of stasis rather than indicators of a living emotional state" (120). The novel renders the characters emotionally alienated, devoid of a depth of feeling—"flat" characters searching for emotional connection.

The remapping of the progressive energetic in Ali's novel thus stages a refusal of the progressive imaginary that we witnessed in the previous chapters at the level of form. Couched within this representation of the emotive energetic is a deep distrust of the kind of stimulants and energetics of the body that emerge from the longings that precipitate a nationalist fervor, the rage of a retributive politics, as well as the very historical teleology they engender. Ali reworks the progressive novel form so that the logic of "progressive" emotions, as the engine of the nationalist consciousness, is defused through the temporal dislocation of the novel, surfacing a critique of the emotions that emerge on its watch. *Twilight in Delhi* thus stages a powerful critique of both structures of longing as affects of national belonging on the level of literary form, either through the utopic temporality of the national narrative, the imaginary we find in *Untouchable*, or that of the separatist, communalist narrative of grievance surrounding the loss of Indo-Islamic life. Written in 1940, just a few years before independence and partition, *Twilight in Delhi* is an extraordinary exploration of the forms of longing and the structures of feeling during this transition to Indian independence, one that rejects the teleology of progressivism and its relationship between the novel and the imagined nation, without espousing a communal narrative of loss or retribution. As Padamsee argues, *Twilight*'s "textual mourning speaks to a new form of postnational and post-communal subjectivity in the rapidly decolonizing subcontinent" (41). My focus, in what follows, is how the performative temporalities of Ali's novels come to comment on their own role in structuring the feelings and genres of longing on display to theorize the pitfalls of both of these national longings, urging us to question not only how the nation is being imperfectly imagined, but also how it is *desired*.

It is precisely this structure of desire that is brought under further interrogation, I argue, in Ali's postpartition novel, *Ocean of Night* (1964). *Ocean of Night* reveals a vested interest in exploring the forms of longing and belonging that undergird the sentiments of Indian nationalism, ones that structure the thematic through line of *Twilight*'s novel of extinction. Within *Ocean of Night*'s reworking of this plotline, Ali uses the romance plot—staged this time, however, with the figure of the courtesan—to further explore the kinds of affective economies that interpolate the national citizen through the bourgeois fantasies of the family. This filial fantasy, predictably, is cemented in the fiction of the marriage plot. But, like *Twilight*, *Ocean of Night* is invested in staging the failure of the bourgeois romance, revealing the illusory nature of the dream to which both male and female characters have fallen victim. As Snehal Shingavi writes, "[The] problem of the desires of women, and specifically how they measure up to the fantasies of modern Muslim men, becomes the axis on which the sensibilities of Ali's politics turns, and which—more clearly than anything else—exposes the contradictory resolution he arrives at to the competition between nationalism and Islam" (111).[4] In turning to *Ocean of Night*, I contend that it is not simply the emotive lives of the male and female characters that undergo the decay and demise of the era under question, but their aesthetic forms, as well, in what I call an aesthetics of evisceration.

The Aesthetics of Evisceration

Given the uncanny repetition in thematics, tropes, characters, narrative structures, and even literal phrases, I propose we read *Ocean of Night* as a postpartition rewriting of *Twilight in Delhi*. Reworking *Twilight in Delhi*'s dual plotline, the two generations of Muslim patriarchs explored in *Ocean of Night*, rather than running in parallel, are embedded within each other. The romance narrative of the younger generation is folded into that of the older one; thus, while we begin and end with the romance of a wealthy nawab of the old Muslim world with his favorite courtesan, "still a voice from the past which spoke a familiar idiom, heir to the old culture now fallen prey to industrialism and machines," at the center of the novel is the story of a young lawyer of the modern world, Kabir, and his romantic affair with a young courtesan called Huma (Ali, *Ocean of Night*, 71). The novel focuses the dreams of the romantic love of Huma against the backdrop of a modernizing India, where elite patronage of the courtesans of the old world is rapidly diminishing just as the taste and appreciation for their art is in decline.

While the landscape of city ruins and the historical palimpsests of urban Delhi within *Twilight* function as the melancholic repositories of a lost Muslim past, cultural loss is consolidated in *Ocean of Night* through the figure of the Muslim courtesan, or tavaif, who, Mufti has argued, functions metonymically within the representational economy of Indian nationalism to mark the lost high cultural artistic world of a dying Muslim elite (195). As Mufti argues, the tavaif inhabits the ambivalent symbol in Indian literary and popular culture of the excessive and improperly sexual courtesan while also acting as the "guardian of at least some high cultural forms—as saloniere, arbiter of literary and musical taste, and instructor in elite social manners." The courtesan, Mufti writes,

> belonged in very concrete ways to the pre-colonial social elites of cities like Lahore and Lucknow. So if by the end of the nineteenth century she provided a compelling representation of the problematic of being Muslim in the emergence of the Indian modern ... this is owing at least in part to

her ability to stand in metonymically for the culture of the pre-modern elites of North India. (195)

Mufti examines this figure through its meta-allegorical rendering in the short stories of an infamous member of the Progressive Writers' Movement, Saadat Hasan Manto, and in so doing brings to critical focus a central literary trope for the gendered semiotics of the nation within the movement. For Mufti, if it is the asexual and domestic mother that represents the nation within the Indian national imaginary—an "organization of affect" that interpolates the citizen through the filial logics of maternal love and devotion—it is the duplicitous, improperly sexual, and capricious figure of the tavaif that represents the Muslim as "minority" within Manto's short stories (Mufti, 2). In other words, the duplicitous figure of the tavaif comes to represent the ambivalence of the Muslim to Indian national culture, "the equivocal allegiance of the Muslim to the emerging Indian national narrative ... an indication of the unassimilability of these elite cultural practices marked as Muslim to the emerging narratives of India's national existence" (Mufti, 196).

I turn to *Ocean of Night* as it stages the romance between the modern Muslim male subject and this densely coded metonymic figure of the tavaif, drawing on Mufti's insightful readings of Manto, to further examine Ali's interrogations of the structures of longing and desire embedded within his allegorical romance. How are we to read the novel's failed romance, staged between the modern Muslim subject and the courtesan, a figure already inscribed within an analytic of failure? As rendered in the very plot of *Ocean of Night*, it is precisely through her incapacity to become a proper woman—mother and wife—within the logics of bourgeois respectability, that the courtesan cannot be rendered legible within the familial fantasy of the nation.[5] How, precisely, this chapter asks, are we to read the narrative energy invested in this failed romance through its sociohistorical register?

In a book-length analysis of the poetry of T. S. Elliot published in 1942 under the title *Mr. Eliot's Penny World of Dreams*, Ali writes:

> Capitalism always tries to make an appeal of the most superficial order, only of the surface, for it has no real human depth; and so has the poetry of Eliot. Inside it is hollow, it is like a tree on whose roots the worm has already set; only the form remains, still beautiful, but how long will it last? Let us not answer the question.... Capitalism has found its poet in Eliot, who unconsciously interprets for it its last stages, and its impotence. How

ironical that its greatest poet cannot but sing its swan-song without realizing it himself. (9)

In his fascinating Marxist critique of Eliot, Ali draws on what we will find to be a dominant set of aesthetic tropes that appear within his novels: surface and depth. As I argued in my analysis of *Twilight in Delhi*, Ali's novels trace a trajectory in which the experience of character emotion is depicted as attenuating, flattening, hollowing out "like a tree on whose roots the worm has already set." As I argue about *Ocean of Night*, it is not simply the emotive life of his characters that flatten but the vitality and meaning of the emotive form.

The self-conscious staging of sentimentality in both *Twilight in Delhi* and *Ocean of Night* render—and, indeed, perform—the romantic and sentimental feelings of the characters through clichés and hackneyed phrases. If in these novels we read a sentimentalism and melodrama depicting the character romances, as I demonstrated for *Twilight in Delhi*, we do so precisely because the novel is both deploying and commenting on the ideological hold of these generic codes, as well as on its investment in the familial fantasy of the nation at this critical moment in India. We find a proliferation of overly sentimental phrases in *Ocean of Night* to describe the love affair between Kabir and Huma, such as "Her heart was full of emotion," "Her eyes were full of emotion" (47), "He felt the same emotion as when he had held her in her arms" (53), "She held her breath, lest the emotion went out" (59), "The stars felt the emotion she felt" (59), "She felt new emotion that surged within her" (60), "The emotion of her body was in her eyes" (62), and "They felt exhausted with emotion" (62). Both of Ali's novels seem to repeat these phrases endlessly, with the vast range of emotive states subsumed—and, indeed, homogenized—under the clumsy sign of "emotion." *Ocean of Night* further amplifies this move. Refusing particularity or categorization, or the kinds of somatic details we witness in the other novels of this study, the sign of emotion is rendered *as* cliché, as a diminishing and empty signifier, hollowing out, as it were, where "only the form remains" as Ali's characters grasp unsuccessfully for an experience of emotional "depth." As Ali's characters grasp unsuccessfully for an experience of emotional depth, emotion is thus rendered a sign that ceases to mean altogether.

Tracing the sign of emotion in Ali's novels, as both placeholder for experience and petrified linguistic form (in repetition), I argue that the novel performs the very evisceration it stages—both disemboweling and evacuating of "vital meaning." Shifting from the stage of progressive emotions to that of reactionary ones, the visceral aesthetics (the engine of progress in the former novels) is erased under this obstinate sign of "emotion." As I argue, the gendered figure of the courtesan around which *Ocean of Night* is organized becomes the site of this emotive and semantic evisceration. I thus turn to *Ocean of Night* to further probe the aesthetics of evisceration at play, as well as the politics of its semantic refusals.

The space of the brothel in *Ocean of Night*, the world of the courtesan, where those "who daily buy and sell in the marketplace of beauty," is explicitly represented in the novel through its logics of exchange (20). The women of the brothel are trained in the art of trading on the commodities of beauty and men's desire. Couched in the economics of commodity exchange, the narrator tells us about Huma's mother: "If the face speaks for the heart, hers showed that she had lost this commodity in the market of life long ago" (Ali, *Ocean of Night*, 11). The tavaif is thus overtly represented as a figure for the commodification not only of men's desire, but also of the "heart" of the courtesan—the commodification of her emotion. Trained by her mother, Huma learns to feel little for those she entertains; her patrons "did not rouse any deep emotion.... To her love had become a habit even as letting her head-cloth slip at appropriate moments" (Ali, *Ocean of Night*, 30). Huma, however, longs for a love that functions outside the logic of exchange that circumscribes her world.

It is with the philosopher-poet that Huma falls instantaneously in love and on whom she places her dreams of escaping the life of the courtesan and attaining true love in freedom, like the "emancipated women of the middle class" (Ali, *Ocean of Night*, 101). Did these women, Huma wonders, "love differently too?" (Ali, *Ocean of Night*, 95). Mirroring the emplotment of the romance in *Twilight*, the narrative investment in the buildup of the young romance in *Ocean of Night*—the obsessive longing and restless pining—is symmetrical with that of the heartbreak, suffering, and then longing for the past that follows when the dreams are broken. Like the story in *Twilight*, the first half of the narrative explores the obsessive longings for Huma's object of desire. However, as soon as the object of obsessive longing is attained for the male character, Kabir, he loses interest, and the young courtesan is left heartbroken.

The romance plot of *Ocean of Night* is initiated at a party. Huma is dancing for the guests of the wealthy nawab of the older generation when she locks eyes with Kabir, a lawyer by trade, but a philosopher-poet at heart. Kabir parallels the young protagonist of *Twilight*, Asghar, in many ways—notably, in his poetic and philosophical nature and tendencies toward sentimentality and nostalgia. Kabir also resembles the progressive writer in his philosophical and political leanings: "a love of literature and poetry ... Marx and Freud, and Eliot and the modern poets ... [of contemplating] the problems of sex and psychology" (103). The dance performance where Huma and Kabir first meet initiates a lengthy, drawn-out, Bollywood-style pining session in which the two obsessively long for each other. This has led critics to read the novel as a shift from both the social realism and modernism of *Twilight* to a more a sentimental register. However, if one reads the novel as self-consciously performing this sentimentality, *Ocean of Night* imbues both Huma and Kabir with far more psychological detail in its interrogation of their feelings and structures of desire. Furthermore, a number of fascinating parallels are consistently drawn between the two lovers. In fact, at times they become strange mirrors of each other—the poet and the prostitute. However, it is in their inability to feel "deeply" with previous lovers that Huma and Kabir suffer in common.

The scene of the dance performance, the home of the nawab, is not a mere plot device but an ekphrastic dip into the world that the figure of the tavaif represents. Ali indulges in the aesthetics of these scenes, representing the art form in fine detail and with great reverence, even as he critiques the emotive form through which this cultural world is being remembered. Against the landscape of cultural decline and the waning of emotional depth and intimacy in the novel, Huma's performance, through the detailed ekphrastic dance scenes, becomes one of the only places where a dynamic, invigorated body emerges in the text. The aesthetic energy of the scene is directed not only toward the subtlety and grace of bodily movement and gesture—the movement of the eyebrow and the neck or the positioning of the fingers—but also, more precisely, toward how these movements become the gifted modality through which Huma interprets the subtleties of emotion. Thus, the artistry depicted in the scene presents the tavaif as privileged narrator and interpreter of emotion, as well as the agent of emotive transfer to her audience. The scene is thus invested in not only the subtleties of her graceful movement but, simultaneously, how the spectators are being "moved" by them.

This use of the dance scene is particularly interesting given that it is the gestural vocabulary of classical dance that becomes the privileged example of progressive and reactionary art in Ali's "A Progressive View of Art," the essay with which I opened the chapter. In the essay, Ali contrasts classical Bengali dance with that of the Balinese dancer through a lengthy discussion of their artistic form and gesture, rendering the Bengali dance reactionary because of the emotions it imparts, as opposed to the Balinese dancer, who is seen to impart the invigorating emotions of progressive art. As Ali discusses, the "effect" of the Balinese dancer "was revolutionary, and one felt the highest degree of elation and stimulation which is the highest function of art":

> The themes of the Bengali and the Balinese dancers were similar. But the technique and method of representation were as different as a dead language is from one current. The symbols employed by the Bengalis were pedantic and dead.... [T]he Bengalis were trying to throw themselves into the past and thus resuscitate a dead art; the Balinese were dealing with something which is alive—the struggle for liberation. The Bengalis were in the highest degree abstract, dry, pedantic and obscure. Their symbols and images had no meaning for us, and could not penetrate into the profoundest layers of sensual thinking. ("A Progressive View of Art," 59).

Ali's assessment of progressive dance is thus grounded in an analysis of the unification of form and content and, furthermore, the alignment of an art with its era, through which progressive emotion can be conveyed to the audience.

Following Huma's dance, Ali stages a dialogue between Kabir and his friend, Raza Ali, in which they discuss and debate the artistic merit of the performances. The question of dance similarly becomes centered on the emotion it evokes:

> The conversation turned to Indian dancing, and Raza Ali waxed eloquent.
> "Have you ever thought that there is a dance within a dance?'" said Kabir.
> "What do you mean?" Raza Ali asked.
> "There is the dance that you see," Kabir explained. "The dancer is interpreting an emotion, and the emotion has a dance of its own. From the world into the mind, then back again." (Ali, *Ocean of Night*, 84)

The art form of the courtesan's dance is thus judged based on her performance as vehicle of emotive interpretation and transfer. I draw attention to the fact that, from a discussion of the emotions of the dance, the language suddenly shifts to the metaphoric dance of the emotion. The sign of emotion attaches itself to the dance here, pivoting between literal and metaphorical registers. This is followed in the novel by a fascinating aesthetic move that renders a series of more abstract registers of this dance within the novel as the representational agent of the work of emotion and the ways in which the subject of that emotion is moved.

The dance of the courtesan thus becomes the central organizing trope and metaphor for the emotive world of this text. It is in this way that the figure of the dancer and the dance hinges on a series of questions surrounding the emotive forms of its characters. I argue that if the stubborn sign of emotion provides the site of evisceration, where the visceral pathways of progressive feeling are displaced by the novel's sentimentality, our search for the trace of the visceral brings us to the gendered figure of the dancer.

In one poignant, self-reflexive moment in *Ocean of Night*, we find a lengthy, meditative lamentation delivered by Huma's mother, Azizan Jan, who was also a courtesan of the older world. Reflecting the very historical arc of the courtesan's world depicted by the novel, Azizan Jan reflects:

> Connoisseurs and real lovers of art were now so few.... Men went after butterflies that flitted from flower to flower, distracted their minds by seeing the passing shows on the screen or the stage, made love in drawing rooms. Life had become disjointed and too fast to allow any leisure for the cultivation of the fine arts of conversation and dancing that centered [on] the courtesan.... The courtesan had become the dancing girl, the dancing girl a common prostitute. (Ali, *Ocean of Night*, 70)

Against the backdrop of the novel's narrative, which charts the fall of this world under the conditions of colonial modernity, Azizan Jan articulates the transformation through the embodiment of the tavaif as cultural artifact—one in which the courtesan is stripped of her artistry and reduced to brute entertainment or functionality, the "dancing girl" or, worse, the prostitute. Thus, not only is the tavaif the key figure in the ekphrastic segments as dancer in the text, but her modern reinscription as the "dancing girl" serves to mark the fall of her high-culture form to cheap dancing for erotic titillation, barely a step above the prostitute who sells her body for sex. Azizan Jan represents this diminishing art form as being under erasure by both the homogenizing culture of an increasingly Hindu India ("saris replacing long beautiful robes"), but also the transformation brought about by the Westernization and industrialization of colonial culture (Ali, *Ocean of Night*,

70). In fact, Azizan Jan's lamentation of the loss of patronage for this world conjoins the frenetic and "disjointed" temporality of colonial modernity with its structures of both aesthetic taste and men's desire.

This degeneration of taste is further described by Azizan Jan as a result of the mechanization of the art of this new era: "Now there were other things to attract men's attention: the radio and the cinema.... Machines had taken away the beauty of handmade things" (Ali, *Ocean of Night*, 70). The tavaif, as a figure of a diminishing art form and cultural world, makes the art form and the erotic form inextricable under these conditions, indexing this historical shift in aesthetics as also the very structure of men's desire. As Azizan Jan laments, "Dancing had become just a painted mask with only ready emotions to show" (Ali, *Ocean of Night*, 70). The degeneration of the tavaif into the dancing girl thus represents this decline of her dance form, through their concomitant structures of feeling, from the subtle emotions of the tavaif to the easily commodified emotions of her modern equivalent.

What is crucial here is that this emotive shift is characterized as a loss of depth: the surface replaces the interior, emblemized by the mask of "ready emotions." The subject of emotional depth thus enters once again through its antitheses, the surface emotions of the "mask," which are all exterior with an empty interior: "Inside it is hollow," as Ali says of Eliot's poetry, "like a tree on whose roots the worm has already set, only the form remains" (*Mr. Eliot's Penny World of Dreams*, 9). This flattening of affect, this evisceration, thus comes to represent the hollowing out of human experience under the conditions of a capitalist modernity in India. As the courtesan turned dancing girl, Huma thus becomes a figure for the evisceration in which her narrative teleology is inscribed. The image with which we are left at the end of the novel is that of the eviscerated human form: "Through [Huma's] numbness the thought of the fleetingness of life filled her mind.... 'Once love flies from the heart ... , only a carcass remains[,] devoid of feeling'" (Ali, *Ocean of Night*, 168). It is here, I argue, that we can read the courtesan as a figure for this evisceration, the very emotive evisceration the novel performs, if we are to understand her as a guardian not only of certain cultural forms but also of particular *emotive* forms under erasure by the homogenizing forces of capitalist modernity and increasingly aggressive Hindu nationalism in India.

It is worth noting, however, that as the courtesan becomes a figure for this flattening of affect, she is not the subject of these emotions in Azizan

Jan's articulation, but the object. In other words, she is the object of this transformation in the nature of men's desire—the object of this flattening of emotion under capitalism; the object, thus, of this evisceration. While Huma and Kabir are configured as characters who suffer from their alienation and an inability to feel deeply, I propose, the eviscerating subject of this novel is, in fact, Kabir. It is thus to the male figure of the text—a figuration of the potential masculine Muslim citizen subject—that I now turn.

In one of the most explicit political critiques in *Ocean of Night*, the novel narrates a particularly heated debate at Kabir's workplace surrounding the politics of revolution and decolonization in India. Delivered through the mouthpiece of the socialist Muslim present at the scene ("Being a Muslim I am international.... Socialism comes naturally"), the lengthy passage in the debate is reserved for the critique of the very form of nationalist nostalgia staged in the novel: "We as a nation are suffering from nostalgia. Go back to the past is your constant cry. But how can you go back to the past? Which past?" (54). While there is no proper socialist realist omniscient narrator in the novel, and while little in Ali's novels can be taken at face value, the impassioned outcry of this position, I argue, functions as a key ideological moment of the novel:

> We cannot ignore the achievements of those centuries, but we cannot revive the atmosphere of those days. The social conditions are different.... That is not the way of bringing about a revolution. Why call it a revolution, then? Call it just a change of heart. (Ali, *Ocean of Night*, 54)

Indeed, what are we to make of this "change of heart" that plagues the male characters in Ali's novels? How do we read the allegorical implications of this propensity of feeling, this phenomenon of desire, under interrogation? This "change of heart" comes to resonate with a heightened gravity in the novel given the fickleness of men's desire, for which the women of Ali's novels continue to suffer. Whereas the modern male subject in *Twilight in Delhi* suddenly loses interest in the object of his obsessive desire once he attains her, in *Ocean of Night* the story revolves much more explicitly around the suffering and alienation that befall both Huma and Kabir once Kabir has had his change of heart. While it is tempting to read this as a commentary on the fleeting nature of men's desire, as this sentiment is surely taken to be the way of the world in the brothel, I would argue that something more interesting is at play here.

Kabir is tortured by his uncertainty regarding his feelings for Huma. In this sense, he is further rendered as a figure for a larger pathology of his generation—a critical disconnect between the male subject and the interiority of his emotions: "Like his generation, he had lost his grip over the inner life of the heart" (Ali, *Ocean of Night*, 106). Kabir, in fact, longs for the kind of intimacy he finds with his best friend, Satish, which is lacking in his romantic life with Huma. In fact, when he is with Satish, he feels no desire to be with Huma and reflects that such intimacy would be impossible in a heterosexual relationship precisely because it is circumscribed by the gendered logics of exchange: "Kabir was sad. Friends were dear because they gave without expecting and received without selfishness. Seldom did this relationship exist between woman and woman or woman and man" (Ali, *Ocean of Night*, 110). When Kabir finds himself falling out of love with Huma, it is by his own emotions that Kabir is deceived.

This plays out in a fascinating way in the climax of the characters' story line, where the charade of Huma and Kabir's romance is dramatically torn down. It cannot be hidden that Huma is an improper—and, indeed, impossible—figure for the romance and marriage plot she and Kabir are attempting to enact. The climax is the inevitable moment of revelation when Kabir goes to visit Huma at the brothel and is forcefully rejected by her mother in a humiliating spectacle precisely because he is not a paying patron. Kabir is overcome with shame and humiliation and vows never to see Huma again. Just as Huma, as a courtesan who trades on her body, makes impossible the romance of bourgeois world, Kabir disrupts the logic of the brothel as one who does not pay for Huma's art and sex. But this inevitable moment of revelation is manipulated in *Ocean of Night* in a way that complicates this narrative of cause and effect.

The reader is informed that Kabir began to lose interest in Huma long before this humiliating event. What motivates him to go to the brothel to see her is his sudden realization that, when he thinks about Huma entertaining other patrons, he feels no jealousy. He feels *nothing*. He thus goes to see Huma out of a lack of jealousy. In a strange layering of emotions, Kabir feels that he should feel jealous because it is the appropriate emotion toward the woman he supposedly loves. In other words, in the form of love dictated by the romance and marriage plot, this feeling of possessiveness—as she is his possession in this configuration—should be instinctual. But it is not, and this lack of feeling that he feels he should feel is what sends him to the brothel.

Further, in the scene of his humiliation by Huma's mother, Kabir is not simply ashamed but further surprised and disturbed by his own latent bourgeois conservatism, on which the shaming is structured. It is a hangover from an earlier generation that he sees himself as having moved past. The novel renders a series of Kabir's internal conflicts: "He was pleased to see Huma, but ... 'if someone sees her, what will he think?' ... But he satisfied himself by saying ... 'it's so bourgeois to think of respectability'" (Ali, *Ocean of Night*, 101). It is of this series of emotive betrayals, the capriciousness of his own feelings, that Kabir finds himself a victim. Mufti reads the courtesan as a figure of betrayal and duplicity in the short stories of Manto. In *Ocean of Night*, however, the courtesan is a figure of such betrayal only as the emotive *object* of Kabir's feelings. In other words, it is only as the object of his eviscerated emotions that the courtesan becomes a figure for this duplicity, for it is Kabir's emotions that are rendered mercurial and capricious—a condition figured by the novel as that of the modern Muslim male subject of the nation.

Ocean of Night opens with a peculiar prologue that centers the trope of its title, the night (no longer the historical "twilight" of Delhi), as the force that conceals the "mysteries" of human emotion and that frames the story to come as enacted on this metaphysical stage of history:

> Night, like the heart of the lover, conceals within it the mystery of life. Shut between the common world of days, it hides the secret of human passion.... Men dance moved by the invisible strings, behind the curtain, dance until they cannot say who are the puppets and who the spectators, enact the stories of their lives and laugh or cry as the plot unravels.... But Night, the captivating *saqi*, brings out its glittering cups and, drunk on the breeze that makes them dream and forget, they care not for the intruders into their lives.... Dancing they go through the courtyards of life, dancing they pass into the halls of death. (7)

Night, the agent of concealment, thus becomes the organizing trope of the very emotions Ali critiques in his novels: those that blind and intoxicate, the opiates that cause one to "dream and forget," and thus the sentimental and nostalgic emotions that "arrest the forces of history" (to invoke Ali's own description of reactionary emotions). Tethered to the invisible strings that move them, Ali thus frames the movement of man through the passage of time, on the "stage of History," to borrow from Frantz Fanon (*The Wretched of the Earth*, 247). As Ali depicts these men as puppets or spectators, "moved" by human passion through this passage of time, he seems to ask of us the kinds of questions Fanon demanded of the potential revolutionary subject surrounding man's capacity to become actors and, indeed, agents of history: "Decolonization ... transforms spectators into actors, with the grandiose glare of history's floodlights upon them" (*The Wretched of the Earth*, 36). It is that this movement through history is staged *as* a dance that I want to bring to view. How are we to read this intriguing gender shift, for here it is men who dance? What is the nature of this dance, couched within this peculiar historical register?

From the abstract metaphysical register with which Ali opens, *Ocean of Night* moves to the distinct historical contours of the novel, portraying the fall of Muslim rule in India to the rise of colonial modernity. This historical narrative continues to be couched not only through the metaphors of performance but through dance and, furthermore, through the shift in the nature of this dance:

> There was Wajid Ali Shah dancing in the hall of the palace, wearing the precious stones inherited from his dead forefathers.... The hall resounded with a chorus of praise. It echoed through the walls down the halls of Quaiser Bagh where his wives and concubines held their little courts.... But the echoes died down as the book fell shut and the page was lost in the mass of pages that followed. The palace was silent, and the successors of Wajid Ali danced to the tune of a band in the same hall. But this dance was different. Here they danced in couples, man and woman. And the tune that came from the instruments was foreign to the air it floated on.... [T]he clapping died down and was lost in the whirr of a foreign tongue. (Ali, *Ocean of Night*, 10)

Now the liminal spaces of the earlier paragraph, "the halls of death" and "the courtyards of life," are elaborated as the palaces of the last Mughal rule. The passage of time charted in the novel is imagined here through the interior spaces of the palace. However, there is an uncanny dissonance between the edifice and its inhabitants—or, more precisely, the way in which the edifice is being inhabited—that comes to represent this historical transition. This dissonance, it seems, can be characterized as one of form and content, of art and its era. And, indeed, it is this dissonance that *Ocean of Night* proceeds to perform: that of the romance form performed by players who simply cannot fit the part.

The issue of emotive *form* is thus coded through the metaphor of what moves man, and how, through the passage of history. This prologue maps the historical arc of the novel itself through the shift in the formal structure of "the dance": the move from the familial organization of the past era to the nuclear family structure of the nation, tracking metonymically its concomitant structures of filial organizations. Indeed, written in English, the novel performs this lack of fit—a kind of semantic disjuncture—between the romance form and the emotional experience of the characters: "lost in the whirr of a foreign tongue." This scene renders these emotive forms as foreign to the historical agents under its spell, puppets to these invisible strings, as Ali stages the Muslim subject of the nascent Indian nation as one caught in the contradictions of these eras. As if the very "tune" that moves the dancer is rendered foreign to the air on which it floats—a remarkable image of the affective disjuncture at play—the emotive lifeworld of the novel's characters are rendered out of sync, out of place, and, indeed, out of time within the era in which they attempt to enact their stories on the stage of history.

Coda.
EXPLOSION

Frantz Fanon opens *Black Skin, White Masks* with the strange and haunting assertion, "The explosion will not happen today" (7). This evasive statement, scripted in taut and tenuous composure, is immediately confounded by contradicting temporalities: "It is too soon ... or too late" (Fanon, *Black Skin, White Masks*, 7). Propelled by the shadowed presence and absence of this "explosion," the fragmented narration of the chapter titled "The Fact of Blackness" oscillates between these uncanny temporalities of anticipation and belatedness. This elusive explosion and its orbiting temporalities propel from within the very first utterances of *Black Skin, White Masks* the narrative undulations of buildup and release within Fanon's theorizing of the colonial subject. These explosions resound with the shattering and fragmentation of the colonized black subject within the chapter's disjointed narrative.[1] Fanon not only writes the colonized black subject into narratives of history but also illuminates the structures and contradictions of a colonial modernity—not as abstract narrative conceptions, but as visceral repositories of lived history.

This chapter meditates on a peculiar constellation of densely affective, explosive encounters in the writings of Fanon, staged between the colonizer and the colonial subject, which illuminate the crises and contradictions of the visceral as I have been theorizing it. Guiding my inquiry into Fanon's somatic prose is how the affective energy of his theorizing makes inextricable the bounds of the sensate body from the time of history. Giorgio Agamben writes of the Marxist concept of history, "The original task of a genuine revolution ... is never merely to 'change the world,' but also—and first of all—to 'change time'" (91). In this coda I explore how the crises of the black, colonized consciousness appear through a range of somatic dramas we have explored throughout this book—muscular, erotic, proprioceptive, digestive. At times, they turn to the tactile interface of the body, and at other times they calibrate the ideal temperature for the rage of the black subject. As we have seen throughout the previous chapters, visceral imaginaries of decolonization are animated by a volatile conjoining of time and feeling: an explosion. This conjugation of Marxist temporality and feeling, I argue, animates the materialist theory of consciousness that underwrites the progressive imaginaries I chart throughout this book.

By concluding with Fanon, this book returns to rethink the anticolonial theories of the most canonized figure in postcolonial studies and studies of decolonization through the alternative genealogy of the visceral opened up by the Progressive Writers' Movement. Fanon's theories of viscerality are both refracted and displaced through the anticolonial imaginaries of the preceding chapters. Since the publication of his writings, Fanon has remained central to the debates of decolonization as well as to the field of postcolonial studies in its various iterations within the American academy.[2] The constellation of explosive bodily figures that I chart in this final chapter emerges, I argue, out of Marxian theories of revolutionary consciousness in Fanon's writings. By drawing out the distinct contours of the visceral grammars shared by Fanon and the Progressive Writers, I seek to frame the visceral within the broader internationalist circulation of a global Marxist political thought, pushing for new ways to read and understand the aesthetic and political projects of this era.

While one cannot conflate the distinct geopolitical particularities that inflect the corporeal aesthetics of Fanon and the Progressive Writers, I return to Fanon to excavate an aspect of the visceral, as a materialist optic of decolonization, that underwrites this book: its volatile and erratic role in the unfolding of history. What links my readings across the canonical writings of Fanon and of the Muslim internationalists of the Progressive Writers' Association is a revolutionary investment in the visceral reflex of the colonial subject. These texts share a somatic poetics of decolonization that centers the energetic life of the racialized subjects' affective response. As with the Progressive Writers, I mine the somatic scenes of his writing for how the racialized subject is "moved" in the moment of visceral expression, and the revolutionary potential invested in it, centering the role these bodily responses play in the unfolding of a revolutionary consciousness.

This chapter explores the volatile temporal contradictions housed in the visceral by foregrounding the figure of laughter and nausea in Fanon's essays. Progressive feeling, the feeling of new feelings, in Fanon's writings is as much a problematic of time as it is of the visceral trigger. My excavation of Fanon's visceral logics, which provides a theoretical spine for this book, relies on reading key essays from both *Black Skin, White Masks* and *The Wretched of the Earth* through and against one another, as these are often considered two distinct "versions" of Fanon. In centering scenes of affective release and transmission, I excavate their temporal logics of immanence, inevitability, impossibility, and *explosion*.

The Time of Laughter (or Too Soon)

I propose that we read the momentum and mounting pressure in "The Fact of Blackness" as energized by a peculiar desire for explosive laughter. The chapter's famous performance of bodily disintegration and tripling under the gaze of a child begins with the verbal command, "Look, a Negro!" as the narrator passes by. Fanon writes,

> "Mama, see the Negro! I am frightened!" Frightened! Frightened! Now they were beginning to be afraid of me. I made up my mind to laugh myself to tears, but laughter had become impossible.[3] (*Black Skin, White Masks*, 112)

The attempted laughter of the narrator in this scene presents us with an ambiguous and wandering signifier. How are we to read this scene of impossible laughter? To refocus this question through its visceral logics, How are we to make sense of this laughter as the object of the narrator's thwarted desire? Is this desire for laughter a wish to diffuse the violence of the aggressive gaze—to counter this hostility through ridicule or mockery? Is this anxious laughter—the nervous spasms of a body suspended, vibrating in this moment of shame and panic? The laughter may also be read as a strategy of identification or disidentification, to borrow from the great

José Muñoz (*Disidentifications*), or a desire to appease the child, to dismiss the words, to laugh them off, or to soothe the moment of pain with one of bodily pleasure. What falls under the sign of failed laughter?

However we read this scene, I contend that we may engage this figure of laughter slightly outside of its narrative boundaries and through a slightly different logic from the one apparently circumscribed by the scene and its players: an eruptive and interruptive corporeal logic that I have anatomized as visceral. Following this scene of failed laughter in the presence of the frightened child, the narrator of "The Fact of Blackness" explains, "I could no longer laugh, because I already knew that there were legends, stories, history, and above all *historicity*, which I had learned about from Jaspers" (Fanon, *Black Skin, White Masks*, 112). The narrator in this moment attempts to command his body to perform the emotive and corporeal eruption of laughter; however, the mental trigger necessary to activate the bodily response is blocked by his knowledge of the operative ideology of colonialism itself. In other words, the narrator's inability to laugh, to access his "sense" of humor, is rooted in a condition of consciousness. As we will find, this scene of failure comes to anticipate one of triumph in the development of the chapter, which occurs later in the narrative. We will find that this laughter—and, more precisely, the narrator's *desire* for laughter—enacts a drama of determinism, a fundamental struggle of the colonized black subject to command his own body and will.

Consider the critical grammatology in which this statement is inscribed: *I could no longer laugh, because I already knew.* This scene of desire and failure contains a series of shifting temporalities. At issue is not simply the narrator's incapacity to find his *sense* of humor in the face of the child's verbal aggression; it is also the narrator's *sense* of belatedness within the colonial narrative that results in the failure of the laughter: Fanon writes that laughter had become impossible "because I *already* knew" (Fanon, *Black Skin, White Masks*, 112, emphasis added)—his inability to laugh inscribed within a critical state of belatedness. As a physiological reaction dependent on a mental and emotional trigger, one's laughter—one's *sense* of humor—cannot be falsely induced. Laughter is involuntary but ideological, and thus deeply historical. Inscribed within the visceral aesthetics of Fanon's writings lies a particular preoccupation not only with the affective, but also with the temporal contours of the colonial subject's experience of lived history.

If we return to the famous scene on the train, we find that what begins as the desire for laughter ends in what Fanon characterizes as the narrator's experience of nausea:

> In the train it was no longer a question of being aware of my body in the third person.... It was not that I was finding febrile coordinates in the world. I existed triply: I occupied space. I moved toward the other ... and the evanescent other, hostile but not opaque, transparent, not there, disappeared, nausea. (*Black Skin, White Masks*, 112)

Nausea here depicts the existential splintering and tripling of the self under the racist gaze of the child. At the same time, it invokes Jean-Paul Sartre's notion of existential nausea and the violent gaze exacted in the ontological encounter. However, we also find a great deal of play with medical and metaphorical meaning. Fanon begins at the ear of the narrator, this auditory "stimulus" of the child's voice, which then inaugurates the extended corporeal drama through this disorder of the inner ear, the site of balance and motion: nausea.

Nausea here quite literally seems to follow from the narrator's sense of disorientation—dramatized in dizzying prose. In other words, this phenomenological staging enacts the radical sense of imbalance and vertigo in this moment of the narrator's occupying both his physiological body and the confines of the train. What sets the scene on the train in "motion" is the narrator's meditation on his kinetic sensations of balance and being within his racialized body: "I thought that what I had in hand was to construct a physiological self, to balance space, to localize sensations, and here I was called on for more. 'Look, a Negro!' It was an external stimulus that flicked over me as I passed by" (Fanon, *Black Skin, White Masks*, 111). The psychic interiority that Fanon attempts to render through these psychosomatic figures moves us from a racialized sense of humor to the aversive reflex of nausea. The narrator's desire for "the explosion" reveals him to be suddenly grappling with a different bodily trigger altogether. The eruptive, cathartic release that he seeks is no longer to laugh in the face of the colonizer but to vomit.

Within the trajectory of this scene, then, what begins as the narrator's desire for laughter, a yearning for the "explosion," ends instead in a state of nausea, yet another frustrated desire for a cathartic release. The narrator finds himself suspended in this anticipatory temporality, the immanent time of the "not yet." The figure of nausea is equated throughout this essay with a liminal and suspended temporality, a state of existential vertigo.

Throughout "The Fact of Blackness," affects of shame and self-loathing are embedded within this figure of nausea, saturated with a sense of tortured anticipation and potentiality awaiting an explosive release. As I read it, then, Fanon's nausea here signifies not "overwhelming emptiness," as Homi Bhabha suggests (51), but a visceral, frustrated desire for its eruptive potentiality.[4] The immanent time of the "not yet" is a suspended, explosive, tense one with which Fanon battles throughout the essay.

Like the figure of laughter, which energizes the recursive scenarios of colonial struggle throughout the essay, the embodied temporalities of Fanon's prose inhabit the oscillating tenses of presentism and belatedness. Fanon's narrative tends to linger in the moments that *anticipate* the explosive release. From within this immanent temporality, Fanon posits a politics of possibility for the colonized subject of history. These paired figures of laughter and nausea draw into relief the simultaneous impossibility and inevitability of affective release—temporal contradictions that underwrite these somatic crises.

With this understanding of the peculiar temporal dimensions of laughter and nausea, we arrive at the narrator's scene of triumphant laughter. When the narrative desire for laughter is at last fulfilled, a small but halting opening occurs for narrative and embodied control of the colonized black self within the recursions of the initial scene of struggle and failure. The narrator's laughter represents an act of vengeance performed through a vindictive speech act inflicted upon the colonizer:

> I put the white man back into his place; growing bolder, I jostled him and told him point blank, "Get used to me, I am not getting used to anyone." I shouted my laughter to the stars. The white man, I could see, was resentful. His reaction time lagged interminably.... I had won. I was jubilant. (Fanon, *Black Skin, White Masks*, 131–32)

The narrator's eruptive laughter hurls the white man into the belatedness he had previously experienced himself: "His reaction time lagged interminably." The explosive laughter's presentism thus bears the mark not only of a liberation, but also of domination: a control over another body that enables a control over one's own, as well as over the discourse that scripts their vital tenses.

As this momentary inversion of colonial power relations allows for the unblocking of the narrator's mental trigger of laughter, colonial subjugation is marked by an intellectual entrapment that translates into an entrapment of the bodily, a thwarting of the reflex. This crucial temporal shift out of a belated ossification and into a tense of possibility transforms the narrator into an agent of his own will and bodily command. Similarly, in an earlier scene of transient victory, the ability to activate the mental trigger of the desired bodily response is performed through vengeance inflicted on the white woman:

> "Look how handsome that Negro is!" "Kiss the handsome Negro's ass, madame!" Shame flooded her face. At last I was set free from my rumination.... *Now* one would be able to laugh. (Fanon, *Black Skin, White Masks*, 114, emphasis added)

The capacity to laugh here is enabled by the control over the woman's emotive and embodied response that activates the control over his own, making possible the ability to command the eruption of his laughter. Laughter becomes possible only when the narrator seizes the place of subjugator, using his position within a gendered hierarchy to subvert a colonial one. His aggression directed at the white woman impels the narrator into the temporality of present and future possibility. "At last," the narrator exclaims, "I was set free from my rumination.... *Now* one would be able to laugh" (Fanon, *Black Skin, White Masks*, 114, emphasis added).

Within these embodied cavities of lived history we find the uncanny temporal configurations of the Fanonian explosion. Reverberating within the laughter of the colonized is the desire to translate one's desire into a neural impulse that will mobilize the fibers of one's own tensed muscle. Laughter as an embodied temporality of the present tense enacts a possibility of determinism not only over the colonized body, but over the narrative of history itself, of which the black subject is a pre-scripted embodiment within these scenarios of struggle. This desire for laughter becomes the site of the colonized subject's grappling with historical agency and presentism. This peculiar desire animates a scenario not only of corporeal loss and control but also of historical agency: to become the subject rather than the object of one's history, of one's time.

Explosion (or Too Late)

"The Fact of Blackness" predictably ends, as it begins, with explosion. However, like the bursting of the self with which the narrative opens, it is not the liberatory explosion of the colonized subject's laughter, but the bursting of the self—the violent disintegration and fragmentation of the black colonized subject. In other words, "the explosion" happens, but it does not hurl the colonized subject out of the pre-scripted narrative that he attempts to escape; rather, it imprisons him within it. In a fascinating move, Fanon stages this explosion by dramatizing the historically overdetermined erotic dynamic between the black man and the white woman, a well-known preoccupation of his essays within *Black Skin, White Masks*.

Like the scene of laughter, this encounter enacts a drama of control and domination entangled in the logics of race and gender—but here on the grounds of the erotic "pathology" of the colonized male subject. In this move, the explosion takes us from the visceral reflexes of laughter and vomiting to the libidinal terrain of the narrative subject. Instead of staging this moment through the narrative "I," Fanon presents this eruption through his readings of the black American novelists Richard Wright and Chester Himes. Invoking the plot of Wright's *Native Son*, Fanon writes:

> It is Bigger Thomas—he is afraid, he is terribly afraid. He is afraid, but of what is he afraid? Of himself. No one knows yet who he is, but he knows that fear will fill the world when the world finds out. And when the world knows, the world always expects something of the Negro.... In the end, Bigger Thomas acts. To put an end to his tension, he acts, he responds to the world's anticipation. So it is with the character in *If He Hollers Let Him Go*—who does precisely what he did not want to do. That big blonde who was always in his way, weak, sensual, offered, open, fearing (desiring) rape, became his mistress in the end. The Negro is a toy in the white man's hands; so, in order to shatter the hellish cycle, *he explodes*. (*Black Skin, White Masks*, 139–40, emphasis added)

Salient in Fanon's rendering of *Native Son* is the overdetermined "action" of Bigger Thomas. Fanon mobilizes these texts in order to stage the colonized male subject's losing battle with not only the pre-scripted narratives that he cannot escape, but also with his fundamental struggle for bodily agency, for although Bigger Thomas "acts," he does "precisely what he did not want to do." This renders him a puppet of the colonizer: "a toy in the white man's hand."

While it is through the frustrated figure of nausea that Fanon stages the anticipatory temporality of the "not yet," it is through the erotic release of the male colonized subject, a different site of bodily appetite, that Fanon stages the time of the "too late." The libidinal eruption that Fanon stages here is not embedded in the anticipatory temporality of nausea; rather, the eruption *has already been anticipated*: "the world always expects something of the Negro.... [H]e responds to the world's anticipation." In his readings of these texts, Fanon stages the monopoly over the erotics of the colonized subject—the involuntary reflex through which the colonized subject fulfills the story already emplotted for him, against his bodily will. If nausea, as a figure for an agonizing anticipation, focalizes an inability to access the visceral trigger, to set the body into motion, the violent specter of rape here is a figure for a logic of somatic reflex that refuses to comply with the will of the colonial subject.

In staging the belated temporality of the "too late," however, it is the anticipation of the explosion, once again, on which Fanon's prose lingers in this scene of encounter. Dramatized in the anxious repetitions leading up to this "explosion"—*he is afraid, he is terribly afraid. He is afraid, but of what is he afraid? Of himself*—we find the black subject again "locked in." He anticipates his already being anticipated and fears himself becoming the object of fear—the fear through which the supposed savagery of the black man will be, and already has been, confirmed. As rendered in this passage, the temporality that the anxious subject inhabits is one not simply of anticipation and immanence, but also of swelling and mounting, a tumescent temporality accumulating in pressure and intensity. In fact, as this staging of *Native Son* proceeds, we move rapidly from the explosion back to the anxious anticipation of the narrative "I," awaiting his fate: "The Negro is a toy in the white man's hands; so, in order to shatter the hellish cycle, *he explodes*. I cannot go to a film without seeing myself. I wait for me. Just before the film starts, I wait for me. The people in the theater are watching me, examining me, waiting for me" (Fanon, *Black Skin, White Masks*, 140).

Like the dizzying buildup within the compressed space of the train, this scene dramatizes the mounting anxiety within the body of the narrator in the confines of the movie theater, the space where he awaits the very image that he seeks to escape—or, rather, explode. Foregrounded in this scene, staged through the libidinal logics of the colonized black male subject, is the volatile, accumulating potentiality of this immanent time. In this sense, the "explosion" of the black subject that Fanon stages here not only represents the existential shattering of the colonized subject. It further codes the sexual release of this overdetermined encounter. Attending to this immanent time, which drives and is driven by the inevitability of the Fanonian explosion, we continually arrive at the affective release valves of the colonized body on the terrain of the affective and the visceral.

Like the shadowed figure of vomiting, the body logic of the scene simultaneously traces the mounting sexual energy, as well as its dreaded, inevitable release—here, another psychosomatic figure inextricable from the colonized consciousness and involuntary reflex. As the subject ultimately fulfills the prescribed narrative of savagery that he seeks to escape, it is this involuntary response that then hurls the black subject into the temporality of his belatedness: "Too late. Everything is anticipated, thought out, demonstrated, made the most of. My trembling hands take hold of nothing; the vein has been mined out. Too late!" (Fanon, *Black Skin, White Masks*, 121).

Historical Catharsis

The logic of the visceral in these scenes of Fanonian encounter are fundamentally bound up in the snares of history. The scenes I have amplified map the affective release of the racialized subject onto the inevitability (or impossibility) of a historical rupture. This is what animates a series of visceral "crises" and historical impasses. Returning to Agamben's call to "change time" as the project of Marxist revolution, in a remarkable essay, Cesare Casarino responds to this call by revealing where it "butt[s] up against the intractable matter of corporeality" (195). Casarino writes, "The question of corporeality [is] inescapable for any historical-materialist and revolutionary theory of time—and vice versa" (194). Casarino here addresses Agamben's call to elaborate a revolutionary temporality against a "the homogenous empty time" of bourgeois historicism. As Casarino writes, against a Hegelian historical teleology of lack and negation Agamben searches (only partially successfully) within the forgotten vestiges of the Western philosophical tradition "for those forgotten, marginalized, yet always latent temporalities of interruption, discontinuity, and undeferred fulfillment that might be recuperated and marshalled in the service of a revolutionary theory of time" (186). Casarino's search for a revolutionary theory of time brings him to "the intractable matter of corporeality," while my search for the revolutionary energy of the racialized body ensnares my theory of the visceral in these thorny questions of time.

I agree with Darieck Scott that the fact "that temporality is repressed in Fanon shapes his representations of history and its effects in profound ways" (43). Scott draws on Ato Sekyi-Oto's discussion of Fanon's writings as "haunted by" a "repressed" discourse of temporality in order to counter criticisms of Fanon's ahistoricism, writing that "it may be the case not that Fanon ignores or merely wishes history away but that his theory of the historical, his way of thinking of its presence in the ongoing emergency of the now, involves an attempt to organize the information of history along nonlinear axes and in ways that frame its effects as not fully determinative" (43).[5] One of the key places that this repressed temporality emerges, I would argue, is in these visceral figures, where Marxist and Hegelian temporalities emerge "stretched" in Fanon's theory of black political consciousness. Against a time of negation and emptiness, the visceral inhabits an eruptive and disruptive temporality of potentiality, like Agamben's latent temporalities of interruption and fulfillment, but also of destruction. But for Fanon, theorizing from the lens of racial capitalism, there is no historical time outside corporeality: history is housed in the visceral. Within Fanon's concept of a revolutionary history, time and corporeality must be found "embedded and pulsating in each other" (Casarino, 202). The Fanonian explosion profoundly problematizes corporeal and historical agency for the revolutionary subject. This crisis of colonial consciousness can be found throughout the diverse writings of this study in the struggle for control over the visceral trigger and reflex—a struggle that, Fanon posits, is fundamentally temporal in nature. The liberatory potential of the visceral reflex is housed in the drama over *the time* of its cathartic release: to laugh, to vomit, to ejaculate, or, in the case of Fanon's later revolutionary writings, to which I now turn, to kill.

As in the prose of "The Fact of Blackness," the laughter of the colonized subject in the "Concerning Violence" chapter of *The Wretched of the Earth* is imbued with insurgent energy. Predictably, during Fanon's phenomenological description of "the native's" dream, the discourse of the essay slips suddenly into the psychoanalytic stylistic of "The Fact of Blackness," the narrative voice shifts from the ethnographic "they" to the autobiographical "I," and the figure of laughter appears:

> The first thing which the native learns is to stay in his place, and not to go beyond certain limits. This is why the dreams of the native are always of *muscular prowess*; his dreams are of action and of aggression. I dream I am jumping, swimming, running, climbing; *I dream that I burst out laughing,*

that I span a river in one stride.... During the period of colonization, the native never stops achieving his freedom from nine in the evening until six in the morning. (*The Wretched of the Earth*, 52, emphasis added)

Embedded within this series of present-tense action verbs—"jumping, swimming, running, climbing"—the subject's dream of explosive laughter appears once again. What is intriguing about the figure of laughter in this essay is the way in which it becomes equated with not just the corporeal agency we witness in "The Fact of Blackness," but also with the muscular mobility of the colonized subject and, by metonymic extension, the violent physicality of liberatory action. Within this essay, as a generalized condition of the body, the native's muscles, Fanon declares, are in a "state of permanent tension." Fanon writes,

The native's muscles are always tensed.... That impulse to take the settler's place implies a tonicity of muscles the whole time; and in fact we know that in certain emotional conditions the presence of an obstacle accentuates the tendency toward motion. (*The Wretched of the Earth*, 53)

The tension of the native's muscles, he explains, results from the vital impulse to reverse the colonial order, manifesting in the increasingly intensifying "emotional condition" of the subject. The accumulation of this emotive energy is conceptualized as heightening "the tendency toward motion," amassing the emotive energy and revolutionary momentum of the colonized subject. The accumulation of revolutionary time and the historical momentum of the nation are imagined as intensifying in the very musculature of the colonized subject. The Fanonian explosions, which erupt from within the visceral figures in "The Fact of Blackness," are thus located instead within what Fanon refers to as "tensions of the muscle" in the discourse of "Concerning Violence." Such a relocation of the Fanonian bursts, like Benjaminian blasts, from the realms of nausea and laughter to the musculature of the black subject thus shift and layer questions of historical agency from scenes of desire to those of aggression and violence on the stage of revolutionary history.[6] The condition that Fanon calls the tensions of the colonized subject is not simply a corporealization of this immanent state. Rather, it is a muscular manifestation of the subject's revolutionary consciousness, housed within a critical emotive condition, for the stiffness of the muscles, Fanon tells us, is simply a somatic manifestation of the "impulse to take the settler's place" articulated through the envy of the native. The immanent temporality of affective release is now the horizon of national liberation.

Within the binary structure of the colonized world, the native's envy houses the revolutionary desire and muscular potential to overturn the social order. Fanon writes:

> When the native is confronted with the colonial order of things, he finds he is in a state of permanent tension. The settler's world is a hostile world, which spurns the native, but at the same time it is a world of which he is envious. We have seen that the native never ceases to dream of putting himself in the place of the settler—not of becoming the settler but of substituting himself for the settler. (*The Wretched of the Earth*, 52)

Envy here is symptomatic of the critical recognition of the Manicheism of the colonial system, as Sianne Ngai articulates "as an ability ... to recognize and antagonistically respond to potentially real and institutionalized forms of inequality" (129). Like the trope of laughter, the native's envy becomes the vehicle of the revolutionary consciousness of the subject: "He is overpowered but not tamed. He is treated as an inferior but he is not convinced of his inferiority. He is patiently waiting until the settler is off his guard to fly at him. The native's muscles are always tensed" (Fanon, *The Wretched of the Earth*, 53).[7]

Fanon, for example, theorizes the eruptions of civil war as the diffusion of this revolutionary energy housed in the muscles of the subject, which keeps the subject complicit with the colonial order: "The settler keeps alive in the native an anger which he deprives of outlet.... The native's muscular tensions find outlet regularly in bloodthirsty explosions.... Thus collective autodestruction in a very concrete form is one of the ways in which the native's muscular tension is set free" (Fanon , *Wretched of the Earth*, 55). Similarly, Fanon writes famously on the rituals of ecstatic dance and possession through which, he argues, the colonized subject canalizes this aggression instilled by the anger deprived of outlet. What I have tracked in *Black Skins, White Masks* as the time of "not yet" appears in *The Wretched of the Earth* in Fanon's discourse on violence in the process of decolonization and national liberation. Thus, this affective energy accumulating in the colonized subject manifests in what Fanon refers to as the "muscular tensions" of the body, awaiting its inevitable explosive release. These muscular tensions stage the volatile possibility of both historical agency and "autodestruction" as a result of their explosive release. Within Fanon's discussion of the inevitability of violence in the process of decolonization, the possibility of historical agency is centered through the tensed muscles of the colonized subject and the inevitable release of this tension.[8]

Linking the black consciousness of *Black Skin, White Masks* with the revolutionary consciousness of *The Wretched of the Earth* through the trope of muscular tension, Scott writes, "The power of the blackened body—the colonized's body in its defeat—seems to lie in its mimes, its gestural and postural possibilities, which loop, rather than align or stack on a pyramid, the past, present, and future" (*Extravagant Abjection*, 71). In focusing on the repetitive and renewed action of muscular tension, most explicitly seen "exhausting itself" in ecstatic dance, Scott reads muscular tension metaphorically to ask "what it is to live in defeat when you must (as you inevitably do, although not constantly or indefinitely)?" (*Extravagant Abjection*, Scott, 83).[9] However, reading Fanon's muscles alongside Scott's brilliant readings, and in light of the psychosomatic figures I have traced in Fanon's writing, I also share with Mel Chen a set of questions about the materiality of the racialized body in Fanon's writings that "Scott precisely does not ask" in his largely metaphorical reading of the politically agitated subject.[10] What happens when we read Fanon's muscular tension, and its violent release, as a visceral logic of decolonization as I have been theorizing it in this book?

In mining the trope of muscular tension, Scott shares with me an interest in how the colonized consciousness (black consciousness) becomes the resource for emancipation, or national consciousness, in *The Wretched of the Earth*. A suggestive resonance in our readings is in our understanding of muscular tension as fundamentally wrapped up in questions of historicity, the "repressed" temporality of Fanon's historical materialism. The visceral response of the colonized subject, as I have been tracking it, is a crucial pivot or catalyst in Fanon's writings in transforming the colonized consciousness into a vehicle of liberation.[11] In a resonant inquiry, Zahid Chaudhary narrows in on Fanon's use of the term "instinct" in *A Dying Colonialism* as the site of what he calls phenomenological reassembly or "overcoming." Fanon's use of "instinct," as Chaudhary argues, is in this context not an ahistorical essence but, rather, "a historically situated phenomenological experience" that becomes a conceptual pivot in describing "both the body that is in his account overcome, threatened, and inundated with racial typologies and the new body that sublates the meanings and traumas inflicted upon it" (169). As Chaudhry states, "The 'moment' (to use Hegelian language) between these two bodies is one of a radical transformation and the proper place of what Fanon would call 'instinct' in *A Dying Colonialism*" (171).[12] My reading of muscular tension *as* visceral, however, focuses on the volatility—or what Jane Bennett might call the "vitality"—of visceral response, which traffics in the materiality and metaphor of bodily life set in motion by the colonial encounter on the stage of (a revolutionary) history. Specifically, my emphasis on the energetic buildup of somatic reflex in the moment of encounter focuses on the politics of affective release and transmission, bodily catharsis—or what I posit in this section as *historical* catharsis.

What Fanon calls the muscular tensions of the native, I argue, is a visceral logic of the colonized subject, inextricably linking the antagonistic affects, somatic responses, and oppositional consciousness of the subject that we witness in "The Fact of Blackness" with the time of national liberation in *The Wretched of the Earth*. The Fanonian explosion thus comes to function at the core of his writings on violence and revolution, for it is the inevitable release of these tensed muscles, and their emotive and historical energy, through which Fanon theorizes the possibilities and pitfalls of decolonization. Bound up with these Fanonian explosions is thus a rather complex notion of historical agency and determinism. The question of whether the native becomes the subject or object of these violent eruptions haunts his essays throughout *The Wretched of the Earth*. As Chaudhary writes, "The revolutionary act remains a fragile opening ... 'playful' in Benjamin's sense, and it is bound to succeed or fail with no guarantees" (171). My reading of muscular tension focuses on one of the central problematics of the visceral as a logic of decolonization, one that must reconcile the psychiatric condition of colonization with the political action needed for national liberation: the double-edged character of the volatile and erratic drive to cathartic release and transmission, through which one may become either the subject or the object of history.

As Gerard Aching writes, "It can be argued that the complexity of [Fanon's] use of the term *decolonization* emerges precisely from his powerful combination of psychoanalysis, political philosophy, strategies of national liberation, and the critique of political elites" (25).[13] One of the most poignant sites of this tension is seen in how the warfare glorified in "Concerning Violence" is strikingly counterbalanced in the final essay, "Colonial War and Mental Disorders." In his descriptions of torture victims and victims of war, Fanon's medical diagnoses of a number of pathologies reveal a suggestive tension in the way he is thinking violence and the affects of revolution through the loss of corporeal control. Of particular interest in the chapter on mental disorders are the cases of Algerian victims who lose corporeal and even muscular control and whose muscles sometimes control them. In writing about the Algerian War for Independence, Fanon describes a psychosomatic condition he calls "Generalized Contraction with Muscular Stiffness," in which a series of male patients suffer "nervous tension" and "find it increasingly difficult to execute certain movements: going upstairs, walking quickly, or running.... [They are] constantly tense, waiting between life and death" (*The Wretched of the Earth*, 292; *Les damnés de la terre*, 282). Echoing the muscular tensions Fanon theorizes in "Concerning Violence," these conditions inhabit the immanent temporality, suspended between life and death. As Scott writes about muscular tension as a figure for life-in-death and death-in-life, they "are ... modes whereby the colonized subject wrestles in the temporal field with his political and cultural subjection" (71).

Recent scholarship has brought renewed attention to Fanon's psychiatric and clinical writings, once overlooked in favor of his more overtly political writings. In a special issue on the contemporary exigencies of Fanon studies for the present, for example, Aching and Ranjana Khanna think provocatively about the way in which Fanon's clinical case notes "disrupt" the Hegelian paradigm of political consciousness in his essays on national liberation in *The Wretched of the Earth*, leaving us with the challenge of reconciling something that Fanon distinguishes and draws into unresolved tension: "the task of curing the mental pathologies that colonialism induces and those of resolving political challenges to the emergence of the postcolonial state" (Aching, 26). Khanna, for example, provocatively reads the "asylum" of Fanon's psychiatric notes as the Derridean remainder or supplement to the French colonial and independent state, a site of "pre- and postrevolutionary radical indeterminacy," and argues that "the call for a new form of the nation is equally a call for a psychical structure that is yet to be conceived" (134).[14]

In one particular case study, Fanon describes a young soldier in the resistance movement who, haunted by his violent actions, suffers from an affective disorder that is triggered on the same day every year, coinciding with the day he set off a bomb that killed ten people. On this date, the young man suffers from anxiety and "suicidal obsessions" (Fanon, *Wretched of the Earth*, 242). This pathology, described in a remarkable and lengthy footnote, launches Fanon into a peculiar rumination on the case of existential vertigo from which this man suffers. As Fanon grapples with the place of violence and militancy in the struggle, we find that, once again, questions of colonial affect bring him to questions of time:

> In other words, we are forever pursued by our actions. Their ordering, their circumstances, and their motivation may perfectly well come to be profoundly modified a posteriori. This is merely one of the snares that history and its various influences sets for us. But can we escape becoming dizzy? And who can affirm that vertigo does not haunt the whole of existence?" (*Les damnés de la terre*, 243)

Fanon's ruminations on violence and the explosive affects that impel it thus resurface questions of corporeal and historical agency. Will the colonized subject become the object or the subject of history, Fanon asks, or will he forever suffer from this historical vertigo?[15] Lingering in the anticipatory moments that await these inevitable explosions, Fanon stages the catastrophic unpredictability of the eruption. As Scott writes, muscular tension "trembles on the edge of a future" (71). These anticipatory moments contain not only the potential for the explosion, but also the profound ambiguity of its consequences. Is it, in the inaugural words of *Black Skin, White Masks*, too soon or too late?

Within the scenes I have presented here the visceral is inscribed within a temporality of an activated present and future potentiality, revealing itself to be the scripted substrate of racialized experience and thus also the terrain of its transformation as kind of lubricant for the engine of history. To explore the historical registers of the visceral in the writings of Fanon is also to probe the ways in which history is *a visceral logic*.[16] In "The Fact of Blackness," for example, the capacity for laughter, and its temporal inscription of historical presentism, is figured as a function of domination, while the failure of laughter, as we witness in the initial scene of the chapter, marks subjugation and colonial belatedness. Like Benjaminian blasts, the spontaneous, eruptive figure of laughter within this halting narrative inhabits a volatile realm of subversive potentiality from within the scenes of struggle for self-determination and historical agency. In its transfer of temporal and corporeal energy into the dynamic text of Fanon's theorizing, these explosive realms of laughter stage a dynamic politics of possibility surrounding the colonized subject's ability to rupture the historical text in which his belatedness is inscribed and to attain a presentism that would transform him into the agent of his own embodied history.

The visceral opens up the temporal contradictions that drive the visceral crises I have been tracking throughout this book. From the convulsions and compulsions of Ismat Chughtai and Khwaja Ahmad Abbas to the semantic refusals and suspensions, the eviscerations, of Mulk Raj Anand and Ahmed Ali, these psychosomatic figures emerge not only as an index of racialized feeling, but as a grammar of historical time. The visceral is thus driven toward a moment of *historical* catharsis. This crisis of colonial consciousness can be found throughout the diverse writings of this study in the struggle for control over the visceral trigger and reflex—a struggle that, Fanon posits, is fundamentally temporal in nature. The liberatory potential of somatic agency is housed in the drama over *the time* of its cathartic release.

The anticolonial imaginary I trace in this book is further structured, fundamentally, on the affective release and transmission of the visceral, of the inevitable historical catharsis. The affective reflexes I track throughout this book impel the revolutionary subject, the various protagonists of history, to an "ascendance" of consciousness within its revolutionary teleology, binding the visceral response to the temporal horizons of national liberation, whether in the form of a frustrated suspension or the momentum gained in its drive toward release. From the ecstatic and hysterical suspensions of nationalist ecstasy to the incessant and obsessive recursions of obscene cravings, the visceral emerges within these historical imaginings as both the motor of a progressive temporality and a disruption to it.

As I have argued in this book, the visceral lingers in the moments that anticipate the historical catharsis, the explosive release, not simply to dramatize the agonized suspension but, further, to stage the possibilities of rerouting the visceral ordering of the body. However, for Fanon the visceral as an affective tether within his Manichean imaginary belies the desire for corporeal control and domination over the other, for this is the only way he can gain access to the cathartic trigger of his own agonized suspension. While the visceral in Fanon's writings draws the colonial subject into an affective exchange with the colonized—a game of destroying or being destroyed, in the words of Spinoza—the somato-poetics of the Progressive Writers open up a rich imaginary of corporeal relations and sensorial reconstitutions that arise from these moments of affective exchange, in the low and middle ranges of affective intensity. It is the temporality of anticipation itself in the writings of the Progressives that I find so much more nuanced and full of possibility compared with Fanon, so full of other potential times and spaces, of imaginaries of relations in and of bodily being. This book emerges out of the diverse anticipatory temporalities of this poetic register in tiny somatic arousals—the itch, the craving, the tingling—for this is where the visceral logics of colonial subjects, locked in affective dynamics of power and subjection, are coming undone.

The visceral inhabits an unstable time full of potentiality, of possibility and destruction, the erratic and volatile time of the colonized and the subaltern that Gyanendra Pandey associates with "unreason" and the "unreasonable." This is, according to Pandey, the underside of the Enlightenment narrative of progress, "not readily able or willing to reckon with the contingency and unpredictability, the endless creativity and multiplicity of societal life" (7). The time of the visceral disrupts the linear, homogenous, empty time of bourgeois historicism; it refuses the "spatialized, measurable, quantifiable, homogenous, empty, and teleological time" of capitalist modernity and bourgeois historicism and its sequencing of "always fleeting and inconsequential ... instants," where each gains significance only through its own negation (Casarino, 185). It is not a time motored by the reason of Man. History as visceral logic insists on the inextricability of time from racialized affect in a way that echoes Casarino's call for not only a conception of time but a practice of time "as fully incorporated," for it is only "deep from within the folds of such a temporality," Casarino argues, "that one can begin to ask—as Spinoza does ask in *Ethics*—what the body can do, what a revolutionary and liberated body might be" (202). To this I add that it is also from within these historical folds that we can ask the Spinozan question of what it would mean for a body to "change its shape," recalling the radical reconstitution of the colonial sensorium housed as the promise of the visceral: *to feel new feelings*, in the words of Anand, *to be aware with a new awareness*.[17]

NOTES

Introduction

1. As Berlant, asks: "What makes so many people desperate to live conventionally rather than experimentally, when the prevailing norms generate so much noise and evidence of their failure to sustain life? How do conventional ideas of the good life get implanted in our viscera, and how do we go about enabling changes in our visceral understanding of our objects and our potential flourishing?" (Berlant, "Lauren Berlant")

2. As Anjali Arondekar and Geeta Patel write, "Affect, in however generative a guise, turns into a transposable logic or schema traipsing along from the United States to elsewhere" (156).

3. Brennan writes, "As the notion of the individual gained strength, it was assumed more and more that emotions and energies are naturally contained, going no farther than the skin. But while it is recognized freely that individualism is a historical and cultural product, the idea of affective self-containment is also a production is resisted. If we accept with comparatively ready acquiescence that our thoughts are not entirely independent, we are, nonetheless, peculiarly resistant to the idea that our emotions are not altogether our own" (*Transmission of Affect*, 2).

4. See Jose Muñoz's "Feeling Brown, Feeling Down: Latina Affect, the Performativity of Race, and the Depressive Position," Mel Chen's "Toxic Animacies, Inanimate Affections" and *Animacies*, Arun Saldanha's *Psychedelic White*, Saidiya

Hartman's *Scenes of Subjection*, Rachel Lee's *Exquisite Corpse of Asian America*, Ed Cohen's *A Body Worth Defending*, and Monique Alleweart's *Ariel's Ecology* for some important approaches to what Teresa Brennan terms the "transmission of affect" and the problematic of the bounded body for theorizing race, empire, and sexuality.

5. The authors I examine here have been written on extensively by South Asia–based academics, largely through the frame of Indian nationalism. See the work of Narasimhaiah, Mukherjee, Iyengar, Trivedi, Paranjape, Bhatia, Jalil, and Trivedi. For more on the history of the Progressive Writers' Association, see Gopal (2005), Pradan (1979), Coppola (1988), Ahmed (2009), and Zaheer (2006).

6. The Progressive Writers at times have been misunderstood and dismissed by contemporary critics, as they were by their own contemporaries, as socialist propagandists and didactic Marxists. As Priyamvada Gopal writes, "The dismissal of the Progressive legacy in some influential quarters resonates with a wider disavowal of Marxism within literary theory and postcolonial studies as 'economistic' or 'deterministic,' their literature marked by accusations of 'political orthodoxy and aesthetic tyranny'" (*Literary Radicalism*, 4).

7. Mufti similarly locates the Progressive Writers' Movement within a constellation of internationalist artists and an intellectual culture he terms "Bandung humanism." Mufti joins comparative literature scholars such as Lydia Liu and Stathis Gourgouris in their efforts to recuperate the humanism born out of internationalist thought in order to redirect a potential dead end in the antihumanisms of European theory. These scholars return to the transnational era of nonalignment and anti-imperialist solidarity, formally institutionalized at the 1955 Bandung conference, among the newly liberated nations of African and Asia. I join these scholars in recovering a non-Western legacy of humanist thought born out of the global dehumanization of racial subjection.

8. As Lauren Berlant so brilliantly articulates in an interview: "Most people think of Marxism as antithetical to any sensitivity to affect, as a mode of analysis focusing on capitalist processes of value extraction and exploitation. At the same time, though, Marxist thought has also provided a powerful account of fantasy: of how our senses and intuitions are transformed in relation to property, to labor, to presumptions about being deserving, and to enjoying the world. The [Marxist cultural] theorists I responded to see art as a place that clarifies the subjective and visceral aspects of structural social relations. We read artworks as a space where a variety of forces converge and become visible, including the fantasy resolutions we make to be able to live within contradiction." ("Lauren Berlant")

9. See Gauri Viswanathan's foundational *Masks of Conquest* for an in-depth discussion of British colonial educational practices in India and its role in molding cultural norms and sensibilities, a brilliant extension and use of Gramsci's notion of cultural hegemony.

10. As Roy writes, for Spivak the nineteenth-century colonial imperative of subject constitution "is to be understood as 'soul making,' or 'the imperialist proj-

ect cathected as civil-society-through-social-mission.' For Charlotte Brontë's *Jane Eyre* ... this involved the monumental but necessary task of transforming 'the heathen into a human so that he [could] be treated as an end in himself'" (7).

11. Here I draw on Gopal's phrasing in her reading of Chughtai's novel, *The Crooked Line*, and its central thematic concern with "the way in which the instinctual is subjected to the social, but it is by no means clear where the former ends and the latter takes over," a poignant description of what I term the visceral in this study (71).

12. For two recent English translations, see Snehal Shingavi's "Angaarey" and Vibha S. Chauhan and Khalid Alvi's "Angaraey."

13. As Ben Baer writes, "[the PWA's] locus of operation was primarily in the domain of culture, broadly conceived at the national level, and practically split into region and linguistic units. The PWA considered the national level of cultural work to be a metonymic part of an international whole.... In the India of the mid-1930s, the PWA's culturalist Popular Front anti-facism were among the first to perceive at first hand the connection between fascism and imperialism. Anand wrote in 1939, '[W]e saw the ugly face of Fascism in our country earlier than the writers of the European country, for it was British Imperialism which perfected the method of the concentration camp, torture, and bombing for police purposes'" (583).

14. I am indebted to Elizabeth Povinelli for the term "energetic" in this context (personal correspondence, Wesleyan University, 2011).

15. I am grateful to the anonymous reader at the University of Minnesota Press for helping me to bring this point into greater focus.

16. Posing a provocative and resonant question for this study in her dazzling book *Exquisite Corpse of Asian America*, Rachel Lee writes, "I inquire whether literary criticism and performance studies can still remain humanist if they think in terms of distributed parts rather than organic structures, or, more exactly, turn fragment and substance into patterns—circulations of energy, affects, atoms, and liquidity in its accounting of the soma" (7).

17. I am indebted to conversations with Jesus Hernandez on his brilliant thinking about "illegitimacy" in the context of Cuban American literature and politics.

18. The somato-poetics of the progressive writers index the influence of Freudian psychoanalysis. Even as I do not center psychoanalytic readings (properly speaking) in this book, I position this project as one that builds on and contributes to the invaluable work on colonial affect by psychoanalytic race scholars such as David Eng, Ann Cheng, and Ranjana Khanna and builds on the project of what Khanna terms the "worlding of psychoanalysis" (see "Worlding Psychoanalysis" in Khanna's *Dark Continents: Psychoanalysis and Colonialism*).

19. I also join scholars, Holland, Ochoa, and Tompkins, who in a recent *GLQ* double issue, explore the queer and feminist potential of the visceral. They define "viscerality," at the intersection of food and sexuality studies, as "a phenomenological index for the logics of desire, consumption, disgust, health, disease, belonging, and displacement that are implicit in colonial and postcolonial relations" (395). See the *GLQ* double issue entitled "On The Visceral."

20. Jane Bennett's work with Spinozist affect is particularly apt here. Bennett collapses the distinction between affect and matter in her attempt to surface an obscured political ontology that centers what she calls the "vitality" of matter: "My aim is to theorize a vitality intrinsic to materiality as such, and to detach materiality from the figures of passive, mechanistic, or divinely infused substance.... Not a life force added to the matter said to house it.... I equate affect with materiality, rather than posit a separate force that can enter and animate a physical body" (3). Even as Bennett's vibrant matter attempts to think through the agency of nonhuman matter, a collapsing of the distinction between affect and matter becomes a requisite for rendering legible the life of the somatic within colonial forms of discipline.

21. Here I draw on Mufti's central thesis in *Enlightenment in the Colony*, to which I will return throughout this book: "The crisis of Muslim identity must be understood in terms of the problematic of secularization and minority in post-Enlightenment liberal culture as a whole ..." (2).

Chapter One

1. As Anderson writes, "No matter how banal the words and mediocre the tunes there is in the singing an experience of simultaneity. At precisely such moments, people wholly unknown to each other utter the same verses to the same melody. The image: unisonance.... How selfless this unisonance feels!" (149).

2. *Stedman's Medical Dictionary* (New York: Houghton Mifflin, 2015) defines "shock" as: "Something that jars the mind or emotions as if with a violent, unexpected blow. 2. The disturbance of function, equilibrium, or mental faculties caused by such a blow; *violent agitation*. 3. A generally temporary massive physiological reaction to severe physical or emotional trauma, usually characterized by marked loss of blood pressure and depression of vital processes. 4. The sensation and muscular spasm caused by an electric current passing through the body or a body part."

3. Here I am indebted to Mufti's crucial formulation: "The crisis of Muslim identity must be understood in terms of the problematic of secularization and minority in post-Enlightenment liberal culture as a whole and therefore cannot be understood in isolation from the history of the so called Jewish Question in modern Europe" (2). My reading of Abbas's novel also echoes a similar insight made by Mufti surrounding the poetry of the Progressive Writer and Urdu poet Faiz Ahmed Faiz, whose engagements with modernity reveal "not mere rejection of religious experience but rather a wrestling with it" (222).

Chapter Two

1. I am indebted to Sianne Ngai's writing on irritation as an affect that connotes an "inadequate form of anger" as well as an affect that "bears an unusually close relationship to the body's surfaces or skin" (35).

2. Anand, for example, famously worked for T. S. Eliot's magazine, *Criterion*. See Anand, *Conversations in Bloomsbury*.

3. See Gajarawala's "Marxism, Modernism, Metaphor: The Origins of a Literary Politics of Particularlism" (in *Untouchable Fictions*) for an insightful critique of the pitfalls of Anand's attempts at representing caste within the Marxist modernist framework of class and labor in the novel.

4. Shingavi argues that Anand's experiments in stream of consciousness should be read as the projection of the middle-class racialized sensibility onto the casteized subject, enabling Anand "to take the authentic untouchable consciousness and present it as a mirror of the middle class's reaction to the process of colonization" (54).

5. See especially Ulka Anjaria, Ben Conisbee Baer, Jessica Berman, Toral Gajarawala, Aamir Mufti, and Snehal Shingavi. I am particulary indebted to these authors for opening up the complexity of the novel's representational politics diffused through the subaltern consciousness and interiority as it emerges in a complex relationship to the (socialist realist) omniscient.

6. As Mufti argues, "The Nehruvian, 'Progressive' aesthetics that emerged in the 1930s under the influence of Popular Front conceptions of artwork and society, telling the truth of society in fiction—'realism'—amounted to narrating the emergence of ... the abstract and secular citizen subject ... as the highest form of consciousness possible in a colonial society. The protocols of social realism, first formulated as a program at the Soviet Writers' Congress in 1934 and adopted as official Popular Front policy in 1935, undergo a transformation in being transplanted to a colonial setting. What the language of realist aesthetics now seeks to define is a specific relationship between writing and the nation so that it is more accurate to speak of *national realism* in this context" (183).

7. While a number of critics read the day-in-the-life structure of *Untouchable* through the lens of Bloomsbury modernism, Anjaria compellingly argues that the single-day structure becomes the site through which a classical realist emphasis on contingency (the wanderings of Bakha as internally driven) is metanarratively disrupted by an omniscient narrator who, "in a language that is clearly not Bakha's," attempts to fix the events of the protagonist into broader signifying fields—in other words, to allegorize the subaltern subject for the nation. The protagonist of the novel, as Anjaria argues, is self-consciously drawn into focus as the battleground "between the conflicting registers of symbol and contingency, realism and allegory. The contradictions between acting completely for and from oneself, and as a part of a larger [national] narrative" (61).

8. The wide range of concerns explored in Guru's collection include debates surrounding the forms of humiliation that accompany the reordering of Indian society under colonial modernity (the splitting of private and public spheres and the accompanied politics of "recognition"); the relationship of race humiliation to caste, gender, and class humiliation; the distinctive forms of humiliation of Dalit women that inform Dalit feminism; important forms of exchange and comparison with black studies in the United States; debates surrounding the utility

of phenomenology for humiliation studies in India; and the place of Marxism and its vernacular appropriations in Dalit movements (e.g., *Dalit Studies* outlines how Dalit activists question their marginalized place in Naxalite and Maoist movements in India).

9. Although their work is marginalized in the academy, Dalit scholars and feminists have long theorized the affective contours of caste and gender humiliation. *Dalit Studies* pointedly calls out the blind spot and elitism of Indian scholarship and puts forth a "new historiographic agenda" understood as enabled by the formal disbanding of the subaltern studies collective (Rawat and Satyanarayana, 16). For a poignant reflection on the difficulties of incorporating Dalit studies into the gender studies curriculum in the Indian academy, see Rege, *Writing Caste, Writing Gender*.

10. As Steven Connor writes, "The great age of thermodynamic science and technology brought an equivalent attention to the economies of energy involved in the skin's temperature exchanges: this gave the skin a new function, not only a thermodynamic engine, but reserve and restoration of nervous energy (*The Book of Skin*, 23).

11. For an excellent reading of the subaltern politics of this ambivalent scene in the novel, see also Baer.

12. In one letter, for example, Anand writes to K. V. S. Murti, "Perhaps you know that, from the earlier days, my approach has been to empty myself, receive the full impact of a character, become possessed by him or her, and express the conflicts and ecstasies and exaltations, as well as despairs, from the immediacy of possession" (*Old Myth and New Myth*, 19).

13. Here I join Ulka Anjaria in foregrounding the self-reflexivity and "metatextuality" of the Progressives' experiments in realism (*Realism in the Twentieth-Century Indian Novel*, 5).

14. I would like to thank Peter Lehman here for first bringing this use of the conditional to my attention.

15. This gap may be the site of affect proper, theorized by Brian Massumi as the "autonomy of affect."

Chapter Three

1. See Rakshanda Jalil's recently published *A Rebel and Her Cause: The Life and Work of Rashid Jahan*.

2. For an excellent analysis of Jahan's fiction in the context of the history of the gynecological training of middle-class Muslim women in northern India, see the chapter titled "Gender, Modernity, and the Politics of Space: Rashid Jahan, 'Angareywali,'" in Gopal, *Literary Radicalism in India*.

3. As Lloyd writes, "The subaltern marks the limit of the nation-state's capacity for representation, if, indeed, it marks a limit to representation in every way, the problem of the representation of the subaltern leads postcolonial theory into a

virtual aporia with regard to thinking practical alternatives to nationalist notions of decolonization" (4).

4. Here I have in mind Glissant's notion of "opacity" in *Poetics of Relation*.

5. Chughtai, in fact, worked as a scriptwriter and scenarist for the Bombay film industry, and her literary prose often reveals the influence of this cinematic aesthetic.

6. As Patel notes, "Scripted into the language of another tradition that renders them in metaphors appropriate to the Urdu *gazal* (a genre of lyric poetry), these renditions of the visual are already mediated by Urdu poetics. Both the *begam* and the boys as 'typical' beloveds return to the convention of the *gazal* as their bodies are sensually described: 'fair, slim-waisted boys,' and the *begam* with 'complexion fair ... hair black ... eyebrows like a couple of perfect bows'" (143).

7. As Gopinath writes, "It is precisely through Chughtai's narrative play with disclosure and visibility that fluid forms of homoerotic desire and structures of sexuality elide state discipline in its refusal to make them see-able and thus say-able within dominant discursive frames" (151).

8. This chapter is deeply indebted to the queer feminist scholarship of Gayatri Gopinath and Geeta Patel for opening up rich new channels of reading Chughtai's work. For an important set of interventions in reading the politics of sexuality and same-sex desire in "The Quilt," see the chapter titled "The Transnational Trajectories of *Fire* and 'The Quilt'" in Gopinath's *Impossible Desires* and Patel's "Homely Housewives Run Amok."

9. Begum Jan is also often described as being afflicted with a perpetual itch, thus epidermalizing this insatiable sexual desire and craving for intimacy.

10. This repressed sexual desire literally drives the artist to madness by the end of the story. In fact, when the artist descends into madness, he is said to be found on the side of the road each day drawing rounded, curved lines with dark charcoal.

11. For an excellent discussion of the mapping of domestic, public, emotive, and psychic spaces and the modern gendered *habitus* in *The Crooked Line*, see the chapter titled "Habitations of Womanhood: Ismat Chughtai's Secret History of Modernity" in Gopal's *Literary Radicalism in India*.

12. This is, in fact, a particularly troubling blind spot in Kolnai's discussion, as questions of intimacy lead him to rather homophobic conclusions about sexuality and disgust.

Chapter Four

1. See Carlo Coppola's interview with Ahmed Ali in Mehr Afsan Farooqi's *The Two-Sided Canvas: Perspectives on Ahmed Ali*.

2. As Ali proclaims in the afterword to *The Prison House*: "Sajjad Zahir and his minions had announced over the Pakistan Radio in my absence that I had ceased to be considered a 'progressive,' which was glaringly contrary to 'the right of free expression of thought and opinion' the 1936 Manifesto had stood for and emphasized" (167).

3. See Zaheer's *The Light: The History of the Movement for Progressive Literature in the Indo-Pakistan Subcontinent*.

4. See Shingavi's "The Missing Mahatma: Ahmed Ali and the Aesthetics of Muslim Anticolonialism" in *The Mahatma Misunderstood* for a nuanced reading of the hybrid aesthetics of *Twilight in Delhi* and its gender politics in light of the problematics Ali faced in reconciling Islam and the minoritization of Muslims (to borrow from Mufti) with (Gandhian) anticolonial nationalism and the Progressive Writers' Movement.

5. Nowhere does this become more explicit than at the end of the novel. Even after Kabir breaks off his relationship with Huma, she begs him repeatedly to give her a child, but Kabir refuses. Not only is Huma unable to attain the sign of mother, but, at the novel's conclusion, she learns about the death of the former patron who gave her the home in which she and her mother live. She returns the home to its "rightful" owner, the wife of the nawab, and is rendered literally homeless.

Coda

1. I refer here to Charles Lam Markmann's widely circulated translation of chapter 5 of *Black Skin, White Masks*, whose title, "L'expérience vécue du Noir," is more accurately translated as "The Lived Experience of the Black Man" (see Fanon, *Peau noire, masques blancs*).

2. While many scholars correctly highlight the issue of mistranslation in this text, I draw on Markmann's translation of *Black Skin, White Masks* (1967, because these iterations of Fanon's ideas have been central to the debates of Anglophone postcolonial studies and were the vehicle of their circulation within global Marxist liberation movements in the 1960s. I am grateful to Guilan Siassi and Jeannine Murray-Roman for their invaluable insights on these translations.

3. Notably, Markmann translates the original French *s'amuser* (to enjoy oneself) as "laughter" (see Fanon, *Peau noire, masques blancs*).

4. Bhabha writes, "From that overwhelming emptiness of nausea Fanon makes his answer" (51).

5. In response to Hortense Spillers's question about "how best to interarticulate the varied temporalities that arrive on the space of the now" in Fanon's works, Scott writes, "I would argue that Fanon's temporalities are in fact interarticulated; it is just that he does not map for us the thick web-strands that bind and colocate his often dismissed past, his catastrophic present, and his preferred future" (44).

6. As Casarino briefly mentions in an aside, the fact that the same historical problematic is articulated in one instance as "desire" and in another as "time" speaks to that fact that both are names for Spinoza's substance (193).

7. Markmann translates Fanon's original French *en attente* (in attention, in a state of waiting) as "tension of the muscle" (see Fanon, *Les damnés de la terre*, 54).

8. These articulations of muscular tension carry clear resonances with Marx's own articulations of the "muscular force" of the worker within what Casarino identifies as "a historical-materialist genealogy of affect" that emerges in Marx's meditations on the money form: "Marx repeatedly emphasizes how such a living source of all value exists exclusively as a potential incorporated in the 'bodily existence,' 'bodiliness,' and 'muscular force' of the worker—a corporeal potential for exponential leaps of production, creativity, and liberation that fully came into its own with capitalist modernity" (198).

9. Scott reads this muscular tension as a metaphor for an incomplete or "inauthentic" resistance, moments of opening, "powers amidst debility," although ultimately "defeat." He argues that the trope of muscular tension appears repeatedly throughout *The Wretched of the Earth* as a metaphor for this form of corporeal defeat insofar as it "is inert yet moves by means of miming, acting out in gesture and posture, the resistance it does not yet fully or authentically embody" (Scott, *Extravagant Abjection*, 71).

10. In response to Scott's claim that "muscular tension is the state of flexure that has the appearance of movement but is in substance barely moving and static, in a state of attenuated atrophy" (*Extravagant Abjection,* 66), Chen writes, "Asking questions of embodiment that Scott precisely does not ask, I do wonder about the link between tension and agitation, one as the condition for the other, or where tension is the condition shared between a sedimented rigidity and the movement that is then dubbed insurgency" ("Agitation," 561).

11. For Scott, this transaction, in Fanon's theory, rests on Fanon's "sociogenic understanding of Blackness" (Scott, 25).

12. As Chaudhary writes, "For Fanon, the truth that emerges from black consciousness is possible only via a phenomenological reassembly of the self, a process that is only possible with revolutionary action itself.... Bodily perception necessarily remains central to the self's constitution since it was the access point for the black subject's original trauma" (170).

13. Fanon notes the "out of place or untimely" nature of his own psychiatric case notes alongside his political writings. Aching argues that Fanon, in so doing, "urges us to reconcile 'consciousness' as both object of clinical psychoanalysis and the means by which the subject of political action assumes subjectivity" (25).

14. As Khanna writes, "Marx aimed to rescue the moral force of the proletariat by divorcing it from the lumpenproletariat, and Fanon in a single gesture asserted the mercenary potential of the decolonizing lumpen only to leave us with the remainder of the mental asylum, in which the moral worth and political redeemability of the mad remainders of colonial rule are at least questionable" ("The Lumpenproletariat, the Subaltern, the Mental Asylum," 138).

15. For a fascinating reading of this footnote as a reworking of Sartre's phenomenology, see Scott, *Extravagant Abjection*.

16. I am grateful to the anonymous reader at Duke University Press for urging me to pursue this question.

17. As Spinoza writes in *Ethics*, "Whether it is easy or difficult to force the parts composing an individual to change their situation, and consequently whether it is easy or *difficult for the individual to change its shape*, depends upon whether the parts of the individual or of the compound body lie with less, or whether they lie with greater surfaces upon one another" (60, emphasis added).

BIBLIOGRAPHY

Abbas, Khwaja Ahmad. *An Indian Looks at America*. Bombay: Thacker and Co., 1943.
Abbas, Khwaja Ahmad. *Bread, Beauty, and Revolution: Being a Chronological Selection from the Last Pages, 1947 to 1981*. New Delhi: Marwah, 1982.
Abbas, Khwaja Ahmad. *Face to Face with Khrushchov*. New Delhi: Rajpal and Sons, 1960.
Abbas, Khwaja Ahmad. *I Am Not an Island: An Experiment in Autobiography*. New Delhi: Vikas, 1977.
Abbas, Khwaja Ahmad. *Inquilab* [Revolution]. New Delhi: India Paperbacks, 1977.
Abbas, Khwaja Ahmad. *Mad, Mad, Mad World of Indian Films*. New Delhi: Hind Pocket Books, 1977.
Abbas, Khwaja Ahmad. *Rice, and Other Stories. With an Introductory Letter by Mulk Raj Anand*. Bombay: Kutub, 1947.
Abbas, Khwaja Ahmad. "Social Realism and Change." In *Aspects of Indian Literature: The Changing Pattern*, edited by Suresh Kohli, 145–54. Delhi: Vikas, 1975.
Aching, Gerard. "No Need for an Apology: Fanon's Untimely Critique of Political Consciousness." *South Atlantic Quarterly* 112, no. 1 (2013): 23–38.
Adorno, Theodor W. *Aesthetic Theory*, edited and translated by Robert Hullot-Kentor. Minneapolis: University of Minnesota Press, 1997.
Adorno, Theodor W. *Minima Moralia: Reflections from Damaged Life*. London: Verso, 1978.
Adorno, Theodor W. *Negative Dialectics*. New York: Continuum, 1983.

Adorno, Theodor W., and J. M. Bernstein. *The Culture Industry: Selected Essays on Mass Culture*. London: Routledge, 1991.

Adorno, Theodor W., Walter Benjamin, Ernst Bloch, Bertolt Brecht, and Georg Lukács. *Aesthetics and Politics*. London: NLB, 1977.

Agamben, Giorgio. *Infancy and History: Essays on the Destruction of Experience*, translated by Liz Heron. London: Verso, 1993.

Ahmed, Sara. "Orientations Matter." In *New Materialisms: Ontology, Agency, Politics*, edited by Diana Coole and Samantha Frost, 234–57. Durham, NC: Duke University Press, 2010.

Ahmed, Sara. "Orientations: Toward a Queer Phenomenology." *GLQ* 12, no. 4 (2006): 543–74.

Ahmed, Sara. *Queer Phenomenology: Orientations, Objects, Others*. Durham, NC: Duke University Press, 2006.

Ahmed, Sara. *Strange Encounters: Embodied Others in Post-coloniality*. London: Taylor and Francis, 2000.

Ahmed, Sara. *The Cultural Politics of Emotion*. Edinburgh: Edinburgh University Press, 2004.

Ahmed, Talat. *Literature and Politics in the Age of Nationalism: The Progressive Episode in South Asia, 1932–56*. New Delhi: Routledge India, 2009.

Aijaz, Ahmad. *Lineages of the Present: Ideology and Politics in Contemporary South Asia*. London: Verso, 2000.

Aijaz, Ahmad. *Theory: Classes, Nations, Literatures*. London: Verso, 1994.

Ali, Ahmed. "A Progressive View of Art" (1936). In *Marxist Cultural Movement*, vol. 1, edited by Sudhi Pradhan, 67–83. Calcutta: Santi Pradhan, 1979.

Ali, Ahmed. *Mr. Eliot's Penny World of Dreams: An Essay on the Interpretation of T. S. Eliot's Poetry*. Bombay: Neo, 1942.

Ali, Ahmed. *Ocean of Night*. London: Peter Owen, 1964.

Ali, Ahmed. *The Prison House: Short Stories*. Karachi: Akrash, 1985.

Ali, Ahmed. *Twilight in Delhi* (1940). New York: New Directions, 1994.

Alleweart, Monique. *Ariel's Ecology: Plantations, Personhood, and Colonialism in the American Tropics*. Minneapolis: University of Minnesota Press, 2013.

Ambedkar, Bhimrao Ramji, and Mulk Raj Anand. *Annihilation of Caste: An Undelivered Speech*. New Delhi: Arnold, 1990.

Anand, Mulk Raj. "Amended Manifesto." In *Marxist Cultural Movement*, vol. 1, edited by Sudhi Pradhan,. Calcutta: Santi Pradhan, 1979.

Anand, Mulk Raj. *Author to Critic: The Letters of Mulk Raj Anand*, edited by Saros Cowasjee. Calcutta: Writers Workshop, 1973.

Anand, Mulk Raj. "A Writer in Exile." In *Voices of the Crossing*, edited by Ferdinand Dennis and Naseem Khan, 77–82. London: Serpent's Tail, 2000.

Anand, Mulk Raj. *Conversations in Bloomsbury*. New Delhi: Arnold-Heinemann, 1981.

Anand, Mulk Raj. *Lament on a Death of a Master of Arts*. Delhi: Hind Pocket Books, 1938.

Anand, Mulk Raj. *Old Myth and New Myth: Letters from Mulk Raj Anand to K. V. S.* Calcutta: Writers Workshop, 1991.
Anand, Mulk Raj. "On the Progressive Writers Movement." In *Marxist Cultural Movement in India, Chronicles and Documents*, edited by Sudhi Pradhan, 1–22. Calcutta: Pustak Bipani, 1985.
Anand, Mulk Raj. *Roots and Flowers: Two Lectures on the Metamorphosis of Technique and Content in the Indian-English Novel.* Dharwar: Karnatak University Press, 1972.
Anand, Mulk Raj. *Untouchable.* New York: Penguin, 1940.
Anand, Mulk Raj. *Two Leaves and a Bud.* London: Lawrence and Wishart, 1937.
Anand, Mulk Raj. *The Village: A Novel.* London: J. Cape, 1939.
Anand, Mulk Raj. *The Sword and the Sickle: A Novel.* London: J. Cape, 1942.
Anand, Mulk Raj. *Homage to Tagore.* Lahore: Sangam Publishers, 1946.
Anand, Mulk Raj. *The Tractor and the Corn Goddess and Other Stories.* Bombay: Thacker, 1947.
Anand, Mulk Raj. *The King-Emperor's English, or, the Role of the English Language in the Free India.* Bombay: Hind Kitabs, 1948.
Anand, Mulk Raj. *Lines Written to an Indian Air: Essays.* Bombay: Nalanda Publications, 1949.
Anand, Mulk Raj. *The Indian Theatre.* London: D. Dobson, 1950.
Anand, Mulk Raj. *Apology for Heroism: A Brief Autobiography of Ideas.* 2nd ed. Bombay: Kutub-Popular, 1957.
Anand, Mulk Raj. *The Road: A Novel.* Bombay: Kutub-Popular, 1961.
Anand, Mulk Raj. *Is There a Contemporary Indian Civilisation?* New York: Asia Pub. House, 1963
Anand, Mulk Raj. *The Humanism of M. K. Gandhi: Three Lectures.* Chandigarh: University of Panjab, 1967.
Anand, Mulk Raj. *Coolie.* Delhi: Hind Pocket Books, 1972.
Anand, Mulk Raj. *The Bubble: A Novel.* New Delhi: Arnold-Heinemann, 1984.
Anand, Mulk Raj. *A Pair of Mustachios and Other Stories.* New Delhi: Orient Paperbacks, 2002.
Anand, Mulk Raj, and Atma Ram. *Anand to Atma.* Calcutta: Writers Workshop, 1994.
Anderson, Benedict. *Imagined Communities: Reflections on the Origin and Spread of Nationalism.* London: Verso, 2006.
Anjaria, Ulka, ed. *A History of the Indian Novel in English.* Cambridge: Cambridge University Press, 2015.
Anjaria, Ulka. *Realism in the Twentieth-Century Indian Novel: Colonial Difference and Literary Form.* Cambridge: Cambridge University Press, 2012.
Arondekar, Anjali. "Caste, Sexuality, and the *Kala* of the Archive." *Gender, Caste and the Imagination of Equality* (ed. Anupama Roy). New Delhi: Women Unlimited, 2018, 109–35.
Arondekar, Anjali. *For the Record: On Sexuality and the Colonial Archive in India.* Durham, NC: Duke University Press, 2009.

Arondekar, Anjali. "In the Absence of Reliable Ghosts: Sexuality, Historiography, South Asia." *differences* 25, no. 3 (2015): 98–122.
Arondekar, Anjali, and Geeta Patel, eds. "Area Impossible: The Geopolitics of Queer Studies." *GLQ* 22, no. 2 (2016): 151–171.
Baer, Ben Conisbee. "Shit Writing: Mulk Raj Anand's *Untouchable*, the Image of Gandhi, and the Progressive Writers' Association." *Modernism/Modernity* 16, no. 3 (2009): 575–95.
Bakhtin, Mikhail. *Rabelais and His World*, translated by Helene Iswolsky. Bloomington: Indiana University Press, 1984.
Bakhri, Deepika. *Postcolonial Biology: Psyche and Flesh after Empire*. Minnesota: University of Minnesota Press, 2017.
Barthes, Roland. *Camera Lucida: Reflections on Photography*. New York: Hill and Wang, 1981.
Bartolovich, Crystal, and Neil Lazarus, eds. *Marxism, Modernity, and Postcolonial Studies*. Cultural Margins, vol. 10. Cambridge: Cambridge University Press, 2002.
Benjamin, Walter, and Hannah Arendt. *Illuminations*. London: Pimlico, 1999.
Bennett, Jane. *Vibrant Matter: A Political Economy of Things*. Durham, NC: Duke University Press, 2010.
Berlant, Lauren. *Cruel Optimism*. Durham, NC: Duke University Press, 2011.
Berlant, Lauren."Intimacy: A Special Issue." Critical Inquiry 24, no. 2 (1998): 281–288.
Berlant, Lauren. *Intimacy*. Chicago: University of Chicago Press, 2000.
Berlant, Lauren. *The Queen of America Goes to Washington City: Essays on Sex and Citizenship*. Durham, NC: Duke University Press, 1997.
Berlant, Lauren. "Lauren Berlant on Her Book *Cruel Optimism*" [online interview], *Rorotoko*, June 4, 2012.
Berman, Jessica. "Toward a Regional Cosmopolitanism: The Case of Mulk Raj Anand." *Modern Fiction Studies* 55, no. 1(2009): 142–62.
Bhabha, Homi K. *The Location of Culture*. London: Routledge, 1994.
Bhalla, Alok, and Indian Institute of Advanced Study. *Life and Works of Saadat Hasan Manto*. Shimla: Indian Institute of Advanced Study, 1997.
Birla, Ritu. *Stages of Capital: Law, Culture, and Market Governance in Late Colonial India*. Durham, NC: Duke University Press, 2009.
Brennan, Teresa. *The Transmission of Affect*. Ithaca, NY: Cornell University Press, 2004.
Burton, Antoinette M. *Dwelling in the Archive: Women Writing House, Home, and History in Late Colonial India*. Delhi: Oxford University Press, 2003.
Butalia, Urvashi. *The Other Side of Silence: Voices from the Partition of India*. Durham, NC: Duke University Press, 2000.
Butalia, Urvashi, and Ritu Menon. *In Other Words: New Writing by Indian Women*. Boulder, CO: Westview, 1994.

Carter, Mia, and Barbara Harlow. *Archives of Empire*. Durham, NC: Duke University Press, 2003.
Casarino, Cesare. "Time Matters: Marx, Negri, Agamben, and the Corporeal." *Strategies* 16, no. 2 (2003): 185–206.
Chakrabarty, Dipesh. *Provincializing Europe: Postcolonial Thought and Historical Difference*. Princeton, NJ: Princeton University Press, 2000.
Chakravarty, Sumita. *National Identity and Indian Popular Cinema, 1947–1987*. Austin: University of Texas Press, 1993.
Chandalia, Hemendra Singh. *Ethos of Khwaja Ahmad Abbas, Novelist, Film Maker, and Journalist: A Study in Social Realism*. Jaipur: Bohra Prakashan, 1996.
Chatterjee, Partha. *The Nation and Its Fragments: Colonial and Postcolonial Histories*. Princeton University Press, 1993.
Chatterjee, Partha. *The Nationalist Resolution of the Women's Question*. Calcutta: Centre for Studies in Social Sciences, 1987.
Chatterjee, Partha. *Nationalist Thought and the Colonial World: A Derivative Discourse*. London: Zed, 1993.
Chatterjee, Partha. *A Possible India: Essays in Political Criticism*. Delhi: Oxford University Press, 1997.
Chatterjee, Partha. *Wages of Freedom: Fifty Years of the Indian Nation-State*. Delhi; New York: Oxford University Press, 1998.
Chatterjee, Partha, and Centre for Studies in Social Sciences. *Caste and Subaltern Consciousness*. Calcutta: Centre for Studies in Social Sciences, 1989.
Chatterjee, Partha, and Pradeep Jeganathan. *Community, Gender and Violence*. Subaltern Studies, vol. 11. New York: Columbia University Press, 2000.
Chaudhary, Zahid R. "Subjects in Difference: Walter Benjamin, Frantz Fanon, and Postcolonial Theory." *Differences* 23, no. 1 (2012): 151–83.
Chauhan, Vibha (editor) and Alvi, Khalid (translator). *Angarey: Nine Stories and a Play*. New Delhi: Rupa Publications India, 2014.
Cheah, Pheng, Bruce Robbins, and Social Text Collective. *Cosmopolitics: Thinking and Feeling beyond the Nation*. Minneapolis: University of Minnesota Press, 1998.
Chen, Mel Y. "Agitation." *South Atlantic Quarterly* 113, no. 3 (2018): 551–66.
Chen, Mel Y. *Animacies: Biopolitics, Racial Mattering, and Queer Affect*. Durham, NC: Duke University Press, 2012.
Cheng, Ann Anlin. *Melancholy of Race: Psychoanalysis, Assimilation, and Hidden Greif*. New York. Oxford University Press, 2000.
Cheng, Ann Anlin. *Second Skin: Josephine Baker and the Modern Surface*. New York. Oxford University Press, 2011.
Cheng, Ann Anlin. *Ornamentalism*. New York. Oxford University Press, 2019.
Chow, Rey. *Writing Diaspora: Tactics of Intervention in Contemporary Cultural Studies*. Arts and Politics of the Everyday.Bloomington: Indiana University Press, 1993.

Chowdhry, Prem. *Colonial India and the Making of Empire Cinema: Image, Ideology and Identity*. Manchester, U.K.: Manchester University Press, 2000.

Chughtai, Ismat. *A Chughtai Collection*, translated by Tahira Naqvi and Syeda S. Hameed. New Delhi: Women Unlimited, 2003.

Chughtai, Ismat. *The Crooked Line* (1944), translated by Tahira Naqvi. New York: Feminist Press, 2006.

Chughtai, Ismat. "Lihaaf" [The Quilt]. In *A Chughtai Collection*, translated by Tahira Naqvi and Syeda S. Hameed, 7–19. New Delhi: Women Unlimited, 2003.

Chughtai, Ismat. "Til" [The Mole]. In *A Chughtai Collection*, translated by Tahira Naqvi and Syeda S. Hameed, 110–26. New Delhi: Women Unlimited, 2003.

Chughtai, Ismat, and M. Asaduddin. *Lifting the Veil: Selected Writings of Ismat Chughtai*. New Delhi: Penguin, 2001.

Chughtai, Ismat, and Tahira Naqvi. *My Friend, My Enemy: Essays, Reminiscences, Portraits*. New Delhi: Kali for Women, 2001.

Clough, Patricia Ticineto, and Jean Halley. *The Affective Turn: Theorizing the Social*. Durham, NC: Duke University Press, 2007.

Connor, Steven. *The Book of Skin*. Ithaca: Cornell University Press, 2009.

Coole, Diana, and Frost, Samantha. *New Materialisms: Ontology, Agency, Politics*. Durham, NC: Duke University Press, 2010.

Coppola, Carlo. "The Angare Group: The Enfants Terribles of Urdu Literature." *Annual of Urdu Studies* 1 (1981): 57–69.

Coppola, Carlo. *Marxist Influences and South Asian Literature*. East Lansing: Asian Studies Center, Michigan State University, 1974.

Coppola, Carlo. *Marxist Influences and South Asian Literature*. Delhi: Chanakya, 1988.

Cvetkovich, Ann. *An Archive of Feelings: Trauma, Sexuality, and Lesbian Public Cultures*. Durham, NC: Duke University Press, 2003.

Cvetkovich, Ann. *Depression: A Public Feeling*. Durham, NC: Duke University Press, 2012.

Deleuze, Gilles. *Spinoza: Practical Philosophy*, translated by Brian Massumi. San Francisco: City Lights, 1988.

Deleuze, Gilles, and Félix Guattari. *A Thousand Plateaus: Capitalism and Schizophrenia*, translated by Robert Hurley. Minneapolis: University of Minnesota Press, 1987.

Derrida, Jacques, Kamuf, Peggy (trans). *Spectres of Marx: The State of the Debt, The Work of Mourning, and the New International*. New York: Routledge, 1994.

De Souza, Eunice, and Lindsay Pereira. *Women's Voices: Selections from Nineteenth- and Early-Twentieth Century Indian Writing in English*. New Delhi: Oxford University Press, 2004.

Devy, G. N. *After Amnesia: Tradition and Change in Indian Literary Criticism*. Bombay: Orient Longman, 1995.

Dirks, Nicholas B. *Castes of Mind: Colonialism and the Making of Modern India*. Princeton, NJ: Princeton University Press, 2001.
Eng, David. "The End(s) of Race" PMLA 123.5 (2008); 1479–1493.
Eng, David. "Colonial Object Relations" Social Text 34.1 (2016); 1–19
Eng, David. *The Feeling of Kinship: Queer Liberalism and the Racialization of Intimacy*. Durham: Duke University Press, 2010.
Fabian, Johannes. *Time and the Work of Anthropology: Critical Essays, 1971–1991*. Philadelphia: Harwood Academic, 1991.
Fanon, Frantz. *Black Skin, White Masks*. New York: Grove, 1967.
Fanon, Frantz. *Les damnés de la terre*. Paris: La Découverte, 2002.
Fanon, Frantz. *A Dying Colonialism*. New York: Grove, 1967.
Fanon, Frantz. *Peau noire, masques blancs*. Paris: Seuil, 1952.
Fanon, Frantz. *Toward the African Revolution; Political Essays*. New York: Monthly Review, 1967.
Fanon, Frantz. *The Wretched of the Earth*. New York: Grove, 1963.
Farooqi, Mehr Afsan. *The Two-Sided Canvas: Perspectives on Ahmed Ali*. New Delhi: Oxford University Press, 2013.
Fleissner, Jennifer. *Women, Compulsion, Modernity: The Moment of American Naturalism*. Chicago: University of Chicago Press, 2004.
Flemming, Leslie A. *Another Lonely Voice: The Urdu Short Stories of Saadat Hasan Manto*. Berkeley: Center for South and Southeast Asia Studies, University of California, 1979.
Flemming, Leslie A. "Progressive Writer, Progressive Filmmaker: The Films of Rajinder Singh Bedi." *Annual of Urdu Studies* 5 (1985): 81–97.
Forbes, Geraldine Hancock. *Women in Colonial India: Essays on Politics, Medicine, and Historiography*. New Delhi: Chronicle, 2005.
Forbes, Geraldine Hancock. *Women in Modern India*. Cambridge: Cambridge University Press, 1996.
Forster, E. M., Mulk Raj Anand, and Sayyid Hamid Husain. *Only Connect: Letters to Indian Friends*. New Delhi: Arnold Heinemann, 1979.
Foucault, Michel. *Discipline and Punish: The Birth of the Prison*. New York: Vintage Books (Random House), 1995.
Foucault, Michel, *The Order of Things: An Archealogy of the Human Sciences*. New York: Vintage Books (Random House), 1994.
Foucault, Michel. *History of Sexuality, Volume 1: An Introduction*. New York: Vintage Books (Random House), 1978.
Foucault, Michel. *"Society Must Be Defended": Lectures at the College de France 1975–1976*. New York: Picador, 1997.
Gajarawala, Toral Jatin. *Untouchable Fictions: Literary Realism and the Crisis of Caste*. New York: Fordham University Press, 2014.
Geetha, V. "Bereft of Being: Untouchability and Humiliation." *Humiliation: Claims and Context*. Ed. Gopal Guru. Delhi: Oxford University Press, 2011.

George, Rosemary Marangoly. *Indian English and the Fiction of National Literature*. New York: Cambridge University Press, 2013.

Glissant, Édouard. *Poetics of Relation*. Ann Arbor: University of Michigan Press, 1997.

Gokulsing, K., and Wimal Dissanayake. *Indian Popular Cinema: A Narrative of Cultural Change*. Sterling, U.K.: 2004.

Gopal, Priyamvada. "Concerning Maoism: Fanon, Revolutionary Violence, and Postcolonial India." *South Atlantic Quarterly* 112, no.1 (2013): 115–28.

Gopal, Priyamvada. *Literary Radicalism in India: Gender, Nation and the Transition to Independence*. Routledge Research in Postcolonial Literatures, vol. 11, London; New York: Routledge, 2005.

Gopalan, Lalitha. *Cinema of Interruptions: Action Genres in Contemporary Indian Cinema*. London: British Film Institute, 2002.

Gopinath, Gayatri. *Impossible Desires: Queer Diasporas and South Asian Public Cultures*. Perverse Modernities. Durham, NC: Duke University Press, 2005.

Gordon, Lewis. *What Fanon Said*. New York: Fordham, 2015.

Gramsci, Antonio. *Prison Notebooks*, vols. 1–3. New York: Columbia University Press, 2011.

Guha, Ranajit. *Dominance without Hegemony: History and Power in Colonial India*. Cambridge, MA: Harvard University Press, 1997.

Guha, Ranajit. *Elementary Aspects of Peasant Insurgency in Colonial India*. Delhi: Oxford University Press, 1992.

Guha, Ranajit. *History at the Limit of World-History*. Italian Academy Lectures. New York: Columbia University Press, 2002.

Guha, Ranajit. *An Indian Historiography of India: A Nineteenth-Century Agenda and Its Implications*. Calcutta: K. P. Bagchi, 1988.

Guha, Ranajit. *A Subaltern Studies Reader, 1986–1995*. Oxford: Oxford University Press, 2000.

Guha, Ranajit. *Writings on South Asian History and Society*. Subaltern Studies, vol. 1. Delhi: Oxford University Press, 1982.

Guha, Ranajit. *Writings on South Asian History and Society*. Subaltern Studies, vol. 2. Delhi: Oxford University Press, 1983.

Guha, Ranajit. *Writings on South Asian History and Society*. Subaltern Studies, vol. 3 Delhi; New York: Oxford University Press, 1985.

Guha, Ranajit, and Merrill College. *A Disciplinary Aspect of Indian Nationalism*. Santa Cruz: Merrill College, University of California, Santa Cruz, 1991.

Guha, Ranajit, and Gayatri Chakravorty Spivak. 1988. *Selected Subaltern Studies*. New York: Oxford University Press.

Guru, Gopal. *Humiliation: Claims and Context*. New Delhi: Oxford University Press, 2011.

Halberstam, Jack. *In a Queer Time and Place: Transgender Bodies, Subcultural Lives*. New York: New York University Press, 2005.

Halberstam, Jack. *The Queer Art of Failure*. Durham: Duke University Press, 2011.

Hall, Stuart. "The After-life of Frantz Fanon: Why Fanon? Why Now? Why Black Skin, White Masks?" In *The Fact of Blackness: Frantz Fanon and Visual Representation*, edited by Alan Read, 12–37. London: Institute of Contemporary Arts and International Visual Arts, 1996.

Hall, Stuart. *Policing the Crises: Mugging, the State and Law and Order*. New York: Palgrave, 1978.

Hartman, Saidiya. *Scenes of Subjection: Terror, Slavery, and Self-Making in Nineteenth-Century America*. New York: Oxford University Press, 1997.

Holland, Sharon P., Marcia Ochoa, and Kyla Wazana Tompkins, eds. "Introduction: On the Visceral." *GLQ* 20, no. 4 (2014): 391–406.

Hurley, E. Anthony. "Power, Purpose, and Presumptuousness of Postcoloniality and Frantz Fanon's *Peau noire, masques blancs*." In *Postcolonial Theory and Francophone Literary Studies*, edited by H. Adlai Murdoch and Anne Donadey, 21–36. Gainseville: University of Florida Press, 2004.

Ilaiah, Kancha. *Post-Hindu India: A Discourse in Dalit-Bahujan, Socio-spiritual, and Scientific Revolution*. New Delhi: Sage, 2010.

Ilaiah, Kancha. *Why I Am Not a Hindu: A Sudra Critique of Hindutva Philosophy, Culture, and Political Economy*. Kolkata: Samya, 2005.

Jahan, Rashid. "Woh" [That One]. In *Women Writing in India: 600 B.C. to the Present*, vol. 2, edited by Susie Tharu and K. Lalita, 119–22. New York: Feminist Press, 1993.

Jalil, Rakshanda. *A Rebel and Her Cause: The Life and Work of Rashid Jahan*. New Delhi: Women Unlimited, 2014.

Jameson, Frederic. *The Political Unconscious: Narrative as a Socially Symbolic Act*. Ithaca, NY: Cornell University Press, 1982.

Joshi, Priya. *In Another Country*. New York: Columbia University Press, 2002.

Judy, Ronald A. T. "Fanon's Body of Black Experience." In *Fanon: A Critical Reader*, edited by Lewis R. Gordon, T. Denean Sharpley-Whiting, and Renée T. White, 53–73. Oxford: Wiley-Blackwell, 1996.

Keeling, Kara. *The Witch's Flight: The Cinematic, Black Femme, and the Image of Common Sense*. Durham: Duke University Press, 2007.

Khan, Mahmuduzzafar. "Intellectual and Cultural Reaction." In *Marxist Cultural Movement*, vol. 1, edited by Sudhi Pradhan, 84–89. Calcutta: Santi Pradhan, 1979.

Khan, Naseem, and Ferdinand Dennis. *Voices of the Crossing: The Impact of Britain on Writers from Asia, the Caribbean and Africa*. London: Serpent's Tail, 2000.

Khanna, Ranjana. *Dark Continents: Psychoanalysis and Colonialism*. Durham, NC: Duke University Press, 2003.

Khanna, Ranjana. "The Lumpenproletariat, the Subaltern, the Mental Asylum." *South Atlantic Quarterly* 112, no. 1 (2013): 129–143.

Khilnani, Sunil. *The Idea of India*. London: H. Hamilton, 1997.

Kolnai, Aurel. *On Disgust*, edited by Barry Smith and Carolyn Korsmeyer, 408–409. Chicago: Open Court, 2004.

Korsmeyer, Carolyn, and Barry Smith. "Visceral Values." In *On Disgust,* edited by Barry Smith and Carolyn Korsmeyer, 1–25. Chicago: Open Court, 2004.

Lee, Rachel. *The Exquisite Corpse of Asian America: Biopolitics, Biosociality, and Posthuman Ecologies.* New York: New York University Press, 2014.

Lloyd, David "Representation's Coup." *Interventions* 16, no. 1 (2014): 1–29.

Loomba, Ania. "Race and the Possibilities of Comparative Critique." New Literary History 40, no. 3 (2009): 501–22.

Lorde, Audre. "The Uses of Anger." *Women's Studies Quarterly* 9.3 (1981): 7–10.

Lowe, Lisa. *Intimacy of Four Continents.* Durham, NC: Duke University Press, 2015.

Lukács, Georg. *The Meaning of Contemporary Realism.* London: Merlin, 1962.

Lukács, Georg. *The Theory of the Novel: A Historico-Philosophical Essay on the Forms of Great Epic Literature.* Cambridge, MA: MIT Press, 1989.

Mankekar, Purnima. *Unsettling India: Affect, Temporality, Transnationally.* Durham, NC: Duke University Press, 2015.

Manto, Saadat Hasan. *Kingdom's End and Other Stories.* London; New York: Verso, 1987.

Manto, Saadat Hasan. *Mottled Dawn: Fifty Sketches and Stories of Partition.* New Delhi; New York: Penguin Books, 1997.

Manto, Saadat Hasan, and Mohammad Asaduddin. *For Freedom's Sake: Selected Stories and Sketches.* Karachi: Oxford University Press, 2001.

Manto, Saadat Hasan, M. Asaduddin, and Muhammad Umar Memon. *Black Margins: Stories.* New Delhi: Katha, 2003.

Marriott, David. *Whither Fanon? Studies in the Blackness of Being.* Palo Alto: Stanford University Press, 2018.

Marx, Karl, Engels, Friedrich. *The Communist Manifesto.* New York: Penguin, 2002.

Marx, Karl, Fowkes, Ben (trans.). *Capital: A Critique of Political Economy, Volume 1.* Hamondsworth: Penguin Books, 1976.

Marx, Karl. *Grundrisse: Foundations of the Critique of Political Economy.* New York: Penguin, 1993.

Marx, Karl, Engels, Friedrich and Robert C. Tucker. *The Marx-Engels Reader.* New York: Norton, 1978.

Marx, Karl, Engels, Friedrich. *The German Ideology.* New York: International, 1984.

Mbembe, Achille. *On the Postcolony.* Berkeley: University of California Press, 2001.

Mbembe, Achille. *Critique of Black Reason.* (tr. Lauren Dubois). Durham, NC: Duke University Press, 2017.

Mbembe, Achille. "Necropolitics." *Public Culture* 15.1 (2003): 11–40.

Menon, Ritu, and Kamla Bhasin. *Abducted Women, the State, and Questions of Honour: Three Perspectives on the Recovery Operation in Post-Partition India.* Canberra: Gender Relations Project, Research School of Pacific Studies, 1993.

Menon, Ritu, and Kamla Bhasin. *Borders and Boundaries: Women in India's Partition*. New Delhi: Kali for Women, 1998.
Mishra, Vijay. *Bollywood Cinema: Temples of Desire*. New York: Routledge, 2002.
Mishra, Vijay. "Towards a Theoretical Critique of Bombay Cinema." *Screen* 26, nos. 3–4 (1985): 133–51.
Morris, Rosalind. *Can the Subaltern Speak? Reflections on the History of an Idea*. New York: Columbia University Press, 2010.
Moten, Fred. *In the Break: The Aesthetics of the Black Radical Tradition*. Minneapolis, MN: University of Minnesota Press, 2003.
Mufti, Aamir R. *Enlightenment in the Colony: The Jewish Question and the Crisis of Postcolonial Culture*. Princeton, NJ: Princeton University Press, 2007.
Mufti, Aamir R. *Forget English! Orientalisms and World Literature*. Cambridge, MA: Harvard University Press, 2018.
Muñoz, José. *Disidentifications: Queers of Color and the Performance of Politics*. Minnesota: University of Minnesota Press, 1999.
Muñoz, José. "Feeling Brown, Feeling Down: Latina Affect, the Performativity of Race, and the Depressive Position." *Signs* 31, no. 3 (2006): 675–88.
Muñoz, José. "Theorizing Queer Inhumanisms: The Sense of Brownness." *GLQ* 21.2–3 (2015): 209–210.
Muñoz, José. *Cruising Utopia: The Then and There of Queer Futurity*. New York: New York University Press, 2019.
Nandy, Ashish. *The Intimate Enemy: Loss and Recovery of Self under Colonialism*. Delhi: Oxford University Press, 2009.
Ngai, Sianne. *Ugly Feelings*. Cambridge, MA: Harvard University Press, 2005.
Padamsee, Alex. "Postnational Aesthetics and the Work of Mourning." *Journal of Commonwealth Literature* 46 (2011): 27–43.
Pandey, Gyanendra. *Unarchived Histories: "The Mad" and "The Trifling" in the Colonial and Postcolonial World*. New York: Routledge, 2014.
Patel, Geeta. "Homely Housewives Run Amok: Lesbians in Martial Fixes." *Public Culture* 16, no. 1 (2004): 131–58.
Povinelli, Elizabeth. *Geontologies: A Requiem to late Liberalism*. Durham, NC: Duke University Press, 2016.
Pradhan, Sudhi. *Marxist Cultural Movements in India: Chronicles and Documents, 1936–1947*. Calcutta: Santi Pradhan, 1979.
Prasad, M. Madhava. *Ideology of the Hindi Film: A Historical Construction*. Delhi: Oxford University Press, 1998.
Prasad, Vijay. *The Darker Nations: A People's History of the Third World*. New York: The New Press, 2007.
Prasad, Vijay. *Red Star Over the Third World*. New Delhi: LeftWord Books, 2019.
Puar, Jasbir. *The Right to Maim: Debility, Capacity, Disability*. Durham, NC: Duke University Press, 2017.
Rajan, Rajeswari Sunder. *The Scandal of the State: Women, Law, and Citizenship in India*. Durham, NC: Duke University Press, 2003.

Rajadhyaksha, Ashish, and Paul Willemen, eds. *Encyclopedia of Indian Cinema*. London: British Film Institute, 1999.

Ramachandran, T. M. *Seventy Years of Indian Cinema, 1913–1983*. Bombay: Cinema India-International, 1985.

Rao, Anupama. *The Caste Question: Dalits and the Politics of Modern India*. Berkeley, CA: University of California Press, 2009.

Rao, Anupama, ed. *Gender, Caste, and the Imagination of Equality*. New Delhi: Women Unlimited, 2018.

Rao, Anupama. *Gender and Caste (Issues in Contemporary Indian Feminism)*. London: Zed, 2005.

Rawat, Ramnarayan S., and K. Satyanarayana, eds. *Dalit Studies*. Durham, NC: Duke University Press, 2016.

Ray, Bharati. *From the Seams of History: Essays on Indian Women*. Delhi: Oxford University Press, 1995.

Ray, Sangeeta. *En-gendering India: Woman and Nation in Colonial and Postcolonial Narratives*. Durham, NC: Duke University Press, 2000.

Rege, Sharmila. *Against the Madness of Manu: B. R. Ambedkar's Writings on Brahmanical Patriarchy*. New Delhi: Navayana, 2013.

Rege, Sharmila. *Writing Caste, Writing Gender: Reading Dalit Women's Testimonios*. New Delhi: Zubaan, 2006.

Robinson, Cedric. *Black Marxism: The Making of the Black Radical Tradition*. Chapel Hill, NC: University of North Carolina Press, 2000.

Roy, Arundhati. *God of Small Things*. Toronto: Vintage Canada, 1997.

Roy, Parama. *Alimentary Tracts: Appetites, Aversions, and the Postcolonial*. Durham, NC: Duke University Press, 2010.

Rushdie, Salman. *Midnight's Children*. London: Jonathan Cape, 1981.

Said, Edward W. *Culture and Imperialism*. New York: Vintage, 1994.

Said, Edward W. *Orientalism*. London: Penguin, 2003.

Said, Edward W. *Representations of the Intellectual: The 1993 Reith Lectures*. New York: Vintage, 1996.

Said, Edward W. *The World, the Text, and the Critic*. Cambridge, MA: Harvard University Press, 1983.

Sahai, Malti. "Raj Kapoor and the Indianization of Charlie Chaplin." *East West Film Journal* 2, no. 1 (1987): 62–76.

Saldanha, Arun. *Psychedelic White: Goa Trance and the Viscosity of Race*. Minneapolis, MN: University of Minnesota Press, 2007.

Sangari, Kumkum, and Sudesh Vaid. *Recasting Women: Essays in Colonial History*. New Delhi: Zubaan, 2006.

Scott, Darieck. *Extravagant Abjection: Blackness, Power, and Sexuality*. New York: New York University Press, 2010.

Scott, David. *Conscripts of Modernity: The Tragedy of Colonial Enlightenment*. Durham, NC: Duke University Press, 2004.

Sedgwick, Eve. *Touching Feeling: Affect, Pedagogy, Performativity*. Durham, NC: Duke University Press, 2003.

Sedgwick, Eve, and Adam Frank. "Shame in the Cybernetic Fold: Reading Silvan Tomkins." *Critical Inquiry* 21, no. 2 (1995): 496–522.
Sharpe, Christina. *In The Wake: On Blackness and Being*. Durham, NC: Duke University Press, 2016.
Sharpe, Jenny. *Immaterial Archives: An African Diaspora Poetics of Loss*. Chicago: Northwestern University Press, 2020.
Sharpe, Jenny. *Allegories of Empire: The Figure of Woman in the Colonial Text*. Minneapolis, MN: University of Minnesota Press, 1993.
Sharpe, Jenny. *Ghosts of Slavery: A Literary Archeology of Black Women's Lives*. Minneapolis, MN: University of Minnesota Press, 2003.
Sharpe, Jenny. "The Archive and Affective Memory in M. NourbeSe Philip's Zong!" Interventions 16: 4 (Jul 2014): 465-82.
Shingavi, Snehal (trans). *Angaaray*. New Delhi: Penguin Books, India, 2014.
Shingavi, Snehal. *Mahatma Misunderstood: The Politics and Forms of Literary Nationalism in India*. New Delhi: Anthem, 2013.
Shingavi, Snehal. "When the Pen Was a Sword: The Radical Career of the Progressive Novel in India." In *The History of the Indian Novel in English*, edited by Ulka Anjaria, 73–87. Cambridge: Cambridge University Press (2015): 73–87.
Schuller, Kyla. *The Biopolitics of Feeling*. Durham, NC: Duke University Press, 2018.
Singh, Julietta. *Unthinking Mastery: Dehumanism and Decolonial Entanglements*. Durham, NC: Duke University Press, 2018.
Spinoza, Benedict de. *Ethics*, translated by W. H. White, edited by A. H. Sterling. Hertfordshire, U.K.: Wordsworth, 2001.
Spivak, Gayatri Chakravorty. *A Critique of Postcolonial Reason: Toward a History of the Vanishing Present*. Cambridge, MA: Harvard University Press, 1999.
Spivak, Gayatri Chakravorty. *Death of a Discipline*. New York: Columbia University Press, 2003.
Spivak, Gayatri Chakravorty. *In Other Worlds: Essays in Cultural Politics*. New York: Routledge, 1988.
Spivak, Gayatri Chakravorty. *Outside in the Teaching Machine*. New York: Routledge, 1993.
Spivak, Gayatri Chakravorty, Donna Landry, and Gerald M. MacLean, eds. *The Spivak Reader: Selected Works of Gayatri Chakravorty Spivak*. New York: Routledge, 1996.
Spivak, Gayatri Chakravorty, and Judith Butler. *Who Sings the Nation-State? Language, Politics, Belonging*. Calcutta: Seagull, 2007.
Stewart, Kathleen. *Ordinary Affects*. Durham, NC: Duke University Press, 2007.
Stewart, Susan. *On Longing: Narratives of the Miniature, the Gigantic, the Souvenir, the Collection*. Durham, NC: Duke University Press, 1993.
Stoler, Ann Laura. *Haunted by Empire*. Durham, NC: Duke University Press, 2006.
Stoler, Ann Laura. *Duress: Imperial Durabilities in Our Times*. Durham, NC: Duke University Press, 2016.
Stoler, Ann Laura. *Along the Archival Grain: Epistemic Anxieties and Colonial Common Sense*. Princeton, NJ: Princeton University Press, 2010

Stoler, Ann Laura. *Race and the Education of Desire: Foucault's History of Sexuality and the Colonial Order of Things*. Durham, NC: Duke University Press, 1995.

Sudhir, Chandra. *The Oppressive Present: Literature and Social Consciousness in Colonial India*. Delhi: Oxford University Press, 1992.

Tagore, Rabindranath. *The Home and the World*, translated by S. Tagore. London: Penguin, 1985.

Taussig, Michael. "Tactility and Distraction." *Cultural Anthropology* 6.2 (1991): 147–153.

Taylor, Diana. *The Archive and the Repertoire: Performing Cultural Memory in the Americas*. Durham, NC: Duke University Press, 2003.

Terada, Rei. *Feeling in Theory: Emotion after the "Death of the Subject."* Cambridge, MA: Harvard University Press, 2001.

Tompkins, Kyla Wazana. *Racial Indigestion: Eating Bodies in the 19th Century*. New York: New York University Press, 2012.

Tompkins, Kyla Wazana. "On the Limits and Promise of New Materialist Philosophy." *Lateral* 5, no. 1 (2016).

Trotter, David. "Fanon's Nausea." *Parallax* 10, no. 2 (1999): 32–50.

Uberoi, Patricia. *Social Reform, Sexuality, and the State*. New Delhi: Sage, 1996.

Vasudev, Aruna. *Frames of Mind: Reflections on Indian Cinema*. New Delhi: UBS, 1995.

Vasudev, Aruna, and Philippe Lenglet. *Indian Cinema Superbazaar*. New Delhi: Vikas, 1983.

Vasudevan, Ravi. "Addressing the Spectator of a 'Third World' National Cinema: The Bombay Social Film of the 1940's and the 1950's." *Screen* 36, no. 4 (1995): 305–24.

Vasudevan, Ravi. *Making Meaning in Indian Cinema*. New Delhi: Oxford University Press, 2000.

Virdi, Jyotika. *The Cinematic Imagination: Indian Popular Films as Social History*. New Brunswick, NJ: Rutgers University Press, 2003.

Viswanathan, Gauri. *Masks of Conquest: Literary Study and British Rule in India*. New York: Columbia University Press, 2014.

Weheliya, Alexander G. *Habeus Viscus: Racializing Assemblages, Biopolitics, and Black Feminist Theories of the Human*. Durham, NC: Duke University Press, 2014.

Williams, Linda. "Film Bodies: Gender, Genre, and Excess." *Film Quarterly* 44, no. 4 (1991): 2–13.

Williams, Raymond. *Marxism and Literature*. Oxford: Oxford University Press, 1977.

Wilson, Elizabeth. *Gut Feminism*. Durham, NC: Duke University Press, 2015.

Wynter, Sylvia. "Unsettling the Coloniality of Being/Power/Truth/Freedom: Towards the Human, After Man, its Overrepresentation—An Argument." *CR: The New Centennial Review*, 3.3 (2003): 257–337.

Zaheer, Sajjad. *The Light: The History of the Movement for Progressive Literature in the Indo-Pakistan Subcontinent*, translated by Amina Azfar. Karachi: Oxford University Press, 2006.

INDEX

Abbas, Khwaja Ahmad, 16, 44, 47, 54, 58; aesthetics of, 32, 41, 51; agitated subject of, 48, 50, 51; artistic experiments and forms of, 37–39; Bombay film industry and, 40, 59; Fanon and, 52–53; on Indian independence, 35–36; Indian nationalism depicted by, 42, 46, 51; narrative and, 45; politicization and, 56–57; revolutionary subject of, 43; social realist novel and, 39; in US, 39. *See also Inquilab*

Aching, Gerard, 2, 146–47

aesthetics, 30; of Abbas, 32, 41, 51; of agitation, 51, 53–54, 57; of Anand, 75, 77; of decolonization, 4, 25; of disgust, 94; of empire, 10; of evisceration, 34, 108, 119, 122, 125–27; of Fanon, 135; of Indian progressive writers, 2–4, 10, 17, 27; of *Inquilab*, 51, 57, 59; of Marxism, 8, 31; Mufti on, 155n6; of political agitation, 37; PWA and, 17; of skin, 67; as visceral, 1, 57, 75, 77, 122, 135

agency, 23–25, 47–48, 138–39, 142, 149; of agitated subject, 57; of subaltern figure, 90

agitated subject, 48, 50, 51, 56–57

agitation, somatic logic, 27, 32, 35, 50; aesthetics of, 51, 53–54, 57; of decolonization, 38; of ecstatic body, 49; in politics, 11, 37, 42–43, 49, 56, 88

Ali, Ahmed, 3, 34, 109–10, 114, 158n4; *Mr. Eliot's Penny World of Dreams* by, 120, 126; *Twilight in Delhi* by, 111–19, 121–23, 127. *See also Ocean of Night*

All-India Progressive Writers' Association (PWA), 3, 10, 99, 109, 111, 120; aesthetics and, 17; Ali and, 114; Anand and, 73–74, 76; anticolonial ideology of, 18; artistic experiments and forms of, 16, 38–39; manifesto of, 14–15, 73, 110; modernism of, 14; Mufti on, 152n7; subaltern figure and, 28; Urdu writers and, 13

Anand, Mulk Raj, 1, 13–16, 27, 31, 32, 61, 78–83; poetics of, 33, 62, 63, 65, 67; progressivism of, 73, 75; psychoanalysis and, 16; PWA and, 73–74, 76; social realism and, 40; subaltern figure of, 33; visceral aesthetics of, 75, 77. *See also Lament on the Death of a Master of Arts*

Angarey (Burning Coals, or Embers), 13, 87

anger, 19–20, 33, 144; explosion of, 68, 72; fire metaphorizing, 6, 68–69, 71; in *Inquilab*, 50; in politics, 16, 61

anticolonial authors, 5, 18, 32, 34, 60; feminism of, 85–87; Marxism of, 2, 86–87

anticolonial imaginary, 7, 133, 149

anticolonialism, 5; archival materials of, 25; biopolitics of, 8; of Chughtai, 94, 99, 102; corporeal states of, 32; ecstatic terror of, 38; feminism and, 19; imaginary of, 7, 133, 149; Indian nationalism and, 20, 37; Marxism and, 10–13; as masculine, 20; PWA and, 18

Anwar Ali (fictional character), 43, 58; as bastard, 40, 45; bodily response of, 54–55; colonial violence witnessed by, 52; education of, 50, 58; masculinity and, 49–51; nausea of, 56; politicization of, 41, 54; qawaali watched by, 45–46, 50; social order and, 49; transformation of, 41–42, 44–45, 48–49

appetite, 31, 33, 86, 102, 104, 106–7; politics of, 29; Roy on, 12; sexual desire depicted by, 96–97

archival materials, 1, 2, 7, 9, 25, 31–32

artistic experiments and forms, 4, 14, 30; of Abbas, 37–39; as archival materials, 31–32; power in, 19–20, 97; of progressive writers, 31–32; of PWA, 16, 38–39; somatic theory and, 20; subaltern figure in, 19–20

ascendance, of consciousness, 16, 64–65, 75, 83

Association of Writers for the Defense of Culture, 14

attraction, and revulsion, 33, 85–86, 97–98

Baer, Ben Conisbee, 10, 64, 66, 153n13

Bakha (fictional character), 62, 65, 68–69, 74, 83; caste and, 63–64, 66–67, 70

Bakha's body, 65, 67–68, 71

Bakhtin, Mikhail, 8, 65, 90

bastard (*haramazada*), 28, 40, 45

begumati zuban, 86

Begum Jan (fictional character), 94–97

Bennett, Jane, 146, 154n20

Berlant, Lauren, 9, 23, 89, 151n1, 152n8

biological realism, 42, 64, 65, 69, 80

biology, 29–30

biopolitics, 8, 21, 29, 30

Black Skin, White Masks (Fanon), 3, 5–7, 132–41, 145, 148, 158n2

Blitz Magazine, 35, 38

bodily appetite, 29, 31, 33, 86, 96–97

bodily life, 2, 29, 61, 66, 75, 146

bodily matter, 11, 21, 22, 29

bodily response, 2–7, 54–55

bodily texture, 1, 26, 28, 31, 92, 97

body logics, 24, 48, 65, 69, 141

Bollywood, 40, 123

Bombay film industry, 40, 59

Brennan, Teresa, 9, 151n3

British colonialism, 2–4, 25, 33, 62, 65; education and, 12; power in, 6–8, 29; race and, 9, 27

British colonization, 2, 21, 24, 29, 143, 146

Burning Coals, or Embers (*Angarey*), 13, 87

capitalism, 9, 30, 120, 127, 142

caste, 39, 75–76, 87; humiliation through, 66; liberation and, 12, 28; *Untouchable* addressing, 63–64, 66–67, 70

caste alienation, 66–67

casteized subject, 12, 31, 67, 70, 76

caste oppression, 33, 61–62
cathartic release, 5, 16, 22, 24, 54
chanting, 41–43, 46, 54, 58, 76
Chen, Mel Y., 25, 145
Chughtai, Ismat, 19, 21, 33, 86–87; anticolonialism of, 94, 99, 102; *The Crooked Line* by, 92, 98–105, 107, 153n11; feminism of, 20–22, 99, 107–8; masculinity and, 28; obscenity and, 33, 93–94, 98, 106; poetics of, 94, 106, 108; "The Quilt" by, 92–98, 102, 104–5, 157n8
colonial affect, 5–7, 11, 18, 27
colonial government, 13, 33, 87–88, 93
colonial hygiene, 12, 26, 33, 85, 96–97, 102
colonialism, British, 2–4, 25, 29, 33, 62, 65; education and, 12; imaginary of, 8; power in, 6–8, 29; race and, 9, 27
colonial order, 53, 67, 143–44
colonial power, 6–8, 29
colonial subjugation, 3, 4, 7
colonial violence, 6–7, 12, 27, 29, 54; ecstatic terror of, 52; trauma of, 2–4
colonized black subject, 5–7, 132, 143
colonized body, 2, 12, 22
colonized subject, 1, 8, 29, 53, 144
communal violence, 32, 37, 45
compulsion, somatic logic, 21, 27, 33, 34, 85, 107
consciousness, 3, 12, 34; ascendance of, 16, 64–65, 75, 83; of human collective, 14; transformations of, 39
contagion, 20, 23, 32, 43–44
convulsion, somatic logic, 20–21, 37; of nationalist ecstasy, 13; spasms of, 48, 55; visceral crises of, 23–24
convulsive logics, 11, 32, 48
corporeal imaginary, 21, 32
corporeality, 4, 7, 21, 23, 24, 32; poetics of, 65, 73, 82
courtesan (*tavaif*), 28; Mufti on, 119–20, 133
Cowasjee, Saros, 75–77, 83

The Crooked Line (Chughtai), 92, 98–105, 107, 153n11
Cvetkovich, Ann, 23

Dalit subject, of India, 12, 63, 66–67, 156n9
Les damnés de la terre. See *The Wretched of the Earth* (Fanon)
dance, as metaphor, 47, 52–53, 64, 123–26, 129–31, 144–45
decolonization. *See specific topics*
Deleuze, Gilles, 21, 25
desire and disgust, 12, 26, 87, 92, 97–98, 104; dialectic of, 85–87; as energetic forces, 33, 107
dialectics, 12, 33, 74, 76, 85–87
disgust, 31, 82, 88, 91–92, 102–3; aesthetics of, 94; as energetic force, 33; erotics of, 13, 34, 85, 93, 104–7; queer feminist critique of, 33; texture and, 12; touch and, 91–92
A Dying Colonialism (Fanon), 145–46

ecstasy, 16, 27, 33; as contagion, 43–44; of Indian nationalism, 38–44, 49, 51, 54, 57, 149; of religion, 45–51; of revolutionary subject, 43; spasms of, 29
ecstatic body, 38, 48; agitation of, 49; religion and, 45–51; somatic agitation of, 49; spectacle of, 44, 47, 55
ecstatic excess, 37, 50, 55
ecstatic spectacle, 44, 48
ecstatic terror: of anticolonial violence, 38; of colonial violence, 52; in *Inquilab*, 27, 52–59; of Jallianwallah Bagh Massacre, 54; spasms of, 13
education, 12, 61, 78–79, 87; of Anwar Ali, 50, 58
Eliot, T. S., 120–21, 123, 126
embodied experience, 1, 9, 42, 61
emergent nation, 36, 41, 53, 64, 90, 111
"emotional complex," 35–37, 41, 46, 57–58

emotionalism, of masses, 32, 36, 37, 46, 47, 50
emotive contagion, 1, 7, 9, 23
emotive response, 3, 4, 7, 12
emotive transfer, 44, 48–49, 123
emotive transformation, 16, 42, 44, 69, 71
empire, 10, 21, 29
energetic force, 6, 16, 20, 25, 33, 107
Eng, David, 10
enlightenment, 43, 64, 65, 69, 71
erotics: of disgust, 13, 34, 85, 93, 104–7; of power, 19–20; of queer theory, 31; texture and, 26, 33, 85
Ethics (Spinoza), 150, 160n17
euphoria, of masses, 11, 32, 38
European modernism, 11, 14, 17
evisceration, somatic logic, 21, 27, 75, 109; aesthetics of, 34, 108, 119, 122, 125–27
explosion, somatic logic, 21, 27, 53–54, 132–33, 136, 144; of anger, 68, 72; emotionalism as, 36; Fanon and, 138–41, 143, 146, 148; of laughter, 56, 134, 137, 143; Marxism and, 34
explosive laughter, 56, 134, 137, 143
The Exquisite Corpse of Asian America (Lee), 152n4, 153n16

Fanon, Frantz, 2, 4, 20, 133, 142, 149; Abbas and, 52–53; *Black Skin, White Masks* by, 3, 5–7, 132–41, 148, 158n2; cathartic release theorized by, 54; on colonial affect, 5–7, 11, 27; colonized black subject and, 132; on colonized subject, 144; on decolonization, 34; *A Dying Colonialism* by, 145–46; explosion and, 138–41, 143, 146, 148; laughter and, 134–35; as masculine, 21; musculature tension, 147; Muslim internationalists and, 8; nausea and, 134, 136–37, 139–40, 143; racialization depicted by, 5–6; revolutionary subject of, 11; visceral aesthetics of, 135; *The Wretched of the Earth* by, 3, 38, 51–53, 134, 142–47
Fanonian explosion, 138–41, 143, 146, 148
Fanonian figurations, 11, 23
Fanonian train scene, 5–6, 18, 21, 24
feel new feelings (concept), 1, 13, 31, 32, 108
female body, 26, 31, 93–96, 107–8; compulsion and, 34; materiality of, 86, 106; texture of, 28, 34, 92, 95–96, 105; violence upon, 85–87
feminism, 4, 9, 27, 31, 90; of anticolonial authors, 85–87; anticolonialism and, 19; of Chughtai, 20–22, 99, 107–8; in postcolonialism, 30; queer theory and, 30, 31, 33; representationalism in, 20; social realism and, 86; in South Asia, 10; of US, 31
femme cravings, 28, 33, 86
film industry, of Bombay, 17, 32, 39, 40, 44, 123; Abbas and, 40, 59; *Inquilab* influenced by, 44
fire, as metaphor, 6, 67–69, 71
Freud, Sigmund, 11, 27, 86, 92, 123, 153n18

Gajarawala, Toral, 17
Gandhi, Mahatma, 40, 60, 63, 70, 90
Geetha, V., 66–67
gender, 3, 5–8, 21, 27, 139; humiliation and, 67
gender and sexuality, 3, 9–10, 30, 107; decolonization grounded in, 20, 28; Indian Muslims and, 13
gendered figure, 28, 122, 125
Gopal, Priyamvada, 3, 28, 38
Gopinath, Gayatri, 28
government, colonial, 13, 33, 87–88, 93
Guru, Gopal, 66–67, 155n8

haramazada (bastard), 28, 40, 45
Hegelian dialectic, 141–42, 145, 147
historical agency, 142–44, 146–48

Huma (fictional character), 119, 121–23, 126–29
human collective, 36, 46; consciousness of, 14; revolutionary consciousness of, 3, 13; revolutionary feeling within, 32
humiliation, 66–67, 128, 155n8
hygiene, colonial, 96; regimes of, 12, 26, 97; sexual discipline and, 12, 33, 85, 102; violent regimes of, 12

imaginary, 16, 22, 56, 106, 111; of anticolonialism, 7, 133, 149; of British colonialism, 8; of corporeality, 21, 32; of decolonization, 4, 15; of gender, 21; of Indian nationalism, 49, 58, 120; of postcolonialism, 36; of progressivism, 86, 117, 133; of the racialized body, 31; in *Untouchable*, 118
imperialism, 12, 14, 152n7, 153n13
independence, of India, 4; Abbas on, 35–36; narrative of, 40, 54, 57; in social realist novel, 40
India. *See specific topics*
Indian Muslim, 11, 33
Indian nationalism, 2, 3, 17; Abbas depicting, 42, 46, 51; anticolonialism and, 20, 37; ecstasy of, 38–44, 49, 51, 54, 57, 149; "emotional complex" of, 35–37, 41, 46, 57–58; emotionalism and, 46, 50; imaginary of, 49, 58, 120; in *Ocean of Night*, 118–19; religion and, 41; simultaneity and, 37, 41–42, 44, 49; teleology of, 110; violence and, 34
Indian national politics, 10–11
Indian People's Theater Association (IPTA), 3, 38
Indian protests, 32, 40–43, 52–55, 57
Indo-Islamic life, 58, 112–13, 118
Inquilab (Abbas), 39–43, 45, 113–14; aesthetics of, 51, 57, 59; anger in, 50; Bombay film industry influence on, 44; ecstatic terror in, 27, 52–59; masculinity in, 49–51; narrative of, 42, 49; nationalist ecstasy depicted in, 43–44, 49, 51, 54, 57; teleology in, 47; trauma in, 52, 55
"Inquilab Zindabad" (Long live the revolution), 41–43, 46
internationalism, 11, 13, 61
IPTA. *See* Indian People's Theater Association
irritation, somatic logic, 21, 27, 32, 72, 73, 83; poetics of, 11, 61; of revolutionary subject, 33; in *Untouchable*, 60–71
Islamic orthodoxy, 4, 15, 33, 87, 114

Jallianwallah Bagh Massacre, 40, 52; ecstatic terror of, 54

Kabir (fictional character), 119, 121–24, 127–29

Lament on the Death of a Master of Arts (Anand), 62, 74–76, 84; narrative of, 77–82; nausea in, 78, 80–83
laughter, 5–6, 11, 135; explosion of, 56, 134, 137, 143
Lee, Rachel, 30–31, 152n4, 153n16
liberation, 2–4, 12, 28
literary intelligentsia, 2–4
Loomba, Ania, 26–27

Manto, Saadat Hasan, 28, 93, 120
Marxism, 3, 22, 152n8; aesthetics of, 8, 31; of anticolonial authors, 2, 86–87; anticolonialism and, 10–13; consciousness in, 12; in decolonization era, 8; as explosive, 34; Indian progressive writers tainted by, 152n6; muscular tension and, 159n8; revolutionary consciousness and, 11, 12, 34, 38; revolutionary subject in, 15
Marxist literature, 2, 12, 32
masculinity: of anticolonialism, 20; Anwar Ali and, 49–51; Chughtai and, 28; of colonial violence, 27; of Fanon, 21; in *Inquilab*, 49–51; patriarchy and, 27–28

mass euphoria, 11, 32, 38
materialism, 9, 11, 21, 25, 29, 145; poetics of, 87; racialized emotions and, 2, 7
materialist imaginary, 6, 8
materiality, 25, 104; of bodily life, 61, 66, 146; of colonized body, 2, 22; of embodied experience, 9, 42, 61; of female body, 86, 106; of racialized body, 145; Spinozist affect and, 154n20
Mbembe, Achille, 8
minoritization, 26, 51, 58, 62, 111
modernism, 18; Ali and, 111; in Europe, 11, 14, 17; of PWA, 14; realism and, 66; of *Twilight in Delhi*, 123
"The Mole" (Chughtai), 19, 21
Mr. Eliot's Penny World of Dreams (Ali), 120, 126
Mufti, Aamir, 28, 58, 64; minoritization and, 26, 51; Muslim identity and, 154n3, 154n21; on PWA, 152n7; realism and, 16–17, 155n6; on *tavaif* (courtesan), 113, 119–20
musculature, 38, 53, 143, 147; Marxism and, 159n8
Muslim identity, 154n3, 154n21
Muslim internationalists, 8, 34, 38, 133
Muslims, of India, 13, 26, 33, 34; minoritization of, 26, 51, 58, 62, 111. *See also specific topics*

narrative, 22, 45, 126; of Indian independence, 40, 54, 57; of *Inquilab*, 42, 49; of *Lament on the Death of a Master of Arts*, 77–82; "The Quilt" and, 94–96, 98; of *Untouchable*, 63, 65, 71–72
narrative gaze, 63, 79, 82, 95
national consciousness, 18, 51, 66; revolutionary subject and, 57; in *The Wretched of the Earth*, 145
nationalism. *See* Indian nationalism
nationalist ecstasy, 16, 27, 33, 38–42, 149; convulsions of, 13; in *Inquilab*, 43–44, 49, 51, 54, 57

nationalist imaginary, 49, 58, 120
nationalist teleology, 110
national realist novel, 16, 22, 39, 64, 66, 74
native figure, 52–53, 99, 142–44, 146
Native Son (Wright), 139–40
nausea, 1, 94, 96; of Anwar Ali, 56; as cathartic release, 5, 24; Fanon and, 134, 136–37, 139–40, 143; Fanonian train scene staged by, 24; in *Lament on the Death of a Master of Arts*, 78, 80–83; of Sartrean figures, 5, 8, 24, 80, 136; visceral crises staged by, 24
Nehru, Jawaharlal, 40, 75–76
Ngai, Sianne, 9, 10, 37, 47
Nur (fictional character), 77–84

obscenity, 19; Chughtai and, 33, 93–94, 98, 106; regimes of, 28, 87; texture and, 87–92
Ocean of Night (Ali), 113–14, 120–21, 123–24, 126–31; gendered figure in, 122, 125; Indian nationalism in, 118–19
oppression, 27, 33, 61–62, 67
orthodoxy, Islamic, 4, 15, 33, 87, 114

Pandey, Gyanendra, 22, 150
patriarchy, 27–28
poetics, 13–18, 37, 79, 133, 149; of Anand, 33, 62, 63, 65, 67; of Chughtai, 94, 106, 108; of corporeality, 65, 73, 82; of Deleuze, 25; of irritation, 11, 61; of materialism, 87; of political agitation, 11; of touch and feeling, 33, 62, 73
political agitation, 11, 42–43, 49, 56, 88; aesthetics of, 37; of revolutionary subject, 23–24, 38; somatic unconscious of, 38
politicization, 41, 54, 56–57
politics: agitated subject and, 56–57; agitation in, 11, 37, 42–43, 49, 56, 88; anger in, 16, 61; of appetite, 29; Marx-

ist aesthetics and, 31; visceral grammars of, 10
Popular Front policy (1935), 17
postcolonialism, 1, 4, 6, 10, 36, 91; queer theory in, 30; race and, 25, 30
power, 21, 25, 30, 58, 137; in art, 19–20, 97; in British colonialism, 6–8, 29; colonial violence and, 6–7; erotics of, 19–20
progressive imaginary, 86, 117, 133
progressive teleology, 115, 118
progressive transformation, 2, 116
Progressive Writers, of India, 3–4, 14–15, 20, 111, 134; aesthetics of, 2–4, 10, 17, 27; archiving, 25; artistic experiments and forms of, 31–32; decolonization during, 31; in film industry, 17; Freudian psychoanalysis influencing, 153n18; Marxism tainting, 152n6; sensory aesthetics of, 30; somato-poetics of, 28, 30, 149; visceral grammars of, 133
Progressive Writers' Movement. *See* All-India Progressive Writers' Association (PWA)
progressivism, 63; of Ali, 109–10, 114; of Anand, 73, 75; decolonization and, 13; imaginary of, 86, 117, 133; teleology of, 115, 118
protests, in India, 32, 40–43, 52–55, 57
psychic logics, in somatic actions, 8, 18
psychoanalysis: Anand and, 16; decolonization and, 4; of Freud, 11; Indian progressive writers influenced by, 153n18
psychoanalytic unconscious, 4, 29
PWA. *See* All-India Progressive Writers' Association (PWA)
PWA manifesto, 14–15, 73, 110

qawaali, religious spectacle, 47–48, 51, 53–55, 57–58; Anwar Ali watching, 45–46, 50
queer feminism, 33, 157n8

queer theory, 9, 28; erotics of, 31; feminism and, 30, 31, 33; in postcolonialism, 30
"The Quilt" (Chughtai), 92–98, 102, 104–5, 157n8

race, 5, 7, 26, 29, 39, 94; British colonialism and, 9, 27; gender and, 139; humiliation and, 67; postcolonialism and, 25, 30
racial capitalism, 30, 142
Racial Indigestion (Tompkins), 29
racialization, 26, 30; of colonized subject, 1; Fanon depicting, 5–6; materialism and, 2, 7; trauma of, 3
racialized body, 31, 67, 107, 136, 141, 145
racialized consciousness, 27, 30
radical transformation, 4, 13, 60, 62, 68
realism, 11, 17–18; as biological, 42, 64, 65, 69, 80; modernism and, 66; Mufti and, 16–17, 155n6
realistic dimensions, 19–20
regimes: of colonial hygiene, 12, 26, 97; of colonial violence, 12; of obscenity, 28, 87
relations, of power, 25, 30, 137
religion, 10, 13, 15, 26, 40, 41
religious ecstasy, 45–51
religious spectacle, 46–48, 51, 53–55, 57–58
representationalism, 10, 20
revolutionary, 32, 41–43, 46, 53–54, 58
revolutionary consciousness, 2, 4, 8; of human collective, 3, 13; Marxism and, 11, 12, 34, 38; for transformation, 16
revolutionary feeling, 1, 15, 27, 31, 32
revolutionary subject, 58, 61, 71, 74, 149; of Abbas, 43; agency of, 142; cathartic release for, 16; ecstasy of, 43; of Fanon, 11; irritation of, 33; in Marxism, 15; in Marxist literature, 32; musculature of, 38, 53; national consciousness and, 57; political agitation of, 23–24, 38; somatic actions of, 23; transformation of, 39; visceral logics of, 66

revulsion, and attraction, 33, 85–86, 97–98
Roy, Parama, 12, 28–29, 70

Saldanha, Arun, 7
Sartre, Jean-Paul, 5, 6, 8, 24, 80, 136
Scott, Darieck, 141–42, 145, 147, 148, 158n5, 159nn9–10
Scott, David, 18
sense-making, 62, 66–67, 70, 83
sensory aesthetics, 17–19, 30, 106
sensory poetics, 79, 94
separatism, 111, 116, 118
sexual desire, 19, 92, 96–97, 98, 105
sexual discipline, 12, 33, 85, 102
sexuality and gender, 3, 9–10, 30, 107; decolonization grounded in, 20, 28; Indian Muslims and, 13
sexual repression, 19, 92
Shamshad (fictional character), 99–105
Shingavi, Snehal, 11, 63, 67, 118, 155n4, 158n4
shock, 37, 54, 56–57, 75, 154n2
simultaneity, 37, 41–42, 44, 49, 154n1
skin, 19, 61, 68, 70–73; aesthetics of, 67; as revolutionary feeling, 31; somatics of, 63; tactility of, 33; touch and, 70
social order, 2, 49
social realism, 16, 99; Abbas and, 39; Ali and, 111; Anand and, 40; through feminist lens, 86; Indian independence in, 40; PWA embracing, 17
somatic arousals, 21, 22, 150
somatic logic. *See* agitation; compulsion; convulsion; evisceration; explosion; irritation
somatic unconscious, 28–32; contagion of, 23; of political agitation, 38; touch and tactility and, 31
somatic vitality, 30, 63
somato-poetics, 21–22, 133; of Chughtai, 108; of Indian progressive writers, 28, 30, 149; of race, 26

soul making, 12–13, 27, 152n10
South Asia, 10, 42, 51, 88, 112, 152n5
Soviet Union, 2, 11, 16, 17, 37, 40
spasms, 21, 23, 37, 47, 134; convulsive, 48, 55; of ecstasy, 29; of ecstatic terror, 13
spectacle, 20, 37; ecstasy of, 44, 48; of ecstatic body, 44, 47, 55; as religious, 46, 48, 50; of violence, 52
Spinoza, Baruch, 7, 21, 23, 25, 150, 160n17; materiality and, 154n20
Stoler, Ann Laura, 12, 29
subaltern figure, 16, 17, 28; agency of, 90; of Anand, 33; in art, 19–20

tactility, 33, 62, 70, 72, 75; touch and, 12, 26, 31
tavaif (courtesan), 28; Mufti on, 113, 119–20
teleology, 16, 41, 113–15, 118, 126; as Hegelian, 141; of Indian nationalism, 110; in *Inquilab*, 47; of *Untouchable*, 65–66
texture: of body, 1, 26, 28, 31, 92, 97; colonial disgust and, 12; erotics and, 26, 33, 85; of female body, 28, 34, 92, 95–96, 105; as obscene, 87–92
Tompkins, Kyla Wazana, 25, 29
touch, 63, 65, 70, 91–92; as feeling, 33, 62, 73, 83; tactility and, 12, 26, 31
transformation, 3; of Anwar Ali, 41–42, 44–45, 48–49; of consciousness, 39; as emotive, 16, 42, 44, 69, 71; of racialized consciousness, 30; as radical, 4, 13, 60, 62, 68; revolutionary consciousness for, 16; of revolutionary subject, 39
transformative potential, 52, 73, 83
transmission, of affect, 7, 9, 28, 151n4
trauma, 8, 30, 145; of colonial violence, 2–4; in *Inquilab*, 52, 55; of racialization, 3; in *Untouchable*, 77–78; from violence, 26
Twilight in Delhi (Ali), 111–19, 121–23, 127

United States (US), 31, 39
Untouchable (Anand), 1, 27, 33, 79; caste addressed in, 63–64, 66–67, 70; imaginary in, 118; irritation in, 60–71; narrative of, 63, 65, 71–72; teleology of, 65–66; trauma in, 77–78
Urdu literature, 13, 19, 28, 86–87, 112–13, 157n6
utopia, 24, 40, 70, 113, 118
utopic visions, 4, 16, 111, 113

violence, 53, 117, 134, 142–46, 148; as communal, 32, 37, 45; upon female body, 85–87; spectacle of, 52; trauma from, 26. *See also specific topics*
violence, colonial, 2, 29, 54; Anwar Ali witnessing, 52; bodily response within, 6; of colonial subjugation, 3, 7; ecstatic terror of, 52; hygiene and, 12; of Indian nationalism, 34; masculinity and, 27; postcolonialism lodged in, 4; power of, 6–7; regimes of, 12
visceral aesthetics, 27, 51, 57, 122, 135; of Anand, 75, 77
visceral crises, 32; of convulsion, 23–24; nausea staging, 24; of postcolonialism, 6, 10
visceral grammars, 8, 10, 52, 133
visceral logic. *See specific topics*
"viscerally manipulated," 50, 59

Williams, Linda, 38, 43–44, 48, 50, 55–56
Williams, Raymond, 5, 10
women's sexuality, 85, 93–98, 101
Woolf, Virginia, 62, 66
The Wretched of the Earth (*Les damnés de la terre*) (Fanon), 3, 38, 51–53, 134, 142–47
Wright, Richard, 139–40

www.ingramcontent.com/pod-product-compliance
Lightning Source LLC
Chambersburg PA
CBHW031834230426
43669CB00009B/1342